Jesus
A Colloquium in the Holy Land

The Colloquium on the Historical Jesus,
June 9–19, 2000, sponsored by
The Cardinal Suenens Program
in Theology and Church Life,
at John Carroll University,
was made possible by grants from
the Fidelity Charitable Trust
and
Margaret F. Grace

JESUS

A COLLOQUIUM
IN THE HOLY LAND

With
James D. G. Dunn
Daniel J. Harrington
Elizabeth A. Johnson
John P. Meier
E. P. Sanders

Edited by
Doris Donnelly

Continuum
New York London

2001
The Continuum International Publishing Group Inc
370 Lexington Avenue, New York, NY 10017

The Continuum International Publishing Group Ltd
The Tower Building, 11 York Road, London SE1 7NX

Printed in the United States of America

Library of Congress Cataloging-in-Publication Data

Jesus : a colloquium in the Holy Land / with James D.G. Dunn . . . [et al.] ; edited by Doris Donnelly.
    p.   cm.
  Includes bibliographical references.
  ISBN 0-8264-1307-2
  1. Jesus Christ—Biography—Congresses. 2. Catholic Church—Doctrines—Congresses. I. Dunn, James D. G., 1939– II. Donnelly, Doris.

BT303 .J47 2001
232.9'08—dc21

2001028477

Contents

INTRODUCTION
  Doris Donnelly   1

1. Jesus in Galilee
     E. P. Sanders   5

2. Jesus and the Dead Sea Scrolls
     Daniel J. Harrington, S.J.   27

3. From Elijah-like Prophet to Royal Davidic Messiah
     John P. Meier   45

4. Jesus in Oral Memory: The Initial Stages
   of the Jesus Tradition
     James D. G. Dunn   84

5. The Word Was Made Flesh and Dwelt Among Us:
   Jesus Research and Christian Faith
     Elizabeth A. Johnson   146

The Colloquium
on the Historical Jesus

PARTICIPANTS

Rosemary Bensman
Daniel Earl Bond
Annette L. Brandin
Jane Brooks
Bonnie M. Brunelle
Alyce M. Cafaro
Judith Cetina
George T. Deas
Joseph Divis
Doris Donnelly
James D. G. Dunn
Meta Dunn
Judith Enterlin, C.S.J.
Sandra M. Estanek
Daniel R. Fickes
Victoria Fuster de la Riva
Stanley Gedaminsky
Ann Marie Gedaminsky
Carol A. Gura
Timothy Hanchin
Daniel J. Harrington, S.J.
Linda E. Hill
Alice Hinkel
Angela M. Howell
Paul Hritz
Antoinette Iadarola
Elizabeth Johnson, C.S.J.
Virginia S. Jones
Rosemarie Keiffer, O.P.
Mark A. Latcovich
Neal Laurance
Anne Laurance

Patricia A. Love
Claire Markham, R.S.M.
Elizabeth M. Markham
John P. Meier
Joan Nuth
Consolata O'Connor
Karen O'Hara
Sarah O'Malley, O.S.B.
Mary Kay Oosdyke
Bruce J. Powers
Jeanne W. Ralston
Anthony Randazzo
Barbara Reid, O.P.
Candace A. Rich
Elaine C. Rose
Patricia Scanlan, R.J.M.
Joyce Scardiglia
Frank Scardiglia
Nicholas J. Scolaro
Donald Senior, C.P.
Priscilla M. Shields
Brian Sinchak
Marianne Slattery
John J. Sudol
Mary Sudol
Guillaume Theys
Jan Van der Veken
Susan VanBaalen, O.P.
Joachim Viens
Joseph Warner
Patricia Wilson

Introduction

Doris Donnelly

*A*NYONE FAMILIAR WITH THE LIFE of Leon-Josef Cardinal Suenens, for whom the Cardinal Suenens Program in Theology and Church Life at John Carroll University in Cleveland, Ohio, is named, would find it hard to believe that he visited the Holy Land only once. So many of his pastoral and theological interests were bound up with this special geographical location: his appreciation for serious biblical study and the development of scholarship surrounding the historical Jesus; his devotion to the Christ of faith, whose message was first preached in towns around the Galilee; his deep commitment to inter-religious dialogue between Christians and Jews; and his conviction concerning the power of God's Spirit to reconcile differences. It would have seemed natural to find him a frequent visitor in Nazareth, Tiberias, Caesarea, Joppa, Bethany, Capernaum, or at the Western Wall or along the banks of the Jordan.

While it is likely that Suenens made the pilgrimage frequently in his heart, he did not actually set foot on Holy Land soil until the fiftieth anniversary of his ordination to the priesthood. Always attentive to symbols and symbolic gestures, Cardinal Suenens arrived in Jerusalem for the first time for the feast of Pentecost in 1977. He came not only with close friends but also with ecumenical traveling companions. And at his fiftieth jubilee eucharistic liturgy, mindful of the suffering caused by separations among Christians, he invited the assembly to pray an "ecumenical Confiteor."

1

When the Cardinal Suenens Program was launched at John Carroll University in the fall of 1998 and its board of advisors set about deciding where to focus its energies, the sponsorship of a colloquium on the historical Jesus seemed a perfect fit. On the one hand, it honored the legacy of Suenens and the agenda of the Second Vatican Council, and, on the other, it valued our mission as a Jesuit university.

In preparing the colloquium, from the very beginning we sought and received unfailingly generous support and counsel from Father John Meier, professor of New Testament at the University of Notre Dame and author of the critically acclaimed volumes entitled *A Marginal Jew.* The plan of the colloquium was to combine study with visits to actual sites connected with the historical Jesus and with the tradition surrounding him. The complementarity of a study-tour appealed to us, and we extended invitations to Father Donald Senior, C.P., and Sister Barbara Reid, O.P., preeminent scripture scholars in their own right, to guide us for the first six days of our colloquium. Presenters and participants journeyed together, ate together, prayed together, and even swam together in the salt-rich Dead Sea.

When we assembled in the Galilee for the conference part of our program, the Sea of Galilee and the surrounding rolling hills formed a breathtaking backdrop for us. For four days we listened to presentations on historical Jesus research and engaged in conversation with papers from James D. G. Dunn, Daniel J. Harrington, S.J., Elizabeth A. Johnson, C.S.J., John P. Meier, and E. P. Sanders. In addition to their roles as "shepherds" of our group, Donald Senior was a respondent to papers, and Barbara Reid moderated the colloquium.

Beginning with "Jesus in Galilee," E. P. Sanders invites us to take a look at Galilee in and around the time of Jesus. Sanders's strength as a historian allows us a glimpse into details the untrained eye might miss: the conditions under which Augustus allowed Herod the Great to be king, the number of wills left by Herod the Great, the endurance of Roman soldiers, who were expected to walk thirty miles a day (we assume sometimes in wretched heat!), and the clear differences between Galilee and Judea during Jesus' ministry.

After visiting Qumran and listening to Dan Harrington's impromptu introduction to the Dead Sea Scrolls *in situ*, conference participants anticipated his formal paper. With uncommon clarity and precision, Harrington offers a sweep of the field in answer to the question raised in the title of his paper, "Jesus and the Dead Sea Scrolls." As it turns out, we learned a lot about direct and indirect connections with the baptism of Jesus by John the Baptist, the kingdom of God theme, the emphasis on community, ritual meals, family values, attitudes toward enemies, and model teachers.

John Meier's paper, "From Elijah-like Prophet to Royal Davidic Messiah," drew a warm response. With an exciting combination of sleuthing and scholarship, Meier offered a surprising and original theory of coherence between what might at first glance seem to be an irreconcilable identity crisis for Jesus.

Readers will find in James D. G. Dunn's paper, "Jesus in Oral Memory: The Initial Stages of the Jesus Tradition," a rich extrapolation of *Dei Verbum*, the Constitution on Divine Revelation of the Second Vatican Council, and in particular its supposition that there are three stages in the history of the Gospels: Jesus' life and teaching, the apostles' preaching, and the evangelists' writing. Dunn's paper touches on all three stages, although perhaps the middle stage more than the others, and his model of oral tradition goes a long way to explain some of the mysteries of synoptic parallels.

In the planning for the colloquium it seemed evident that we needed a systematic theologian to reflect on how modern biblical scholarship shaped our relationship with the mystery of the living God mediated through Jesus Christ. This was a formidable responsibility, and Elizabeth Johnson was certainly up to the task. In her paper, "The Word Was Made Flesh and Dwelt Among Us: Jesus Research and Christian Faith," Johnson grappled with the significance that historical Jesus research may have for what Christians believe and how they act today. She challenges images of Jesus in the popular, homiletic, and even theological arenas that deny him a human nature, and she reinterprets salvation, seeing the passion and death of Jesus as a free, faithful, and loving act.

Like the Gospels themselves, our experiences in the Holy Land have an opportunity to live on for future generations through both oral and written traditions. Months later, we find ourselves recalling and retelling stories connected with the colloquium to others near us and sometimes, in quiet moments, to ourselves.

But the written word allows the gift we experienced to be shared more widely—perhaps with those who could not be with us but for whom these essays will open up fresh insights and the wonders of the inexhaustible nature of the living Word of God.

1

Jesus in Galilee

E. P. SANDERS

*T*HE TOPIC "JESUS IN GALILEE" requires us to relate Jesus to his environment or context—what New Testament scholars often call his
"background." Context is essential to understanding. If we have a saying or an event and do not know the context, our fertile minds will
generally make one up. The context that our brain supplies may be
quite inaccurate, and the result may be misleading, but we automatically try to fit new information into what we already know. The historian, of course, ought to do this in a disciplined way by basing the
context on research. This paper is about the Galilean context in which
Jesus lived and worked, and we shall note illustrations of imaginary
contexts that have been supplied in the absence of historical knowledge.

Students of the historical Jesus have been proposing contexts for
him for a long time, and these proposals are remarkably diverse. In
fact, disputes about Jesus often take the form of disputes about his
context. The consequence is that now there are a lot of different
descriptions of Galilee to offer.

"Jesus in Galilee" is closely related to the topic "Jesus and Judaism,"
but the latter topic has produced much more scholarly literature. Most
New Testament scholars, including myself, have not felt confident
about being able to describe Galilee in enough detail to help very
much in the attempt to understand Jesus' relationship to his contemporaries and have thus fallen back on the more general context, Jesus'

5

relationship to the rest of Judaism. Because of recent research, the question now arises whether or not we know enough about Galilee to discuss "Jesus and Galilee" rather than the broader topic "Jesus and Judaism."

GENERALIZATIONS ABOUT PAST AND PRESENT VIEWS ON JESUS' CONTEXT

I shall begin with very brief sketches of three views of Galilee and of Jesus in Galilee. Not long ago, when people thought of the context in which Jesus lived, they thought of three dominant influences: Pharisaic Judaism, apocalypticism, and Roman oppression. The *Pharisees* were thought to govern the country according to their laws, which (it was thought) have been preserved in the Mishnah and other rabbinic literature. Jewish scholars regarded this supposed ruling class as being kind and tolerant, while most Christian scholars held them to be hypocritical and legalistic in the worst sense of the word. The *apocalyptists* were depicted as members of small conventicles, the heirs of a debased form of prophecy that depicted in lurid colors the intervention of God in history; he would send his Messiah, a son of David, who would defeat the Romans. Politically, therefore, many of the apocalyptists were Zealots, people who believed in fighting the enemies of God and paying whatever price was necessary. Though few in number, they were influential, and from time to time they led uprisings. And the *Romans,* of course, governed in the way common to all-powerful empires. They brutalized the people, demanded extra services, such as carrying their burdens, and were ruthless in collecting taxes. The *ordinary people* gathered in synagogues on the Sabbath, where the Pharisees taught them to be meticulous in observing their rules, which were more important than the Bible, and harassed or even persecuted them when they did not do so rigorously enough. Jesus opposed Pharisaic legalism and described a kingdom of God that was present in his own work and that was based on love, not apocalyptic warfare and judgment.

In very recent years competing ways of envisaging life in Jewish Palestine have arisen. One of these is only a modification of the above paragraph. Some scholars emphasize the economic oppression of the Roman system. They maintain that Galileans had to pay double or even triple taxes: the people were taxed by Rome as heavily as if Rome were the only government; by Herod or (after his death) by one of his sons as if he were the only government; and by the temple as if the Jewish priesthood constituted the only government. This led to loss of family farms on a massive scale and the steady increase of homeless and unemployed people who had no choice but to become brigands.[1] One scholar, Dominic Crossan, thinks that colonists had taken a lot of the land away from Jewish farmers, who became not much better than serfs (nn. 9 and 10 below). In the face of massive economic and consequently social devastation, Jesus arose as a prophet who favored economic and social reform.

The second recent description of Jewish Palestine gives it quite a different look. In Galilee, in particular, Gentiles predominated. Lower Galilee—where Jesus lived and worked—was a large urbanized area with the villages serving as suburbs, in which Greek was the major language and Greek culture flourished. The cause of this hellenization was in part a very large influx of Greeks, Romans, and other Gentiles, who heavily populated the cities of Galilee, especially Sepphoris, only a few miles from Nazareth. The Roman army occupied Palestine, and the soldiers demanded to be served in standard ways: they wanted Gentile food, including pork, and their traditional temples, as well as an amphitheater in which they could see games. As a result, the ordinary Jewish population could see Greek dramas and listen to wandering Greek philosophers, the Cynics. They could readily travel to the coastal cities of the province of Syria (Ptolemais, Tyre, and Sidon) to soak up still more Greek culture. The economic implication of this depiction is a great deal of prosperity, since it is a general rule that the arts and philosophy flourish when money permits. Moreover, if Galilean peasants frequently left their villages, eagerly seeking Greek learning and literature, they did not have to work six days a week from dawn to dark. They must have been very prosperous. Jesus was part of this culture; his teaching is to be likened to that of a Cynic philosopher.[2]

If one combs carefully enough through the work of scholars holding these various views, one can find some things of value. But all three of these descriptions of Jesus' context are largely erroneous. They are either completely in error or so badly exaggerated that the net effect is the same. Let me immediately emphasize that I have described extreme views in order to help you fix some issues in your minds. Recent scholarship also includes less extreme and more likely views; I refer especially to John Meier and Sean Freyne.[3] We shall now consider the following topics:

1. Government in Jewish Palestine in general and Galilee in particular; the presence or absence of the Roman army; the presence of non-Jews, in particular Gentile colonists; land ownership; and the extent of hellenization or romanization.
2. The loyalty or lack thereof of Galileans to common Judaism and

especially to the Judaism of Jerusalem: the temple, the priesthood, support of the temple and priesthood, pilgrimage, and the like. Under this heading we shall also consider synagogues and *miqva'ot,* immersion pools.

3. Money, taxes, class divisions, poverty, oppression, and the role of building programs.

We cannot discuss each subtopic in detail, and so in some cases I shall give a very brief indication of how I see this issue.

GOVERNMENT, THE ROMAN ARMY, COLONIZATION, LANDOWNERSHIP, GREEK AND ROMAN INFLUENCE

Many scholars, including some who know better, refer to Jewish Palestine as having been "annexed" and "occupied" by Rome.[4] From time to time scholars take these words literally and suppose that Rome directly governed the country on a day-to-day basis, which involved bringing in Roman bureaucrats, magistrates, and the army. As we have seen, this perception leads to the view that there were pagan temples and numerous pig farms. According to Howard Kee, in Jesus' day Sepphoris was an "important Roman cultural and administrative center."[5] His "evidence" is a sentence in Josephus to the effect that in the period 57–55 B.C.E., shortly after Pompey the Great conquered Palestine (63 B.C.E.), the Roman general Gabinius established five administrative districts (*Antiquities* 14.91; *War* 1.170). Kee imagines that these districts were staffed by Romans and furthermore that this form of government continued for at least the next ninety years. In fact, these districts were governed by Jews, and the arrangement was changed after only one or two years. Under the new arrangement the high priest Hyrcanus II was ethnarch and the Idumean Antipater was second in command.[6] There were to be several other rearrangements of the governmental structure before Jesus' day, but none of them placed Romans in Galilee.

If it is not true that Roman administrators governed Palestine and that Roman legions occupied it, what was the system? An answer to this requires a little information about the Roman empire. We shall then turn to the governance of Judea and Galilee in Jesus' day.

First of all, Rome governed its empire in diverse ways. Shortly after he came to power in 31 B.C.E., Augustus proposed to the Senate, and the Senate accepted, a plan that distinguished between senatorial provinces and imperial provinces. Basically, the senatorial provinces lay to the west of Syria and Palestine and included the more civilized parts of the Roman empire, while the imperial provinces, including much of eastern Asia Minor, Syria, and Palestine, were further removed from Greco-Roman culture and were also less stable politically and militarily. As I shall explain, Rome had two different ways of governing imperial provinces. To secure stability and peace, Rome stationed legions at strategic points in the East. The legions that were ultimately responsible for good order in Palestine were stationed in Syria, not in Palestine. "Good order" was imposed not by the presence of Romans throughout the eastern provinces but by the threat of retaliation by the nearest legions. As Richard Horsley has emphasized, Rome ruled by terror.[7] The legions sometimes lost battles, but never the war, and the retaliation against rebellious subjects was dreadful. Because of the slowness of communication and transportation, retaliation sometimes took a long time, but it was inevitable and the result was catastrophic. Those who can recall the Soviet empire in eastern Europe will have a very good idea of how the Roman empire worked. Think of Hungary in 1956. Compared to the Romans, however, the Soviets were quite mild in their treatment of rebellious subjects.

Rome's interest in Palestine was very limited but nevertheless vital: Palestine lies between Syria and Egypt. Syria is the gateway to the riches of Asia Minor, and Egypt was Rome's granary. The legions in Syria protected Asia Minor against direct invasion from the east, where the Parthians constituted the only military threat to Roman security at the time, but Rome would not like Palestine to fall into enemy hands, since a foe could use it to strike against either Syria or Egypt.

Thus, Roman imperial policy required that Palestine be loyal and peaceful. This was achieved for a long time by permitting Herod to remain as king of Judea. "Judea" has diverse meanings, depending on context. It is a geographical region (south of Samaria and north of Idumea) and also a governmental entity. In Herod's time the governmental entity "Judea" included all of Jewish Palestine: in terms of geography, it included Galilee, Judea, and Idumea, plus Samaria; but it did not include the Greek city Ascalon (north of Gaza on the coast), nor the cities of the Phoenician coast (Dora, Sidon, and Tyre), nor Scythopolis, a pagan city that juts out just south of geographical Galilee (now Bet Shean). Later, Augustus gave Herod some non-Jewish territory north and east of Galilee so that his army could deflect Parthian attacks aimed at the Phoenician coast and Syria. That is to say, Herod was king of the Jews, plus the Samaritans, plus the relatively few Gentiles who lived in basically Jewish territory, plus some thinly settled Gentile land to the north and east (Gaulanitis, Batanea, Trachonitis, Aurantis). This additional territory included what is now called the Golan Heights.

Herod was a client king, one of Rome's "friends and allies." He ruled an imperial Roman province, and thus ruled at the pleasure of the emperor, Augustus, on the basis of well-understood terms and conditions. The first condition was that he defend his borders, especially against the Arabs and Parthians to the east. Herod did this with outstanding success. Second, he must not allow revolt at home. He also kept this part of the bargain; he suppressed dissent ruthlessly, and so Rome never worried about his part of the world (see, e.g., Josephus, *Antiquities* 15.366–69). Third, as an allied king, Herod had to contribute troops to any military activity that Rome wished to carry out in one of the nearby countries.[8]

Herod relied on his own troops and—after he conquered his kingdom —he did not have to ask for help from the legions in Syria. On the contrary, as we have seen, he assisted them.

When he died in 4 B.C.E., he left two wills, which Augustus adjudicated. Augustus gave Samaria, Judea, and Idumea to Archelaus; Galilee to Antipas; and the regions to the north and east of Galilee to Philip. Most of the land immediately to the east of the Sea of Galilee, however, he attached to the province of Syria. Herod's sister, Salome, received Jamnia, Azotus, and Gaza, with some surrounding land. Philip and Salome now drop out of the picture.

Archelaus was not a success. He had the most difficult area to govern, and—to put the matter plainly—he was not equal to the task. He was deposed in 6 C.E., after ruling Judea, Samaria, and Idumea for about ten years.

As I have mentioned, Rome had two ways of governing imperial provinces. Method A was use of a client king such as Herod. When Augustus deposed Archelaus, he went to plan B for the southern part of Jewish Palestine plus Samaria: rule by a Roman governor, supported by a few troops. In 6 C.E. Augustus sent a minor Roman aristocrat to Judea as prefect. (The Roman governors in Judea were called prefects at first, and later procurators.) The prefect had about three thousand infantry and a few cavalry in support. He dwelt in Herod's palace in the great port Caesarea, surrounded by his troops. This miniscule "Roman" army was not actually Roman: it was recruited from local Gentiles, especially from Sebaste in

Samaria and Caesarea on the coast. The prefect was from Rome; we do not know the national origin of the military officers, but it is at least conceivable that they were also from Italy.

Jerusalem and the surrounding area was actually governed on a day-to-day basis by the high priest and his council, the members of which were either aristocratic priests or "powerful" laymen. The Roman prefect and his army came up to Jerusalem only for the three pilgrimage festivals, since the assembly of large crowds sometimes led to tumult and outbreaks of violence. While in Jerusalem, the soldiers took up residence in the Antonia fortress, attached to the temple, and patrolled the temple area from the roofs of the surrounding stoas, or porticoes. Otherwise, the high priest reigned supreme in Jerusalem, and he was supported not only by the other aristocrats but also by a few thousand temple guards, who could serve as local police if needed. Moreover, his role as ruler was supported by Jewish tradition.

People whose knowledge of Judaism is based on the Bible think of the kings David, Solomon, and others, and thus regard the Jews as having been ruled by kings. But in fact the Jews were ruled by high priests as long as they were ruled by kings. A high priest was the ruler beginning sometime shortly after the return from exile in the sixth century B.C.E. The old high priestly family, the Zadokites, was overthrown by the Hasmonean (Maccabean) revolt, and for a while the ruler of the Jews was a Hasmonean high priest. Some of these took the title "king" as well. When Herod became king, he was the first Jewish king who was not a high priest since the Babylonians conquered Judea in the seventh century B.C.E. High priests governed Jerusalem and the surrounding area from (let us say) 515 B.C.E. to 37 B.C.E., a period of 470 years. Thus, when Rome turned Judea over to the high priest, it was simply reestablishing the dominant Jewish tradition. The high priest became a kind of middle man between the populace in Jerusalem and the Roman administrator down on the coast.

It need only be added that there were very small permanent garrisons of Roman troops (raised locally) in the Antonia fortress in Jerusalem and at a few other points in Judea. Roman soldiers were rather like the cavalry in western movies: they stayed behind walls, away from the hostile natives. They did not patrol the streets and roads.

Now, at last, for Galilee. Antipas, Herod's son, ruled Galilee precisely as his father had ruled a larger kingdom. (Antipas is rather confusingly called "Herod" in the Gospels.) Jesus was perhaps two or three years old when Antipas came to power. Antipas was not allowed the title "king"; he was, rather "tetrarch," "ruler of a fourth," that is, a fourth of Herod's kingdom. Antipas ruled on the same terms and conditions as his father: (1) that he protect his borders against invaders hostile to Rome; (2) that he not allow too much civil unrest; and (3) that on request he contribute troops to assist Roman military activities. He met all these conditions reasonably well. Therefore, Rome left him alone. Rome did not send officials to govern Galilee, nor did Roman troops occupy Galilee.

The paper is half over, and we have dealt only with two subtopics in the first of three major topics. The reason for this disproportion is that most readers of the Gospels do not know all this information about imperial provinces, client rulers, and Roman governors who did not actually govern, nor can they trace the movements of the Roman legions. Unhappily, the same is true of many New Testament scholars. But nothing I have said thus far is actually controversial among historians of the period. No historian of the Roman empire thinks that legions were stationed in Palestine in the time of Jesus. They all understand about the use of local rulers and aristocrats, for these were Rome's standard governing procedures.

I shall summarize the government of Jesus' day by naming the actors. *Antipas,* called "Herod" in the New Testament, governed Galilee. He was an independent ruler who was free to govern as he wished, as long as he fulfilled the expectations of his patron, the Roman emperor. His government required the presence of zero Romans, and as far as we know there were none there. He probably did, however, hire some Gentiles to assist him in various ways, especially in his ambitious building program. *Pontius Pilate* was the Roman prefect in the province of Judea, which included Samaria, Judea, and Idumea. He lived in Caesarea, about one hundred kilometers from Jerusalem, which is about sixty miles, or two days' march. With the prefect in Caesarea, the government of Jerusalem and the rest of Judea lay in local hands, especially the hands of *Caiaphas,* the high priest.

Now for colonialism. Many scholars say that Rome "colonized" Palestine.[9] Dominic Crossan, very well known for his work on the historical Jesus, has a colonial image of first-century Palestine, and he parallels first-century Palestine with Ireland under the British empire.[10] "Colonialization" should mean that there were "colonials" or "colonists," people whom the imperial country settled in a foreign land. And, of course, this was true of Ireland, where many of the large landowners were in fact English and had received their land from the British crown.

Colonies were very well known in the ancient world, as is much of the history of colonization. Colonies required the foundation of a new city, which might be merely an old city that was renamed and given a Greek (or "Hellenistic") mode of government. Outside the city, of course, there was farmland, some of which would be given to new residents—the colonists. This sometimes meant that the native landowners were dispossessed. But the founding of a colony required a city, as I shall explain below. The Roman emperors planted no colonies in Jewish Palestine prior to the death of Jesus.

Herod the Great refounded two cities that were already Gentile.[11] The first was Strato's Tower, which he named "Caesarea" and greatly enlarged. Its population remained basically Gentile, though there were some Jewish residents.[12] The second he named "Sebaste" (the Greek word for "Augustus"). It was in Samaria, notably not in the Jewish part of his kingdom. Antipas rebuilt Sepphoris, which had recently been destroyed in the uprisings following Herod's death. Sepphoris had been Jewish in population, and it seems to have remained so; as far as we know Antipas did not draft Gentile colonists. He also built one entirely new city, Tiberias (named after Augustus's successor), but he populated it principally with Jews. These two Galilean cities had some of the trappings of a Greek city, but only a few.[13] They did not have gymnasia, nor did they have pagan temples. It is also noteworthy that they did not have jurisdiction over the surrounding countryside, which remained under the control of Antipas himself; the countryside was administered by Antipas's appointees.[14] Thus Sepphoris was not a Hellenistic city, and Nazareth was not part of greater Sepphoris.

There were Greek or Hellenistic foundations in a sort of semicircle around Galilee. On the west there were the cities of the Phoenician coast, which were in the province of Syria: from south to north, Dora, Ptolemais, Tyre, and Sidon. Jesus is reported to have gone into this region once, where, not surprisingly, he met a Gentile. On the east there were the famous cities called collectively "the Decapolis" (referred to in Matt. 4:25; Mark 5:20; 7:31). One of these, Scythopolis, was, as noted above, west of the Jordan River, but it was in neither Herod's nor Antipas's domain. The Hasmoneans had conquered many of these Greek/Hellenistic cities (Dora on the coast and the Decapolis), but Pompey the Great liberated them from Jewish control and most of them never returned to it. Pompey allowed the Jews to keep only the areas that were predominantly Jewish, except Joppa and the plain of Esdraelon, two very valuable pieces of real estate, which he also took out of Jewish control, though they were largely Jewish. Julius Caesar gave Joppa back to the Jews, and so it was part of Herod's kingdom. Joppa was very valuable, since it was a port and thus a source of revenue.

Herod also regained Esdraelon and even some of the minor cities of the Decapolis. The latter, however, which were predominantly Gentile, were not given to Antipas but rather attached to the province of Syria. Thus Antipas's Galilee contained far fewer Gentiles than had Herod's.

The point of all this is that the Romans (Pompey, Julius Caesar, Augustus, and Tiberius) tended to keep the Jews and the Gentiles in separate governmental compartments. They planted no new colonies in the Jewish parts of the country and they kept the non-Jewish cities out of Jewish control (with the exception of Samaria and some minor areas north and east of Galilee). Herod refounded Gentile cities in non-Jewish parts of his kingdom, and Antipas populated his one new city largely with Jews.

There is further evidence of the fact that both Romans and the Herodians distinguished Jewish from Gentile areas and treated them differently. Herod did not produce pagan coins, bearing an image of Augustus or himself, but rather good Jewish coins. It is noteworthy that he built numerous pagan buildings, including temples honoring Augustus and an amphitheater for Greek games, and he donated gymnasia to territories that he did not govern: Tripolis, Acco/Ptolemais, and Damascus. I spare you the full list of his pagan buildings. But (and this is a very big "but") he put none of these Gentile/pagan buildings in the Jewish parts of his domain. That is to say: Herod, Augustus, and Tiberius all knew that Jews and Gentiles did not mix very well, at least not in what the Jews considered to be their own country, and that they deeply disliked the trappings of paganism. They *resisted* too much contact with the Greco-Roman culture. Gymnasia, theaters, hippodromes, pagan temples, and amphitheaters were essential to the Romanized version of Greek culture, and without them we simply cannot find much hellenization.

Antipas followed in his father's footsteps: he refrained from the worst offenses in the eyes of his Jewish subjects. He struck coins acceptable to the Jews. He decorated his own palace, which was in a new city, with animals, which was offensive to his subjects, but this seems to have been the limit of his use of pagan symbols and decoration. It is possible, though very unlikely, that the marvelous theater in Sepphoris existed during Jesus' lifetime, but if so, we do not know what sort of plays were performed. They could have been Jewish plays, imported probably from Alexandria, or mimes, or many other things. We should not envisage the audience lapping up the Oedipus cycle.

We may contrast the behavior of Herod and Antipas with that of Herod's third male heir, Philip, who governed Gentile territory. Unlike Antipas, Philip struck pagan-style coins. The difference between the coins of Philip and Antipas shows that the sons of Herod understood that the sensitivities of Jewish subjects had to be respected.

Many New Testament scholars think that Jews and Gentiles were mixed throughout all the areas north of Samaria, including lower Galilee, which included Nazareth.[15] I think that in fact not many Gentiles lived in the Jewish parts of Palestine. Even moderates on this issue, such as John Meier, may overestimate the Gentile presence and influence in the cities of Galilee.[16] The evidence of the literature is that the cities Sepphoris and Tiberias were predominantly Jewish. That is also the result of a review of the archaeology of Sepphoris,[17] though we should not come to a completely firm judgment, since archaeological work is continuing. But if one canvasses the reports thus far, one does not find any firm evidence of pagan practices in Sepphoris before or during the lifetime of Jesus. A lot of evidence that scholars cite as proving that Sepphoris was basically a Hellenistic city comes from after the second Jewish revolt, which ended approximately 135 C.E. (a hundred years after Jesus' death), when there was in fact a Roman legion stationed nearby. But with regard to the Sepphoris of Jesus' day, there are lots of signs of Jewish habitation and no, or virtually no, signs of pagan habitation.

Since there were no Roman colonies in Galilee, the land was owned and farmed by Jews. Crossan's model, based on the British empire in Ireland, supposes that a lot of individual Gentiles were given large landholdings in Galilee. Not only is there no evidence for this, but it is also opposed to the Greek and Roman system. Rome did not give individuals plots of farmland in barbaric countries. The farmland had to fall within the orbit of a city that was at least partly populated by colonists. Since there were no colonial cities in Jewish Palestine, there were no colonists. Rome settled colonists in Gaul, southern England, and elsewhere, not in Palestine.

Jews thus populated the cities and owned the farmland in Galilee. We do not have really good evidence for the size of holdings. In the second century C.E., rabbinic literature supposes that "normalcy" is a small farm run by a nuclear family.[18] Josephus attests that before 70 C.E. Galilee was heavily cultivated, densely populated, and prosperous (*War* 3.42f.; 3.517–19). While we must always allow for exaggeration, this slight evidence suggests that there were a lot of small farms.

I think, in short, that the impression of Galilee that one receives from the Gospels is quite accurate. They give no information about the cities Tiberias and Sepphoris, but they lead us to think that there were a lot of small villages populated by Jewish peasants and fisherman. It is reasonable that in the villages on the border—which includes the west side of the Sea of Galilee—one would find Antipas's toll collectors and other officials or military officers. This too agrees with the Gospels. Finally we note that, according to the Gospels, Jesus encountered Gentiles when he walked west toward Tyre and Sidon (Mark 7:24–30) or sailed east across the Sea of Galilee and walked to the territory of one of the cities of the Decapolis (Mark 5:1–20). This seems to me to be correct. (You may be interested in knowing something about time and distance. The walk to the region of Tyre would be about forty miles, which would require two days; from the east coast of the Sea of Galilee to Gerasa is about thirty miles; the walk would require at least one full day.)

I have not discussed every conceivable aspect of "hellenization," nor can I do so. It is of course true that in some respects every place in the Roman empire was "hellenized." My view, however, is that this did not go very deep in Jewish Palestine. Part of the support for the opposite view, that Galilee was heavily hellenized, is based on the erroneous views about government, the Roman legions, and colonization that I have addressed. A second support for the theory of thoroughgoing hellenization is the assumption that proximity equals influence. Since there were Hellenistic cities within two days' travel, or, in case of the Decapolis, only a short voyage and a day's walk away, the Jews (some believe) must have acquired Hellenistic culture by osmosis. This is a dubious assumption. I grew up in a small town near Dallas, and we considered Dallasites to be "city slickers," not to be trusted or emulated. Though the distance was only thirty miles, and most families (though not mine) had cars, we did not get up every day and nip into the city to soak up the culture. Nor did the Dallasites come to my little town to urbanize it. We lived separate existences; I went to Dallas about once each year. Thirty miles by car is a lot closer than twenty miles on foot, and even closer than three miles on foot. Proximity does not necessarily lead to constant interaction and cultural exchange. On the contrary, it can lead to avoidance as well as to imitation,[19] and there is a lot of evidence that Jews abhorred idolatry and deeply distrusted Gentiles and their culture, while the Gentiles found the Jews to be very difficult to get along with, at least in the Jews' own country. After an attempt in the second century B.C.E. to turn Judea Hellenistic, which led to the Hasmonean revolt, these efforts were dropped on all sides—until the time of Hadrian in the second century C.E. The governments, rather, tried to keep Jews and Gentiles apart. Rome separated them, and within his kingdom Herod treated Jewish areas quite differently from the way he treated the few pagan areas. His sons emulated him.

HOW JEWISH WERE THE GALILEANS?

In two recent books, Richard Horsley has proposed that the Galileans were not very Jewish; that is, they were not loyal to the Jerusalem sort of Judaism, as represented by the Mosaic law and the temple. Horsley has put his finger on a problem. We do not know just when or how the Galileans became Jews in the Jerusalem manner. The northern kingdom of Israel, which included Galilee, was destroyed by the Assyrians ca. 722 B.C.E. We do not know what happened to the survivors—the so-called ten lost tribes. The southern kingdom—Judea—survived until approximately 581 B.C.E. (the time of the third deportation), when the leaders were taken into exile in Babylon. When the Persians conquered the Babylonian empire, Cyrus sent some of the exiles back to Judea and allowed them to establish a dependent state and to rebuild the temple (ca. 538 B.C.E.). The Judaism of Jerusalem was a product in part of the Judeans who were taken into exile in Babylon and in part of their descendants who returned from Babylon to Judea. The Jewish state after the exile was tiny, consisting of Jerusalem and the Judean hills. Thus the question: Who were the Galileans and how did they become Jewish in the Judean sense? Horsley's answer, in part, is that they did not become very Jewish in the Judean sense. We know that Galilee came under the control of Jerusalem during the reign of the Hasmonean Aristobulus I, ca. 104 B.C.E. According to Josephus, he forcibly converted the Galileans to Judaism (*Antiquities* 13.318). This would not mean, of course, that they all immediately started following all the customs of the Jews in Judea. Thus far Horsley is correct. But at some point before the lifetime of Jesus they did become more or less fully assimilated into Judean Judaism.[20]

The evidence for the thoroughgoing Jewishness of the Galileans is as follows:

1. As we saw above, Rome, Herod, and Antipas treated the Galileans as Jews. The rulers kept the populations in the north on the whole separate from Gentiles, just as they did in the south. They also assumed that the Galileans had *approximately* the same sensitivities to pagan buildings and pagan-style coins as did the Judeans—though the residents of Jerusalem were especially touchy about any sign of paganism.

2. There is excellent evidence that the Galileans went on pilgrimage. There are stories in Josephus about Galileans passing through Samaria on

the way to the temple and about Galileans participating in riots in Jerusalem (*War* 2.43; 2.232; *Antiquities* 20.118). Horsley seems to think that people would not willingly adopt Jerusalem-style Judaism unless coerced or persuaded from the top. But in fact it was very attractive, as we shall see if we further consider the theme of pilgrimage. Religious festivals were popular throughout the ancient world. They constituted most of the rare occasions on which ordinary people could eat red meat: festivals meant holidays and feasting. It was fun for the Galileans to be free of their ordinary labors, to walk through the streets of Jerusalem admiring the sights of the most brilliant city in the eastern part of the empire, to watch the temple service, as the priests silently and expertly carried out the divine sacrifices, to listen to music, to shake their lulabs at Sukkot, and to visit the shops, if only to look. As the disciples said to Jesus during his last Passover, "What wonderful stones and what wonderful buildings!" (Mark 13:1).

3. Horsley denies that synagogues existed prior to 70 C.E., which eliminates one of the institutions that spread and inculcated Judaism.[21] There were, however, synagogues throughout Galilee. There are explicit references in Josephus to three synagogues in or near Galilee (Tiberias [in Galilee], Dora, and Caesarea [both on the coast]), and the remains of three pre-70 synagogues have been found, one of which is in Galilee (Gamla; cf. Herodium and Masada). Josephus's references to synagogues take them entirely for granted. He wrote, in effect, that "when we met to discuss the revolt in Tiberias, we assembled in the 'house of prayer'" (a common Greek name for synagogue). He did not write, "it is remarkable that the Tiberians had a special building called a house of prayer in which we could assemble." [22] Most of the ancient synagogues whose ruins you can see in Palestine today are no earlier than the third or fourth century. Two observations explain the relative lack of the remains of pre-70 synagogues: (a) Archaeologists can dig up only small bits of Galilee; Tiberias, for example, simply cannot be examined archaeologically, since it is now a thriving city. The three pre-70 synagogues whose remains have been found are all located in areas that have not been occupied since they were destroyed by the Romans during the first revolt. If there were other such places, there would doubtless be evidence of more synagogues. (b) People tend to build new structures on the sites of old, and the small first-century synagogues were probably demolished to make way for the grander structures of later centuries. This sort of explanation, for example, explains why there are relatively few remains of Saxon churches in England: the Normans built on top of them.

4. A lot of immersion pools have been found in Galilee, as in Judea. There are several immersion pools even in far-off Gamla, in the Golan Heights. Purification by immersion seems to have originated in the Hasmonean period, and so is definitely postexilic. The Galileans practiced the same purification rites as the Judeans. Whereas Horsley explicitly denies the existence of synagogues, he simply ignores immersion pools in considering Galilean religion. But they must not be ignored. They prove the existence of standard Palestinian/Judean piety in Galilee.

5. There is also evidence that Galileans accepted the tithing laws that were developed by Judeans during and after the Babylonian exile (Josephus, *Vita* 63, 80).

6. Finally, during the great Jewish revolt, Galilee revolted along with Judea. Some Galileans resisted being told by Jerusalem how to conduct their part of the revolt, it is true, but many Galileans fought against Rome in Galilee, and others fled to Jerusalem after the Roman army pacified Galilee. In Jerusalem they fought until the city fell. According to Josephus (*Vita* 354), two thousand Tiberians were killed or captured. Sepphoris did not join the revolt, but this was neither because the city was Gentile nor because it was not loyal to Judaism. Sepphoris, rather, was the principal city in Jewish Palestine that had previously been visited by the Roman army, which put down riots in 4 B.C.E., when Herod died. It had revolted then, but it was partly destroyed as a result, and so the Sepphorans prudently decided to remain loyal to Rome.

In short, Galilee shared in the common Judaism of Palestine. This agrees with the portrayal of Galilee in the Gospels, according to which there were numerous synagogues, a great deal of interest in the Jewish law, and loyalty to the temple, as indicated by pilgrimage.

MONEY

Some scholars think that desperate poverty and landlessness were rampant in Jesus' Galilee and that the only meaningful message would have been one of economic and social change. They often propose that Palestinian Jewish farmers were taxed more viciously that any other people. On the contrary, they were almost certainly better off than Egyptian peasants, and they were probably better off than Syrian peasants. Modern scholars sometimes seem to slip into an unconscious comparison of ancient peasants with modern middle-class Westerners, with the result that they feel moral indignation against the iniquitous rulers, who imposed poverty on the ordinary people. We shall understand the situation only if we look at the ancient Palestinian peasants on their own terms.

Most people in the ancient world, not just in Palestine, were farmers, whose labor generated very little money after they fed themselves and bought a few essentials. That is, they were either subsistence farmers or only slightly better than that. They were, on average, about as prosperous as sharecroppers in Mississippi before World War I—or perhaps a little more prosperous. They were, however, far too poor, and far too hard work-ing, to allow us to accept one of the views that I listed above, according to which ordinary Galileans had lots of leisure to go to the cities and partici-pate in the higher culture of the Greco-Roman world. Actually, farm-dwelling peasants in Galilee worked six days a week from dawn to dusk, and on the sabbath they rested. More precisely, the men worked from dawn to dusk, while the women had to rise appreciably before dawn in order to prepare the day's bread. In any case, the ordinary people had neither the money, the time, nor the rapid transportation (that is, horses) to nip into a nearby city for the afternoon drama. They may have gone to the city to sell their goods in the market. But afterwards, they seldom had the money to stay overnight and participate in cultural events after sunset. Nor did they have the money to take weekend jaunts to Tyre and Sidon, where there were even greater Hellenistic treats. If they had had the money, such a trip would have transgressed the Sabbath, and very few of them broke the Sab-bath law for the sake of amusement.

What could they afford to do? Galilee was very fertile; it was a lot better to have a small farm in Galilee than in the Judean hills, and Galilean farm-ers were by no means the poorest in the world. The following facts point to the conclusion that Galilean farming peasants were more prosperous than sharecroppers in Mississippi and that they were by no means at the point of destitution presupposed by Horsley and others.[23] (1) Every sev-enth year they could afford to let their land lie fallow. The Jewish farmers observed the sabbatical year as required by biblical law. They could eat things that grew on their own, but they could not cultivate the soil. (2) Once a year, on average, they could afford to spend their second-tithe money in Jerusalem. Space does not permit discussion of some of the numerous errors that some scholars, especially Horsley and Borg, make about Jewish tithes and other taxes.[24] I shall say only that one of the two tithes was not given away.[25] Rather, it paid for the people's annual sacri-fices, for their rare feasts on red meat, and for a week-long or two-week-long outing in the big city, where there was a lot to do and see—some devotional activities, some tourist-type activities. (3) They could afford to support not only the priests but also the Levites, and many of them had a small amount left over for the poor—that is, the unemployed, and especially widows and orphans. Please note that the supposedly destitute ordinary people were better off than "the poor," whom they helped support in various ways.

Were there vast hordes of landless people? In discussing the landless, and blaming Roman and Jewish taxes, Horsley and others show no comprehension of the root problem: that landlessness is God's fault. God often produces more than one son in a family, but he never creates any more land for the extra sons to inherit.[26] The net result is that in each generation some farmers' sons end up landless. Good King Herod, unlike some modern rulers, did something about unemployment: he launched enormous building projects that employed tens of thousands of laborers. In recent United States history, only President Franklin D. Roosevelt attacked unemployment this directly. (It is socialism, only a small step away from godless communism! It is much better to have people live on the streets by begging.) Almost sixty years after Herod's death, his temple was finally completed, and eighteen thousand men suddenly became unemployed (*Antiquities* 20.219). Herod's great-grandson, Agrippa II, promptly hired many of them to pave the city of Jerusalem (*Antiquities* 20.222). This reveals that Agrippa II and other leaders understood the social and political consequences of very high unemployment and that they took steps to counteract it.

In Antipas's Galilee, the situation was basically the same as in his father's kingdom: Antipas built two successive capital cities and thus employed thousands of laborers (*Antiquities* 18.26, 36).[27] There were still people who had to live off of charity or theft, but the unemployment situation was by no means as desperate as Horsley, for example, imagines.

With some reluctance, I shall reduce the rest of my discussion of money to simple propositions:

1. Galileans were not taxed more heavily than other people in the ancient world.

2. Both Herod and Antipas carried out extensive building projects, which largely took care of unemployment.

3. Herod and Antipas had other sources of income in addition to taxation of peasants.

4. In various parts of the empire there were grumblings and uprisings because of poverty and taxation during the period of Jesus' life, but not in Galilee.

To conclude these comments on money, I should explain that I am not a Pollyanna about the life of ordinary people in the ancient world. I know too much about poverty—wearing patched clothing, eating only the cheapest food, moving the bed when it rains—to think that it is fun. But I also know that people who have hard lives are not perpetually miserable because of this and that they do not ruin their lives because of envy and hatred. I think that ancient Galileans found life to be hard and accepted the hardship as simply the way things were. Of course it was nice to think about a world in which they would not have to worry every day about food and clothing, and such words as those we find in Matt. 6.25–33 must have struck a responsive chord. But I do not think that the only meaningful message in Antipas's Galilee was one of social and economic change. The ordinary people were prepared to put up with the difficulties of this life partly because this was the way of the world but also partly because they trusted in God: God would not put on them more than they could bear, and in some way or other God would provide them with all they needed in the present and with a better life in the future. I think that this led many to respond positively to Jesus' message. He prayed for "today's bread," and he also asked that God's kingdom would come.

CONCLUSION[28]

As I cautioned, we have not discussed Jesus, except for a few brief references. I would like, however, to make two comments about the results of this study. The first is that a review of everything that we now know about Galilee—of which I have described only a fraction—generally supports the impression given by the Gospels. The Gospels *allow* readers to supply erroneous contexts—such as that Roman soldiers were thick on the ground. But if you read them carefully, you will see that they do not *require* an erroneous context on any of the subjects I have discussed and that they fit into our other evidence about Galilee perfectly well. I do not come to this conclusion because I am a fundamentalist. The other biblical scholars who are present at this Historical Jesus Colloquium will assure you that I am not even conservative. But with regard to society and population in Galilee, the governmental structure of Jewish Palestine, and several other subjects, I find that the Gospels are quite accurate.

My second comment is that, since Galilee was, on the whole, Jewish in the Judean sense, there is probably not a vast difference between the results of comparing Jesus with average Judaism and comparing him with Galilean Judaism. I shall give one example to clarify this statement. There are some cases in the Gospels in which Jesus is depicted as performing a minor cure of a nonfatal illness on the Sabbath, which leads to criticism of him for working on the Sabbath. Our only information about minor cures on the Sabbath, apart from what is in the Gospels, comes from the *Damascus Document* (one of the Dead Sea Scrolls) and rabbinic literature, especially the tractate *Shabbat* in the Tosefta.[29] The *Damascus Document* implies a firm rejection of such cures, since there are even restrictions on carrying a child in or out of the house on a Sabbath.[30] Rabbinic literature reveals reluctance to allow such cures, together with indications that they could probably be managed.[31] For example, if you have a toothache, you may not treat it with vinegar on the Sabbath, but you can put vinegar on food and eat it (*Shabbat* 14.4). The *Damascus Document* is hard-line; rabbinic literature is fairly permissive. This does not tell us what average opinion and practice were in Galilee, and in fact we have no information about Galilean attitudes, apart from the Gospels. Non-Galilean information, however, should lead us to be prepared to find a range of opinion. The rabbis were more lenient than the Essenes (probably the party behind the *Damascus Document*), and common opinion was probably more lenient than that of the rabbis. That is, if we want to discuss Jesus' minor cures on the Sabbath, we have to discuss them in light of whatever sources we have, none of which are from the Galilee of his lifetime. But since Galilee was Jewish, the sources that we do have may help us understand that there would have been a range of opinion on the subject in Galilee. We still cannot write a full account of Jesus in his Galilean context, but relating him to a broader Jewish context is probably not very misleading, though of course it may be inaccurate in some details. To answer the question posed at the beginning: we know enough about Galilee to *discuss* "Jesus and Galilee" rather than only "Jesus and Judaism," but our knowledge remains quite inadequate to allow us to settle any major topics, and we are a long way from having the ability to put many of Jesus' sayings and deeds into a specifically Galilean context. It will still be necessary to understand him in light of a large body of Jewish material.

NOTES

1. Richard Horsley, *Jesus and the Spiral of Violence* (San Francisco: Harper & Row, 1987); Richard Horsley and John Hanson, *Bandits, Prophets, and Messiahs* (Minneapolis: Winston, 1985), e.g., 60f.; Richard Horsley, *Galilee: History, Politics, People* (Valley Forge, Pa.: Trinity Press International, 1995), 59f.; similarly Marcus J. Borg, *Jesus: A New Vision* (San Francisco: HarperCollins, 1987), 84–86. Though more nuanced, the view of S. Applebaum is basically the same: "Economic Life in Palestine," in *The Jewish People in the First Century*, ed. S. Safrai and M. Stern (Compendia Rerum Iudaicarum ad Novum Testamentum I.2; Assen: Van Gorcum, 1976), 631–700. See my discussion in E. P. Sanders, *Judaism: Practice and Belief 63 BCE – 66 CE* (London: SCM; Valley Forge, Pa.: Trinity Press International, 1992), 157–69.

2. To varying degrees, this is the view of Burton Mack, *A Myth of Innocence* (Philadelphia: Fortress, 1988), 66; Dominic Crossan, *The Historical Jesus: The Life of a Mediterranean Jewish Peasant* (San Francisco: HarperCollins, 1991), 19, quoting and accepting the views of previous scholars; Richard Batey, *Jesus and the Forgotten City: New Light on Sepphoris and the Urban World of Jesus* (Grand Rapids: Baker, 1991). It should be noted, however, that although Crossan joins Mack, Batey, and others in viewing Galilee as strongly hellenized, he joins the scholars in n. 1 above with regard to the economic plight of Galileans: economically, socially, and politically they were exploited, oppressed, and so on. On Jesus as a Cynic or like a Cynic, see F. Gerald Downing, *Jesus and the Threat of Freedom* (London: SCM, 1987); idem, *Christ and the Cynics* (Sheffield: JSOT Press, 1988); Mack, *Myth of Innocence*. Downing's view is that Jesus was a Cynic, while Mack maintains that Jesus was *like* a Cynic. See also Crossan, *Historical Jesus*, 74–88, 340: Jesus established "Jewish and rural Cynicism rather than Greco-Roman and urban Cynicism."

3. John P. Meier, *A Marginal Jew: Rethinking the Historical Jesus*, 2 vols., Anchor Bible Reference Library (New York: Doubleday, 1991, 1994); Sean Freyne, *Galilee from Alexander the Great to Hadrian: 323 BCE to 235 CE* (Wilmington, Del.: Michael Glazier; Notre Dame, Ind.: University of Notre Dame Press, 1980); idem, *Galilee, Jesus and the Gospels: Literary Approaches and Historical Investigations* (Philadelphia: Fortress, 1988).

4. "Annexed" or "occupied": Borg, *Jesus: A New Vision*, 83 (Palestine was annexed in 63 B.C.E.), 137 (Gentile occupiers). Dominic Crossan, *Jesus: A Revolutionary Biography* (San Francisco: HarperCollins, 1994), 89. Even non–New Testament scholars can fall into this error: according to Alan Segal, the Roman "occupation" of the land of Israel began in 63 B.C.E. (*Rebecca's Children* [Cambridge, Mass.: Harvard University Press, 1986], 35.

5. Howard Kee, "Early Christianity in the Galilee: Reassessing the Evidence from the Gospels," in *The Galilee in Late Antiquity*, ed. Lee Levine (New York/

Jerusalem: Jewish Theological Seminary of America, 1992), 15; so also Batey, *Jesus and the Forgotten City*, 56.

6. Correctly Horsley, *Galilee: History, Politics, People*, 113f. Josephus describes Gabinius's actions as creating a government by an "aristocracy" (*War* 1.169f.), by which he means a Jewish aristocracy. Roman senators did not govern these little Palestinian districts. Peitholaus, who was second in command in Jerusalem (probably under Hyrcanus II), was Jewish: see *War* 1.172, 180; *Antiquities* 14.84. Gabinius changed the government to accord "with Antipater's wishes" (*War* 1.178) before he left Syria. Antipater, of course, wished Hyrcanus II to be ethnarch with himself as second in command—as Pompey had previously arranged—and this system was soon restored. A few years after Gabinius's rearrangements of the government, Hyrcanus II and Antipater were in charge (e.g., *War* 1.187; *Antiquities* 14.127–32; ca. 48–47 B.C.E.).

7. Horsley, *Galilee, History, Politics, People*, 116: "Rome . . . did not run its empire by means of occupying troops. . . . The Romans simply terrorized peoples into submission. . . ."

8. See Josephus, *Antiquities* 15.110, where Antony orders Herod to attack the Arabs. The use of client rulers is better seen during the Roman civil wars prior to the battle of Actium: see, e.g., *Antiquities* 14.127–39. When the Jews revolted against Rome, Rome's client rulers contributed troops to aid the Roman cause (*War* 3.68).

9. E.g., Crossan, *Jesus: A Revolutionary Biography*, xii.

10. Crossan illustrates the situation in Jewish Palestine by telling a story about Ireland (*Jesus: A Revolutionary Biography*, 105). Personal conversations have persuaded me that the analogy with Ireland is very important in Crossan's view of first-century Palestine.

11. A. H. M. Jones, *Cities of the Eastern Roman Provinces* (Oxford: Oxford University Press, 1937), 276f.; 2nd ed., revised by various scholars (Oxford: Oxford University Press, 1971), 274f.; more generally, see A. H. M. Jones, *The Greek City From Alexander to Justinian* (Oxford: Oxford University Press, 1940), 79–82.

12. On the population of Strato's Tower and Caesarea, see Josephus, *War* 2.266; *Antiquities* 20.173–76.

13. Crossan claims that Tiberias had "an entirely Greek constitution," though he grants that the population was "primarily Jewish" (*Historical Jesus*, 18). The only element of a Greek city of which we have knowledge is the existence of a council (*boulē*) of several hundred members (Josephus, *War* 2.641).

14. Jones, *Cities* (1937), 277; *Cities* (1971), 276; *Greek City*, 80.

15. There is a review of the literature in Mark Chancey, "The Myth of a Gentile Galilee" (diss., Duke University, 1999), 1–21.

16. Meier, *A Marginal Jew*, 2:721, 1039.

17. Chancey, "Myth," 101–24, esp. 113f., 123f.

18. Martin Goodman, *State and Society in Roman Galilee, A.D. 132–212* (Totowa N.J.: Rowman & Allenheld, 1983), 34–37.

19. So also Meier, *Marginal Jew,* 2:1039f.

20. Numerous scholars have suggested relatively slight differences between Galilean and Judean Jews, e.g., that the Galileans were less strict about the law. This is possible.

21. Horsley, *Galilee: History, Politics, People,* 5, 222–27; idem, *Archaeology, History and Society in Galilee* (Harrisburg, Pa.: Trinity Press International, 1996), ch. 6. In the course of this argument, he misrepresents the view of Lee Levine (*Archaeology,* 133) and declines to discuss the synagogues in Gamla, Herodium, and Masada, all of which must be pre-70, since these areas were not occupied in later years.

22. On the *proseuchē* in Tiberias, see Josephus, *Vita* 227–303; for Dora, see *Antiquities* 19.300–303; for Caesarea, see *War* 2.285–92. There is now a comprehensive account of pre-70 synagogues available in Lee Levine, *The Ancient Synagogue* (New Haven: Yale University Press, 1999), chs. 1–4.

23. For sound remarks on the strength of the Galilean economy, see Douglas Edwards, "The Socio-Economic and Cultural Ethos of the Lower Galilee in the First Century: Implications for the Nascent Jesus Movement," in *The Galilee in Late Antiquity,* ed. Lee Levine (n. 5 above), 55–65, esp. 63.

24. See my *Judaism: Practice and Belief 63 BCE – 66 CE,* ch. 9.

25. Horsley uses my description of the "fourteen tithe system" to imply that Jewish farmers gave fourteen tithes in every seven-year cycle to the priesthood (Horsley, *Galilee: History, Politics, People,* 140).

26. Horsley imagines that once upon a time generation after generation had been supported on the same ancestral land (*Jesus and the Spiral of Violence* [1992], 232).

27. So also Edwards, "Socio-Economic and Cultural Ethos," 62f.

28. Further details regarding some of the topics in this paper will appear in E. P. Sanders, "Jesus' Galilee," in *Pluralism and Conflicts,* ed. Ismo Dunderberg, Kari Syreeni, and Christopher Tuckett (Leiden: Brill, forthcoming 2001).

29. On the Sabbath, see CD 10:14-11:18; *Shabbat* in the Mishnah and Tosefta.

30. CD 10:11; cf. 10:10, on wearing perfume (possibly meaning medicine). In the translation by Michael Wise, Martin Abegg, and Edward Cook (*The Dead Sea Scrolls: A New Translation* [San Francisco: HarperCollins, 1996]), the enumeration is 11:10f.

31. *Shabbat* 14:3f.; *T. Shabbat* 12.8–14.

2

Jesus and the Dead Sea Scrolls

Daniel J. Harrington, S.J.

O NE CAN ARGUE PERSUASIVELY that the two most important topics in biblical studies over the past fifty years have been the quest for the historical Jesus and the Dead Sea discoveries. The two topics have been linked from the late 1940s. A large part of the popular and even scholarly interest in the Dead Sea Scrolls has been due to the expectation that these ancient texts might tell us some very important things about Jesus of Nazareth. In this paper I want to consider what we have learned from fifty years of reflection on Jesus and the Dead Sea Scrolls. After treating the matter in general, I will focus on some particular issues that illustrate what we have and have not learned about Jesus from the Dead Sea Scrolls.

JESUS AND THE DEAD SEA SCROLLS

What we have learned very well is how complex these two topics are and at the same time that it is possible to arrive at some solid results on each topic.

After the Second World War Rudolf Bultmann's position that the historical Jesus is basically unknowable (though Bultmann did write his own Jesus book) and only a presupposition for New Testament theology was challenged by several of his own students. They in turn launched the "new quest for the historical Jesus"—an attempt to recover at least the existential self-consciousness of Jesus. The challenge of the so-called post-Bultmannians was taken up by other scholars, who took as a starting point the research on Jesus' parables done by C. H. Dodd and Joachim Jeremias, and sought to develop criteria for arriving at authentic Jesus material (dissimilarity, multiple attestation, Palestinian coloring, coherence, and so forth).

The nearly contemporary discovery of the Dead Sea Scrolls brought forth in the 1950s many intemperate and even half-baked claims about their significance for Jesus research. Another round of such claims occurred in the early 1990s when the full dossier of Qumran Cave 4 texts was made public.[1] The real contribution of the Dead Sea Scrolls to Jesus research, however, came more slowly and indirectly. The discovery of the Dead Sea Scrolls set in motion a process by which all of Second Temple Judaism has been studied anew and reevaluated. Besides giving us the earliest (by about a thousand years) manuscripts of the Hebrew Bible, the Qumran library provided original Aramaic texts of *1 Enoch* and Tobit, and Hebrew texts of Sirach and *Jubilees* among other works counted among the Old Testament Apocrypha and Pseudepigrapha. Also included among the Qumran scrolls were biblical commentaries (*Pesharim*), previously unknown examples of the rewritten Bible (*Genesis Apocryphon*), and the earliest Targums (of Job and Leviticus). Most startling of all were the previously unknown rules (*Rule of the Community, War Scroll,* etc.) and fragments of the *Damascus Document* (already known from the Cairo Genizah discoveries in the late nineteenth century). These texts pointed to a connection between the Qumran library and the group that inhabited the site between the second century B.C.E. and the First Jewish Revolt (66–73 C.E.).

The discoveries at Qumran and the related sites around the Dead Sea set in motion a marvelously fruitful period of research on Jewish literature and life in the Second Temple period; that is, from the return from exile in the late sixth century B.C.E. to the end of the first century C.E. New editions not only of Dead Sea texts but of practically everything else have been prepared. New handbooks or thorough revisions of old ones have appeared. From this research we have learned about factors that unified Jews in this period (Temple, Torah, and Land) and the diverse ways of being a Jew not only in the Diaspora but also in the Land of Israel.

A second factor that has inspired this great surge of interest in Second Temple Judaism is continuing fascination with the figure of Jesus. Since the

Dead Sea Scrolls have changed scholarly views about Jewish literature and life, it is not surprising that there would be many scholarly efforts at rethinking the place of Jesus within Second Temple Judaism. The emphasis on the Jewishness of Jesus has in turn become the most fruitful area of research on Jesus.

All this attention to the Jewishness of Jesus has yielded some consensus, at least among mainline biblical scholars. That Jesus the Galilean was born, lived, and died in the land of Israel in what we now call the first century C.E. can hardly be doubted. The religious context of his teaching was Judaism in the land of Israel. Jesus was a Jewish teacher. He spoke Aramaic, used the methods of Jewish teachers of his day, and addressed other Jews for the most part (if not exclusively). His teachings about God, God's kingdom, and God's dealings with his people were thoroughly Jewish. About these basic points Jewish and Christian scholars can agree. The further question about precisely what kind of Jew Jesus was tends to fracture the scholarly consensus. Different pictures of Jesus have emerged, depending on what body of literature or historical background he is interpreted against. He has been portrayed in turn as an eschatological prophet against the background of Jewish apocalyptic writings, a political revolutionary against the background of Josephus's reports about rebels against Rome, an Essene against the background of the Dead Sea Scrolls, a Galilean charismatic against the background of rabbinic accounts about Galilean holy men, a Hillelite against the background of the rabbinic Hillel–Shammai debates, and so forth. The point is that our increased knowledge about the diversity of Second Temple Judaism makes it difficult to be certain about Jesus' precise place within Judaism and exactly what kind of Jew he was.[2]

In my opinion the three best Jesus books of the last fifteen years are E. P. Sanders's *Jesus and Judaism,* John P. Meier's *A Marginal Jew,* and N. T. Wright's *Jesus and the Victory of God.*[3] In addition to their great learning and good judgment, these books all are dedicated to emphasizing the Jewishness of Jesus. Sanders places Jesus within Judaism, whereas Meier situates Jesus at the margin of Judaism and Wright goes so far as to present Jesus as the incarnation of Israel's past, present, and future. Those scholars who take Jesus out of Judaism and make him into something like a Cynic philosopher or an idiosyncratic professor of religious studies (as in the Jesus Seminar) do not convince me at all.

If one can speak of something of a consensus in Jesus research, one can also speak of a consensus in Qumran research (though here too there are discordant voices).[4] There is general agreement (on the basis of archaeology, paleography, historical allusions, and Carbon 14 tests) that the Qum-

ran scrolls come from the period between the second century B.C.E. and the
first century C.E. The site of Qumran was most likely a center for a Jewish
religious group rather than a military outpost or a commercial center, and
it is highly probable that there was a relationship between the group that
inhabited the site and the scrolls discovered in the eleven caves surrounding the site. In other words, the Qumran scrolls represent the remnants of
the library of the Jewish religious group that settled there. This group, if we
can judge from the scrolls, was both priestly and apocalyptic in orientation. From the first discoveries the group has been identified as the Essenes
already familiar from the descriptions in the writings of Josephus and
Philo. There are, of course, some discrepancies between what we learn
about the Qumran people and what Josephus and Philo tell us about the
Essenes. And the Essenes may well be an offshoot of the Sadducees. But in
the final analysis the Essene identification has stood the test of some fifty
years of debate. The site of Qumran was most likely an Essene center.
There have been even more precise identifications of it as a "monastery," a
renewal or retreat center, a publishing house, or a cultic center.

Was Jesus an Essene? Again there is a solid consensus (despite some dis-
cordant voices) that Jesus was not an Essene, and certainly not one of the
Qumran type. Galilee is some distance from Qumran, and according to the
Gospels Jesus spent nearly all his life and most of his public ministry in
Galilee. If there was any Essene influence on him, it may have come
through John the Baptist (though this is by no means certain). Moreover,
it is highly unlikely that Jesus read any of the sectarian Dead Sea Scrolls.
And the proposal that fragments of the Mark's Gospel and other New Tes-
tament texts have been found in Qumran Cave 7 has been refuted many
times over, though it has had an unnecessarily long life in some circles.
Jesus was not an Essene.

What significance then do the Dead Sea Scrolls have for Jesus research?[5]
The short answer is that the Dead Sea Scrolls provide parallels to Jesus and
his movement. Being roughly contemporary and in the same general geographical area (the land of Israel), they can help us to know what was "in
the air" in the time of Jesus. So by comparing them with what we know
about Jesus, we can receive some illumination about what were apparently
two independent movements within first-century Palestinian Judaism.

The long answer represents the second part of this paper. Here I will
take ten topics that scholarly research has established as reliable statements
about Jesus, and see how the Dead Sea Scrolls have illumined our understanding of the person of Jesus. Here I will give particular attention to what
many scholars regard as the "sectually explicit" texts in the Qumran

library: the *Rule of the Community* (1QS), the *Thanksgiving Hymns* (1QH), the *War Scroll* (1QM), the *Habakkuk Pesher* (1QpHab), the *Messianic Rule* (1QSa), and the *Damascus Document* (CD). The examples will show how the Qumran scrolls provide pre–New Testament precedents, parallels between two contemporary Jewish movements, and contrasts.

TEN KEY ISSUES

1. Jesus was baptized by John the Baptist.

The historical character of this event is guaranteed not only by the multiple attestations of it in the New Testament but also by the embarrassment that it caused some early Christians (see Matt. 3:14–15). Why would Jesus need to undergo John's "baptism of repentance for the forgiveness of sins" (Mark 1:4)? This event is not something that the early church would have invented.

It appears that Jesus' movement arose from John's movement. While some modern scholars find tensions between the two movements, the evangelists generally present John and Jesus in a close and smooth relationship—to the point that Luke portrays them as cousins. Luke closes off his presentation of John's infancy with a notice that could suggest a link between John and the Qumran community: "And the child grew and became strong in spirit, and he was in the wilderness until the day he appeared publicly to Israel" (Luke 1:80). The mention of "the wilderness"—presumably the Judean Desert—places John at least in the general vicinity of the Qumran community.

John's characteristic ritual of baptism also suggests a link to the Qumran community. Members of the community addressed in the *Rule of the Community* practiced a ritual of spiritual cleansing symbolized by the use of water: "And when his flesh is sprinkled with purifying water and sanctified by cleansing water, it shall be made clean by the humble submission of his soul to all the precepts of God" (1QS 3:8–9). The regular practice of ritual cleansing of body and soul at Qumran is confirmed by the archaeological excavations that uncovered what appears to have been an intricate system of water channels that made these "baptisms" possible.

If there is a historical link between Jesus and the Qumran community, the most likely candidate is John the Baptist. On the one hand, John lived and was active in the same general area and practiced a "baptism" or ritual washing that signified repentance and the forgiveness of sins. On the other hand, Jesus submitted to John's baptism and very likely took John as his mentor. According to John 4:1, Jesus was "baptizing more disciples than John," a point immediately qualified by the evangelist, who claimed that only Jesus' disciples actually baptized. And, of course, John's baptism was surely one of the roots of the early church's baptism "in the name of Jesus."

Nevertheless, the idea that John the Baptist was the conduit between the Qumran community and Jesus is at best an intriguing possibility. The Judean Desert at this time seems to have been home to many Jewish religious movements, and so there is no certainty that John was ever part of the Qumran community or an Essene. And even if he was, John set out on his own path and founded a new movement (see Josephus's description in *Antiquities* 18:116–19). Moreover, John's baptism seems to have been a once-for-all-time moral preparation for the imminent coming of God's kingdom, whereas at Qumran "baptism" appears to have been repeated ritually and was not as closely linked with the eschaton. At any rate, Jesus in turn went his own way from John and practiced a very different style of ministry in the service of the coming kingdom of God (see Matt. 11:16–19// Luke 7:31–35).

However, the possibility of a direct link between Qumran, John, and Jesus has been made a little more plausible by the publication of 4Q521. In this text someone—whether the subject is God, a prophet, or the Messiah is debated—is said to heal the sick, make the blind see, resurrect the dead, and preach good news to the poor. The language clearly reflects Isaiah 35 and 61, with the exception of the added phrase "revive the dead." In responding to the messengers of John the Baptist, Jesus according to Matt. 11:2–6//Luke 7:18–23 also uses the language of Isaiah 35 and 61, with the exception of the added phrase "the dead are raised." It is entirely possible that the added phrase in the Gospels is simply a redactional element to take account of what Matthew and Luke had already said about Jesus in their narratives. But it is intriguing that both 4Q521 and Matt 11:5//Luke 7:22 contain a reference to resurrection not present in their obvious Old Testament sources.

2. *Jesus proclaimed the kingdom of God as both future and present.*
Perhaps the most important result of the quest for the historical Jesus described so well by Albert Schweitzer was the recovery of the apocalyptic nature of the kingdom of God.[6] Through the work chiefly of Schweitzer and Johannes Weiss, scholars of all kinds came to recognize again that the kingdom of God was central in Jesus' teaching and activity, that this kingdom was primarily future (eschatological) and transcendent (God's kingdom), and that his teaching about the kingdom should be understood

against the background of the Second Temple Jewish apocalypses (Daniel, *1 Enoch, Testament of Moses,* 4 Ezra, *2 Baruch,* etc.).

How to interpret the theological significance of Jesus' teaching about the kingdom is another matter. Behind Schweitzer's own analysis seemed to lurk the figure of Jesus as a noble but deluded visionary who mistakenly thought that his death would turn the wheel to bring about God's kingdom on earth. Albert Loisy's famous dictum to the effect that Jesus proclaimed the kingdom but what came was the church has about it a certain truth, whether it be taken as reflecting the process of church history or the persistent attempt by theologians and church leaders to identify kingdom and church. And from Constantine onward there has been a steady stream of kings and political leaders who have sought to identify the kingdom with their empire or state. In our own time, the Jesus Seminar has tried (unsuccessfully in my opinion) to reverse the course of scholarship by systematically separating the historical Jesus from apocalyptic and making Jesus into a nonapocalyptic wisdom teacher.

When Mark came to summarize the preaching of Jesus, he placed the kingdom of God at the forefront: "The time is fulfilled, and the kingdom of God has come near; repent, and believe in the good news" (Mark 1:15). The Lord's Prayer, in which we surely hear the voice (if not the Aramaic words) of Jesus, looks forward to the fullness of God's kingdom in the future: "Your kingdom come" (Matt. 6:10//Luke 11:2). The apocalyptic discourses found in each of the Synoptic Gospels reinforce the future dimension in Jesus' teaching about God's kingdom. Many of the parables, however, give both a future and a present dimension. For example, the parable of the mustard seed (see Mark 4:31-32), while emphasizing the great shrub that the small seed produces, also leaves room for the already present seed and the mysterious process of its growth. Other Gospel sayings affirm the presence of God in Jesus' exorcisms (see Luke 11:20) and in the violence that has been directed at the kingdom of God (Matt. 11:12//Luke 16:16). To those who seek signs of God's kingdom, Jesus proclaims that "the kingdom of God is among you" (Luke 17:21).

The Qumran community shared the hopes of other Jews and of Jesus for the full manifestation of God's kingdom. The presence of multiple manuscripts of Daniel and *1 Enoch* in the Qumran library shows a lively interest in apocalyptic thinking. While none of the "sectarian" works is a full-scale apocalypse, most of these texts contain abundant apocalyptic language and content.

Included in the *Rule of the Community* 3:13–4:26 is what I regard as the best (almost philosophical) analysis of Jewish apocalyptic thinking that I know. It allows us to get behind the poetic images that characterize Jewish apocalyptic literature and helps us to see basic theological assertions of apocalyptic thinking. Intended for the "Master" or Maskil of the community, the discourse concerns God's final visitation (at the last judgment) and explains how humans should act by way of preparation. It establishes at the start the absolute sovereignty of God: "From the God of Knowledge comes all that is and shall be" (1QS 3:15). Next it claims that the world in the present age is under the control of two great figures—the Prince of Light and the Angel of Darkness. Depending on which figure one takes as leader, one is either a "Son of Light" or a "Son of Darkness," and one does the deeds of light or the deeds of darkness accordingly. In the present "the spirits of truth and falsehood struggle in the hearts of men and they walk in both wisdom and folly" (1QS 4:15). At God's visitation, however, there will be vindication for the Sons of Light and destruction for the Sons of Darkness: "God has ordained an end for falsehood, and at the time of the visitation He will destroy it forever" (4:18–19).

This instruction proposes a modified apocalyptic dualism. The dualism extends to the two leaders, all human beings, and all their actions. But it is "modified" in the sense that God's ultimate sovereignty is assumed. It is apocalyptic or eschatological in the sense that the divine visitation will bring the dualism to an end and bring in the fullness of God's kingdom. How the visitation might happen is described in great imaginative detail in the Qumran *War Scroll*, which purports to describe the war between the Sons of Light and the Sons of Darkness.

Within the New Testament the influence of this schema is most obvious in Paul's letter to the Romans and in John's Gospel and letters. But there are at least hints that some elements of it were presuppositions for Jesus' proclamation of the kingdom of God. Jesus surely acknowledged the sovereignty of the God of Israel, whom he called "Father." He surely viewed the present as a time of struggle on a cosmic level in which the authority of God was at stake. And he looked forward to the decisive intervention of God, when his prayer "Your kingdom come" would be answered.

The present or inaugurated dimension of God's kingdom resides in the ministry of Jesus himself. Origen's characterization of Jesus as *autobasileia* ("the kingdom itself") makes the point perfectly. Jesus' claim "I saw Satan fall like lightning from heaven" (Luke 10:18) indicates that the final struggle was already under way and the victory was near. The confession that God raised Jesus from the dead assigns what was regarded as a collective and eschatological event to an individual before the other end-time events might come to pass. And Jesus' wisdom instructions about entering the kingdom concern the kind of behavior that is appropriate against the horizon of the future fullness of God's kingdom.

There are also elements of present eschatology in the Qumran scrolls. The most striking motif is the permeable boundary between heaven and earth. Through prayer (as in the *Songs of the Sabbath Sacrifice*) or through revelatory experiences (as in the *Thanksgiving Hymns,* or *Hodayot*) it is possible for certain humans to enter the heavenly council. And the Qumran wisdom texts—the most prominent of which is 4QInstruction (formerly known as *Sapiential Work A*)—place much of their advice in the framework of "the mystery that is to come/be" (*rāz nihyeh*)—a concept with both eschatological and ethical aspects, and so analogous to the New Testament's "kingdom of God."[7] The Qumran wisdom texts make it clear that, for the Qumran people and other Second Temple Jews, eschatology and ethics went together. These texts caution against efforts at separating the two in the Sayings Source Q and at removing eschatology from the ethical teachings of Jesus (as in the Jesus Seminar).

3. Jesus gathered disciples and formed a community.

From the start the Jesus movement involved a community of disciples. According to the Gospels, Jesus departed from Jewish custom and summoned people to follow him rather than waiting for them to seek him out. These disciples accompanied Jesus and shared his mission of preaching, teaching, and healing in the service of God's kingdom. The Twelve constituted a core group, and within the Twelve special prominence seems to have attached to Peter, James, and John. Beyond this information the Gospels provide little data about the structures and institutions of the earliest Jesus movement.

By contrast, the Qumran *Rule of the Community* (1QS) and the *Damascus Document* (CD) provide much information about the structures and institutions of the Jewish religious movement(s) that they purport to represent. The former text envisions a secluded and almost "monastic" setting, whereas the latter presupposes a community life lived out within the broader society of Jews and Gentiles.

According to the *Rule of the Community,* prospective members presented themselves to enter the group and had to pass through a two-year period of testing before their full acceptance. The Master, or *Maskil,* served as the spiritual leader, and the *Rule* was apparently written for him to use as a handbook. The community had a strong priestly spirituality and practiced frequent ritual purifications and shared meals. The priestly character of the group was reinforced during its meetings and meals, where a strict hierarchical order beginning with the priests was maintained. The penal code deals with offenses ranging from blasphemy to sleeping during the community meetings. Within the group there was an inner circle consisting of twelve men (representing the twelve tribes of Israel) and three priests (representing the three priestly families that traced their ancestry back to Aaron).

The vocabulary and conceptuality of the *Damascus Document* link it to the *Rule of the Community*. But the second part of the work ("the statutes") presupposes a setting in which those who live in the "camps" of the community have contacts with nonmembers. The statutes deal with oaths, lost property, purification, Sabbath observance, and various other topics. The section about the organization of the community (CD 12:19–14:19) gives prominence to the "guardian" of the camp—the official who instructs the congregation, exercises pastoral care, examines candidates, and oversees the affairs of the community. His Hebrew title *mebaqqer* ("overseer") is equivalent to *episkopos* in Greek, the early Christian word for "bishop."

The communities envisioned by the two Qumran rules were stable and structured, whereas Jesus and his disciples were mobile and fluid as they carried out their mission of proclaiming God's kingdom. Thus, in this case there is more contrast than convergence; however, the Qumran rules remind us that Jews in Jesus' time saw no contradiction between lively eschatological expectations and community structures. The two Gospel passages that show the most affinity with these Qumran texts are Jesus' advice to a divided community in Matthew 18 and his farewell discourses in John 13–17. There are even closer affinities with passages in Acts and the Epistles, which presuppose the existence of stable and structured Christian communities.

4. Jesus addressed God as "Father" (Abba).

While this statement has been denied by some feminist interpreters and memorably qualified by James Barr ("Abba isn't Daddy"), it still remains among the corpus of the characteristic teachings of the historical Jesus.[8] Two Qumran texts—neither of which seems to be "sectarian" within the Qumran library—have both illuminated and complicated the matter.

The psalm in 4Q372 1 begins with the address "My Father and my God." The speaker, who seems to be the patriarch Joseph, expresses confidence that God will be kindly disposed toward him and will save him from the hands of the Gentiles. In this text we have solid evidence that in the literature of Palestinian Judaism "my Father" was used as a personal address to God by someone other than Jesus.[9] Moreover, the context is similar to

Jesus' own "*Abba*" prayer in Gethsemane (Mark 14:36), which continues with an expression of confidence in God ("for you all things are possible") and issues in a petition.

Jesus' relationship of special intimacy with God expressed in his address to God as "Abba, Father" has often been regarded as the source of the "Son of God" title. That "Son of God" was not the creation of Greek mythology but rather belongs within Palestinian Judaism has been confirmed by the Qumran Aramaic "Son of God" text (4Q246). In this text someone is described as follows: "The Son of God he will be proclaimed (or: proclaim himself), and the Son of the Most High they will call him." The language sounds very much like the angel Gabriel's annunciation to Mary in Luke 1:32–35.

The problem with 4Q246 comes in identifying the one about whom these statements are being made. It is, of course, hard to resist a "messianic" interpretation or least a reference to the "one like a Son of Man" in Daniel 7 (which is the context of 4Q246). However, it is also possible (given the fragmentary condition of the manuscript) that we are dealing with a historical figure. This possibility in turn raises the question whether the historical figure might be a friend of Israel or an enemy (such as Antiochus IV Epiphanes or Alexander Balas). The ambiguity, however, need not obscure what is most important: the presence of the titles "Son of God" and "Son of the Most High" in a Palestinian Jewish text prior to the composition of the New Testament.

5. Jesus taught: "Love your enemies and pray for those who persecute you."

If not unparalleled, Jesus' teaching about loving one's enemies (Matt. 6:44; Luke 6:27) is unusual and characteristic of his corpus of core teachings. It makes most lists of sayings in the Gospels that can be attributed with confidence to the historical Jesus.

In Matthew's antitheses (Matt. 5:21–48) Jesus' teaching about love of enemies is introduced by a partial quotation of Leviticus 19:18 ("You shall love your neighbor") with a curious addition ("and hate your enemy"), a clause found neither in Leviticus 19:18 nor elsewhere in the Old Testament. When the Qumran *Rule of the Community* was first published, many scholars argued that at last we have an ancient Palestinian Jewish source for "and hate your enemy" in 1QS 1:10. Part of the introduction to the rule and concerned with why candidates should enter the community, the text proposes that by doing so "they may love all the Sons of Light, each according to his lot in God's design, and hate all the Sons of Darkness, each according to his guilt in God's vengeance." In the dualistic framework of the *Rule of the Community* the Sons of Darkness are polar opposites of the Sons of Light and are led by the Angel of Darkness to perform the deeds of darkness. As such they deserve the hatred of God and so the hatred of the Sons of Light.

While it is unlikely that Jesus or Matthew had this specific Qumran text in mind, they may well have been contrasting the love of enemies with the hatred of enemies assumed by those who proposed a rigid separation between the Sons of Light and the Sons of Darkness such as the Qumran people did. Furthermore, if (as seems likely) Jesus himself held elements of the schema of modified apocalyptic dualism, the contrast between his teaching and that of his Qumran contemporaries is all the more striking (though 1QS 10:17–21 does counsel a more tolerant attitude toward enemies). In the context of modified apocalyptic dualism, love of enemies was not a soft universalism ("Can't we all get along?") but rather a challenge to love even those who are profoundly wrong and perpetrate the deeds of darkness.

6. Jesus taught "no divorce."

By the criteria of dissimilarity and multiple attestation, the prohibition of divorce belongs to the corpus of Jesus' authentic sayings. It went against Jewish practice and even against the permission of the scriptures (Deut. 24:1–4), and it appears in Mark (10:2–12), Q (Luke 16:18 and Matt. 5:31–32), and 1 Corinthians (7:10–11). Of course, one must take account of the exceptions introduced by Matthew (see Matt. 5:32 and 19:9) and Paul (see 1 Cor. 7:12–16). One must also ask how Jesus intended this teaching to be taken—whether as an ideal, a legal principle, a protection for women, a temporary measure (in the face of the coming kingdom of God), or whatever else. Nevertheless, it is fair to say that Jesus taught "no divorce."

The famous rabbis Hillel, Shammai, and Aqiba all assumed the validity of divorce and argued about the grounds for divorce (see *m. Gittin* 9:10). However, two Qumran texts are now often cited as background for Jesus' radical teaching about divorce.[10] *Damascus Document* 4:20–5:6 declares that "taking a second wife while the first is alive" is fornication. As in Mark 10:2-12, the biblical justification is the order of creation enunciated in Genesis 1:27: "Male and female He created them." The problem here, however, is that the topic at issue seems to be polygamy rather than divorce and remarriage, as the rest of the passage with its concern to explain David's several wives suggests.

The *Temple Scroll* (11QTemple) contains a long section about the king.

With regard to marriage (57:15–19), the ideal king should marry within the royal household of Israel. The text goes on to say: "He shall not take another wife in addition to her, for she alone shall be with him all the time of her life." Again the "no divorce" interpretation is problematic. The first problem is whether the directive applies to anyone beyond the king. And the second problem is whether it refers to polygamy on the king's part or to divorce and remarriage, though here the evidence for "no divorce" is stronger.

If one or both of these two texts are interpreted as teaching "no divorce," then they supply parallels to Jesus' teaching on the matter. If they refer simply to polygamy, then they highlight once more the distinctive content of Jesus' teaching.

7. Jesus' meals were anticipations of life in God's kingdom.

In Mark's Gospel one of the first complaints made against Jesus by his opponents is that he eats with sinners and tax collectors (see Mark 2:16). There can be little doubt that the opponents were on to something here, since what some call "open commensality" (or inclusive table fellowship) seems to have been a characteristic and controversial feature of Jesus' public ministry. It is against the background of these meals that we have to understand the feedings of the five thousand (Mark 6:35–44 parr.) and the four thousand (8:1–10 parr.), as well as the Last Supper (14:22–25 parr.). The final sentence in the "words of institution" about Jesus not drinking wine again "until that day when I drink it new in the kingdom of God" (14:25) places the Last Supper and all of Jesus' meals in an eschatological context. These meals anticipate life in God's kingdom. Presided over by Jesus the Messiah, they are previews of the messianic banquet.

A Qumran document designated 1QSa and entitled the *Rule for the Last Days*, or the *Messianic Rule*, provides a description of a community meal that features bread and wine, and involves the participation of two anointed figures or "messiahs." In this meal the priestly and hierarchical character of the group is clear. The "Priest"—previously identified as the "Priest-Messiah"—is the first to bless the bread and wine. Then the Messiah of Israel (a David figure) extends his hand over the bread, and all the congregation utters a blessing. In the double messianism presupposed by this text the Priest-Messiah has precedence. The meal itself has a ritual character and serves as a preview or anticipation of the messianic banquet to be celebrated in the fullness of God's kingdom.

The description of the meal is followed by a very important directive: "It is according to this statute that they shall proceed at every meal at which at least ten are gathered together" (1QSa 2:21-22). The directive suggests that every community meal carries messianic significance and eschatological overtones and somehow anticipates and points forward to the fullness of God's kingdom.

And so it appears that the meals of the Messiahs of Aaron and David and of Jesus the Messiah take place as signs or even sacraments of the fullness of God's reign. The fundamental difference, of course, comes in the "open commensality" of Jesus. His meals are open especially to marginal persons such as tax collectors and sinners, whereas the meals described in 1QSa seem to be closed community meals—for members only. Moreover, at Jesus' meals there is only one presiding Messiah, who combines the roles of the priestly and Davidic Messiahs.

One minor but curious point in Mark's account of the feeding of the five thousand (Mark 6:35–44) may also be illumined by comparison with the Dead Sea Scrolls. That Jesus has the crowd "sit down by companies" and "in groups of hundreds and fifties" (6:39–40) is reminiscent of the concern with communal order found not only in the *Rule for the Last Days* but also in the *Rule of the Community* and in the *War Scroll.* I know of no better explanation for this curious and apparently extraneous detail.

8. Jesus displayed ambivalence about the Jerusalem temple.

While Luke presents the Jerusalem temple as the house of Jesus, there are important indications in the Gospels that the historical Jesus stood in tension with the temple. Indeed, these tensions contributed greatly to his death.

Whatever Jesus intended by the incident commonly called the "cleansing of the temple" (Mark 11:15–19 parr.), it surely was viewed as a prophetic commentary on the inadequacy of the present Jerusalem temple: "You have made it a den of robbers." In Jesus' hearing before the Sanhedrin, the first charge against him concerned his stance toward the temple: "We heard him say, 'I will destroy this temple that is made with hands, and in three days I will build another, not made with hands'" (Mark 14:58). These passages suggest some tension between Jesus and the temple.

The conventional explanation for the founding of the Qumran community also involves tension with the Jerusalem temple. According to this widely accepted theory, a Jewish group devoted to the temple took exception to the Maccabean usurpation of the high priesthood and control of the temple, and so went out to the Judean Desert to await the divine intervention that would restore the authentic priesthood and purify the temple.

Even apart from this historical hypothesis, the Qumran texts themselves suggest that tension with the Jerusalem temple led the community to view itself as "the House of Holiness for Israel, an Assembly of Supreme Holiness for Aaron" (1QS 8:5–6), and to substitute prayer and good works for the traditional temple sacrifices: "And prayer rightly offered shall be as an acceptable sacrifice of righteousness, and perfection of way as a delectable free-will offering" (1QS 9:5).

Other manuscripts in the Qumran library reinforce the impression of tension with the Jerusalem temple. The work known as *Miqsat Ma'ase HaTorah* (MMT) contains a list of legal disagreements between the Qumran people and those in charge of the Jerusalem temple in large part about the temple and its rituals. The *Temple Scroll* provides a verbal blueprint for a new, ideal temple and temple city when the right people (God and the Sons of Light) will be in charge of it again. The New Jerusalem texts specify the dimensions of various features of the city. And the Apocalypse of Weeks in *1 Enoch* (chaps. 91 and 93)—a work well represented in the Qumran library—displays disappointment with the Second Temple.

Both Jesus and the Qumran people were critical about the Jerusalem temple. In the case of the Qumran group, the hostility had its roots in their historical experience and constituted one of the major reasons for their existence. In the case of Jesus, the hostility is more difficult to specify. Although some explain it in terms of traditional Galilean resentment against Judea and Jerusalem or Jesus' personal shock at the commercialization of the temple, the Gospels may well also be correct in presenting it as part of Jesus' own theological vision of "worship in spirit and truth" (John 4:24).

9. Jesus was crucified under Pontius Pilate.

At the time of Jesus' death in 30 C.E. Judea was administered by the Roman prefect or governor named Pontius Pilate. He (as well as his predecessors and successors) used crucifixion as a punishment for rebels and slaves. Its cruelty and public character were intended to deter further popular uprisings. While some of the Jewish leaders in Jerusalem ("the chief priests and elders") may have encouraged and collaborated with Pilate, the ultimate legal responsibility for Jesus' death lay with Pilate.

Two texts from the Qumran library supply information about crucifixion. The *Pesher on Nahum* (4Q169) refers to "the furious young lion" (the Seleucid king Demetrius III Eukairos, who ruled from 95 to 75 B.C.E.) as the one who "hangs men alive" and to "a man hanged alive on a tree" (frgs. 3–4 i 6–7). The "hanging" most likely refers to crucifixion. The *Temple Scroll* 64:6–13 prescribes crucifixion as the appropriate punishment for those who betray the Jewish people ("they shall hang him on the tree") and for apostates who had committed capital crimes ("you shall hang him on the tree"). Here we must assume that Jewish officials had some part in these crucifixions. The latter text has led both Jewish and Christian scholars to reopen the discussion about possible Jewish involvement in Jesus' death, though the ultimate legal responsibility of Pontius Pilate for Jesus' crucifixion seems well established.

The claim that 4Q285—a Qumran "holy war" text"—contains a pre-Christian reference to a suffering messiah depended on a faulty translation of the Hebrew text (as "they will kill him") and a neglect of the biblical context (Isa. 10:34–11:1). With a proper translation ("the Br[anch of David] will kill him") and a respect for the biblical context, the Messiah appears to be the agent rather than the subject of violence. He is a piercing messiah rather than a pierced messiah (see John 19:37).

10. The movement initiated by Jesus continued after his death.

The New Testament evidence for the resurrection of Jesus consists of testimonies by Jesus' followers that he appeared to them, the tradition that his tomb was empty, and the remarkable energy displayed by his followers in spreading the gospel and building up the church. The early Christians looked back on the earthly Jesus and proclaimed that their teacher and guide had been raised from the dead.

In many of the "sectarian" texts among the Qumran manuscripts a figure known as "the Teacher of Righteousness" or "the Righteous Teacher" is prominent. According to the *Damascus Document*, God "raised up for them a Teacher of Righteousness to guide them in the way of His heart" (1:11). According to the *Pesher on Habakkuk*, God made known to the Teacher of Righteousness "all the mysteries of His servants the Prophets" (7:4–5) and would deliver the community "because of their suffering and because of their faith in the Teacher of Righteousness" (8:2–3).

The *Hodayot*, or *Thanksgiving Hymns*, may be the most important source for information about the Teacher of Righteousness, if we follow the line of interpretation that their abundant first-person-singular language refers to the Teacher. If that interpretation be allowed, then in the *Hodayot* we would have the spiritual "memoirs" of the Teacher ("I") with their references to his experiences of divine revelation, the opposition from "lying interpreters" and "those who seek smooth things" (probably the Pharisees), his participation in the heavenly council, and his pastoral solicitude for other members of the group.

Jesus and the Teacher of Righteousness were central figures in two Jewish religious movements that flourished in late Second Temple times. Both were regarded (and surely regarded themselves) as recipients of divine revelation about the "mysteries " of God and his kingdom. Both suffered from opponents within the Jewish people. Both provided the wise teaching and spiritual energy that ensured that their memories would be preserved and that their movements would continue.

On the basis of these parallels some have argued that Jesus was really the Teacher of Righteousness, or that the Teacher provided the precedent and pattern for Jesus. There are, however, some important differences. The Teacher of Righteousness was a Jewish priest active in Judea around 150 B.C.E. who shaped a Jewish sect which in turn preserved his memory. Jesus of Nazareth was a Jewish layman active principally in Galilee around 30 C.E. who shaped a religious movement that eventually became open to Jews and to Gentiles which in turn preserved his memory. But Jesus' movement went further and proclaimed "that Christ died for our sins in accordance with the Scriptures, and that he was buried, and that he was raised on the third day in accordance with the Scriptures, and that he appeared to Cephas, then to the Twelve" (1 Cor. 15:3-5). That is a very important difference.

POSTSCRIPT

Raymond E. Brown, S.S., whose memory this colloquium honored, was a pioneer in using the Dead Sea Scrolls wisely and well in his research on the New Testament. His 1958 doctoral dissertation directed by William Foxwell Albright at Johns Hopkins University treated the Semitic background of the term "mystery."[11] It was one of the first scholarly works to incorporate the newly discovered Qumran materials, and after more than forty years it stands up remarkably well. In 1958–59 Brown worked in Jerusalem on preparation of the concordance for the Qumran Cave 4 texts. This tool—a model of accurate and patient labor—has been essential in facilitating the research that has led to the full publication of the manuscripts. In his commentaries on the Johannine writings and on other parts of the New Testament, Brown could always be counted on to compare the pertinent Qumran texts carefully and creatively. In the study of Jesus in the Gospels and the Dead Sea Scrolls as in so many other areas, Brown showed us the way toward responsible and accessible scholarship.

NOTES

1. For basically complete translations of the nonbiblical texts, see Florentino García Martínez, *The Dead Sea Scrolls Translated: The Qumran Texts in English* (Leiden: Brill, 1994); Geza Vermes, *The Complete Dead Sea Scrolls in English* (London: Penguin, 1997); and Michael Wise, Martin Abegg, and Edward Cook, *The Dead Sea Scrolls: A New Translation* (San Francisco: HarperCollins, 1996).

2. See my essay "The Jewishness of Jesus: Facing Some Problems," *Catholic Biblical Quarterly* 49 (1987): 1–13.

3. E. P. Sanders, *Jesus and Judaism* (Philadelphia: Fortress, 1985); John P. Meier, *A Marginal Jew*, vol. 1, *Rethinking the Historical Jesus;* vol. 2, *Mentor, Message and Miracles* (New York: Doubleday, 1991, 1994); and N. T. Wright, *Jesus and the Victory of God* (Minneapolis: Fortress, 1996).

4. For reliable introductions, see Frank M. Cross, *The Ancient Library of Qumran*, 3rd ed. (Minneapolis: Fortress, 1995); Joseph A. Fitzmyer, *Responses to 101 Questions on the Dead Sea Scrolls* (New York/Mahwah, N.J.: Paulist, 1992); Lawrence H. Schiffman, *Reclaiming the Dead Sea Scrolls: The History of Judaism, the Background of Christianity, the Lost Library of Qumran* (Philadelphia: Jewish Publication Society, 1994); Hartmut Stegemann, *The Library of Qumran: On the Essenes, Qumran, John the Baptist, and Jesus* (Grand Rapids: Eerdmans, 1998); and James C. VanderKam, *The Dead Sea Scrolls Today* (Grand Rapids: Eerdmans, 1994).

5. For collections of classic essays on the Dead Sea Scrolls and the New Testament, see Krister Stendahl, ed., *The Scrolls and the New Testament* (1957; New York: Crossroad, 1992); Jerome Murphy-O'Connor, ed., *Paul and the Dead Sea Scrolls* (1968; New York: Crossroad, 1990); James H. Charlesworth, ed., *John and the Dead Sea Scrolls* (1972; New York: Crossroad, 1990); and James H. Charlesworth, ed., *Jesus and the Dead Sea Scrolls* (New York: Doubleday, 1993). See also Joseph A. Fitzmyer, *The Dead Sea Scrolls and Christian Origins* (Grand Rapids: Eerdmans, 2000).

6. Albert Schweitzer, *The Quest of the Historical Jesus* (New York: Scribner's, 1910; Baltimore: Johns Hopkins University Press, 1998).

7. See my *Wisdom Texts from Qumran* (London/New York: Routledge, 1996).

8. James Barr, "Abba Isn't Daddy," *Journal of Theological Studies* 39 (1988): 28–47.

9. Eileen Schuller, "The Psalm of 4Q372 1 Within the Context of Second Temple Prayer," *Catholic Biblical Quarterly* 54 (1992): 67–79.

10 Joseph A. Fitzmyer, "The Matthean Divorce Texts and Some New Palestinian Evidence," *Theological Studies* 37 (1976): 197–226.

11. Raymond E. Brown, *The Semitic Background of the Term "Mystery" in the New Testament* (Philadelphia: Fortress, 1968). For my sketch of Brown's life and achievements, see "Raymond E. Brown: A Teacher for Us All," *America* 179/5 (1998) 5–6.

3

From Elijah-like Prophet to Royal Davidic Messiah

John P. Meier

*I*N A COLLOQUIUM OF DISTINGUISHED SCHOLARS such as this, it is customary for a presenter to hold forth with a ringing defense of
some particular pet theory. Like an academic Jesse Ventura, the presenter challenges any and all comers to dispute his unshakable position. I am afraid that, in this essay, I will appear instead to be an
academic wimp. For, rather than stoutly defending some infallible
position, this essay aims at soliciting suggestions from my colleagues
on how to solve a conundrum that continues to puzzle me as I search
for the historical Jesus. What has put me in this quandary?

In a sense, the ultimate cause of the quandary is the whole approach
taken in my multivolume series *A Marginal Jew*. Instead of starting
with a clearly articulated thesis about the historical Jesus, a grand theory that I then proceed to prove in detail amid gasps of amazement
that my a priori theory should match the empirical data so perfectly, I
have groped along from one specific question to another, slowly con-
structing a mosaic of Jesus one fragment at a time.[1] Now and then I
have found myself humming "Lead kindly light, amid the encircling
gloom, lead Thou me on."

To be sure, my approach has an obvious advantage: one is not
tempted to impose an all-purpose, one-size-fits-all theory on scattered, heterogeneous, recalcitrant data that never quite jibe with the

grand thesis. The downside of my approach, however, became apparent by the end of volume 2 of *A Marginal Jew*. After pursuing clues step by step through the first two volumes, I had stumbled across a portrait of the historical Jesus that I had not expected, a portrait that I was not looking for, a portrait that I did not especially want, and a portrait that I did not know what to do with once I had it. It was the portrait of an itinerant, miracle-working, eschatological prophet from northern Israel, clothed in the mantle of Elijah.[2]

As I worked ever so slowly through volume 3 of *A Marginal Jew* (to be published in the fall of 2001), the portrait of the Elijah-like, miracle-working, eschatological prophet seemed to be confirmed, at least in its basic outlines. Jesus' imperious call to disciples to follow him quite literally, the radical demands made on those disciples, and the overall prophetic and eschatological context of his ministry and message fit the picture I was stuck with at the end of volume 2. To be sure, volume 3, which deals with the various relationships the Jewish Jesus had with different Jewish groups in first-century Palestine, shows that the complex and enigmatic figure called Jesus cannot be reduced in simplistic fashion to this model of the eschatological prophet like Elijah. The tense relations and disputes with rival groups such as the Pharisees and the Sadducees, the detailed teaching on certain aspects of the Mosaic Law, the proverbs and aphorisms that belong to the wisdom tradition of Israel, and the vague intimations of some kind of structure or organization among his followers—all these facets of the historical Jesus remind us that he cannot be conveniently pigeonholed in any single category.

And yet the massive amount of the Gospel record dedicated to Jesus' miracle working, his itinerant prophetic ministry, his eschatological message, and even his narrative parables, which belong more to the prophetic than to the sapiential mode of speaking, argues that the Elijah-like eschatological prophet is probably the best single model for the historical Jesus, however much it must be supplemented by elements from the legal and sapiential traditions of Israel. The Elijah-like prophet is not the total explanation of the historical Jesus, but it is, in my view, the dominant pattern.

But this conclusion, arrived at by a lengthy step-by-step process through the first three volumes, has created major problems for me as I envision the fourth and final volume of *A Marginal Jew*—in other words, as I reach the end of the story. Inevitably, the end of the story forces one to confront a very different portrait of the historical Jesus from that of the Elijah-like prophet: Jesus the royal Davidic Messiah who winds up being crucified by the Romans under the hermeneutically recycled title King of the Jews. So, on the one hand, the Elijah-like, miracle-working, eschatological prophet in the first three volumes; on the other hand, the royal Davidic Messiah in volume 4. How do these starkly divergent portraits of the historical Jesus fit together? Or do they? Is one of these portraits—or possibly both of these portraits—simply wrong?

For the sake of argument, let us accept for the moment the claim that the model of the Elijah-like miracle-working eschatological prophet is a basically correct portrait of the historical Jesus—though obviously not the full portrait. If we accept such a portrait, however partial, the question then must be: How do we get from this portrait to that of a royal Davidic Messiah—or should we? As I try to think through this question in this essay, perhaps it would be helpful to divide this overall question into two distinct questions:

1. Is the image of the royal Davidic Messiah an idea that the historical Jesus or at least some of his historical disciples actually applied to Jesus during his public ministry? Or is it a portrait applied to Jesus only after his death by the faith of the early church? I stress here that the question is put in terms of a claim (explicit or implicit) made by the historical Jesus or his disciples during the public ministry. I am not asking whether Jesus was in biological fact descended from David, and I am not asking primarily whether Jesus' family made such a claim about their genealogy—though that question may be raised secondarily along the way. I emphasize this point because all too often the historical and theological question has been fought out primarily in terms of biological reality or genealogical claims made by Jesus' family—an approach that I think is a methodological mistake.[3]

2. If this image of the royal Davidic Messiah does go back to the historical Jesus or his disciples during the public ministry, how does it cohere—or does it cohere—with the portrait of Jesus as the Elijah-like eschatological prophet?

QUESTION ONE

Does the Idea of Jesus as a Royal Davidic Messiah Reach Back to the Days of the Historical Jesus, or Is It a Creation of the Early Church?

Survey of the Data

Any attempt to claim that the idea of Jesus as the royal Davidic Messiah or the prophesied Son of David of the end-time goes back to the ministry of the historical Jesus must face the firm opposition of eminent scholars such as John J. Collins. To be sure, Collins argues at length in his book *The Scepter and the Star* that the idea of the Messiah as a Son of David or a Davidic king was the picture of the Messiah most commonly held by Palestinian Jews around the time of Jesus.[4] Yet Collins rejects the position that Jesus or his disciples during the public ministry applied such a portrait to Jesus.[5]

Salva reverentia, I think instead that the usual criteria of historicity invoked in Jesus research favor the view that the picture of Jesus as Son of David or royal Davidic Messiah goes back to the historical Jesus. Chief among these criteria is the criterion of multiple attestation of sources and forms. The idea of Jesus as royal Davidic Messiah enjoys wide attestation in many different strata of New Testament material. This wide attestation is all the more striking when one compares it, for instance, to the isolated state of the tradition affirming Jesus' birth in Bethlehem. The latter idea is unambiguously attested only in ch. 2 of Matthew's Gospel and ch. 2 of Luke's Gospel. Curiously, the idea of Jesus' being born in Bethlehem finds no echo, resonance, or repetition later on in these two Gospels or in the Acts of the Apostles. One can easily see how birth in Bethlehem might be judged a theologoumenon arising out of the prior idea of Jesus' Davidic sonship. The reverse process is hardly likely. Son of David is the earlier and much more widely attested motif. To appreciate this point, let us review briefly the varied New Testament venues of the Son of David or royal Davidic Messiah tradition as applied to Jesus.

1. As long as we have been looking at the infancy narratives of Matthew and Luke, let us begin at this unpromising locus.[6] The infancy narratives are the New Testament passages that inculcate most emphatically Jesus' Davidic sonship, but they are also the ones most quickly dismissed as highly legendary and midrashic, yielding next to no reliable historical data. Even if one accepts this judgment in a global way, the presence of the Son of David tradition in the two infancy narratives does contribute to our quest, however indirectly. One may note, for instance, the difference between the Son of David tradition and the birth in Bethlehem tradition even with the narrow confines of the infancy narratives. While birth in Bethlehem is restricted to parts of ch. 2 in both Matthew and Luke, the Son of David tradition permeates the two infancy narratives in such different types of pericopes as Jesus' genealogy, the Benedictus of Zachary in Luke 1 (vv. 69 + 78–79), the annunciations to Joseph and Mary respectively, the birth in Bethlehem traditions of Matthew 2 and Luke 2, and the visit of the Magi with the concomitant wrath of Herod in Matthew 2.

If we grant, as the majority of scholars would, that Matthew and Luke did not know each other's Gospels, and if we grant that behind the infancy narratives in both Gospels lay earlier motifs, traditions, or primitive stories, then one must conclude that the Son of David theme existed in these infancy traditions before they were taken over and developed by the two evangelists.[7] Indeed, when one considers how the Son of David theme pervades and undergirds so much of the infancy traditions in both Gospels, one may wonder whether the Son of David theme acted as the very matrix of the infancy narratives. Be that as it may, we may reasonably suppose that separate traditions about Jesus' birth, already imbued with Davidic motifs, circulated in the Matthean and Lucan communities before the two Gospels were written. Hence these varied infancy traditions, in whatever fragmentary form, existed around or before 70 C.E. Thus, this glance behind the two infancy narratives suggests the presence of the idea of Jesus as Son of David in a special and isolated, not to say unique, stream of early Christian thought, one quite distinct from most other New Testament streams of tradition.

In fairness, I should note that not all critics see the references to David in the infancy narratives as early tradition. Christoph Burger, for instance, tries to show that all the designations of Jesus as Davidic in the infancy narratives are traceable to the redactional activity of Matthew and Luke and hence stem ultimately from the impulse of the references or allusions to Jesus as Son of David in Mark.[8] However, Burger is able to arrive at this conclusion only by the strategic move of treating the two infancy narratives in isolation from each other. Once one examines all the thematic parallels found in the two infancy narratives, Burger's position becomes very dubious. It is difficult to imagine that, simply by a happy coincidence, Matthew and Luke, working independently of each other, both added Davidic references or allusions at exactly the same points in their material: to their genealogies (though Luke's lies outside his infancy narrative proper), to their stories of the angel's annunciation of Jesus' virginal conception, and to their stories of Jesus' birth in Bethlehem. These agreements between the two evangelists' largely divergent infancy narratives argue for the presence of Davidic references in the pre-redactional traditions.

Indeed, even after Burger removes the supposedly redactional references to David, he never supplies a satisfying explanation of why both the pre-Matthean and pre-Lucan infancy narratives, independently of each other, placed the birth of Jesus of Nazareth in Bethlehem. The only reasonable explanation is that, from the beginning of the legend of the birth in Bethlehem, this motif was prompted by the idea of Jesus' Davidic descent. Thus, despite Burger's attempt to avoid the obvious conclusion, the very existence of the pre-Matthean and pre-Lucan infancy traditions testifies that the idea of Jesus as Davidic circulated in Matthean and Lucan traditions prior to the work of the two evangelists and independently of their knowledge of Mark.

2. From these pre-Matthean and pre-Lucan traditions, let us move back to the earliest days of Christianity, soon after Jesus' crucifixion and the church's Easter experience. Thanks to Paul's need to authenticate himself and his gospel to the Christians in Rome, we have access to a remarkable pre-Pauline confessional formula cited in Rom. 1:3–4. The formula, couched in terms and ideas uncharacteristic of Paul, is neatly balanced in the manner of the antithetical parallelism found in Hebrew poetry. In my opinion,[9] the core of this formula tells us that Jesus was

(1) *born of the seed of David according to the flesh*
(2) *appointed Son of God according to a spirit of holiness*

and then the formula adds a clarifying half-line as a concluding comment:

at the resurrection of the dead.

While many an article has been written on this short formula, and much could be said about every single word in it, just a few points interest us here.[10] First, in writing the Epistle to the Romans, Paul is in the unusual and uncomfortable position of writing to a Christian community that he has not founded and has never visited, a community with a strong Jewish background, some of whose members may be wary of an apostle proclaiming a law-free gospel to the Gentiles.[11] Paul is at pains to affirm the authenticity of his gospel and his apostleship. His citation of a primitive Jewish-Christian creedal formula right in the *praescriptio* of the letter displays his diplomatic strategy from the start.[12]

Second, we can draw an intriguing corollary from our first point: in the mid-50s of the first century, some twenty-five years after the crucifixion, Paul can take for granted that a Christian community at some distance from his mission field, a community he has never visited, taught, or addressed by letter, a community with perhaps a different theological orientation than Paul's own churches, would nevertheless recognize a particular creedal formula and see it as a token or guarantee of true Christian faith on the part of a person it had never met. One must therefore suppose that the creed enshrined in Rom. 1:3–4 was formulated quite early on, was disseminated among various churches very quickly, and was generally accepted as a terse summation of faith in Jesus Christ.[13]

All the more striking, then, is the concentration of the first of the two parallel lines on the fact that Jesus was *genomenou ek spermatos Dauid kata sarka*, that is, that Jesus was "born from the seed [literally, 'sperm'] of David according to the flesh." Obviously, this is first of all a theological affirmation: the mortal, earthly life of the Jew named Jesus, his life "according to the flesh [i.e., in the sphere or field of force of the flesh]," is, despite its lowliness, already being evaluated positively as the life of the royal Davidic Messiah. The Old Testament background for this evaluation and for the whole formula is probably Nathan's prophecy to David in 2 Sam. 7:12–14. The correspondence with some Greek words in the Septuagint form of the text (2 Kgdms. 7:12–14) is striking: "I will raise up your seed [i.e., David's seed]" = *anastēsō to sperma sou;* "he shall be my son" = *autos estai moi eis huion.* The pre-Pauline formula thus indicates that death and resurrection are not the absolute beginning of Jesus' theological importance or function in salvation history.

Yet one must attend to how this theological affirmation in the first part of the formula is made. It does not use the title "Son of David," which would have provided a more exact parallel to the corresponding title "Son of God" in the second line. Rather, the first line makes its theological evaluation with the periphrastic and blatantly biological phrase, "born of the seed of David in the realm of weak, corporeal, mortal human existence," that is, the flesh. Thus, in a Jewish-Christian creedal formula reaching back to the earliest days of Christianity, Jesus' Davidic sonship is already understood in biological terms and given positive theological meaning. Needless to say, I am not claiming here that this theological affirmation is actually true in a historical and biological sense. But it is remarkable that such a claim was being made so early on and was so widely known in the pre-Pauline tradition of the early church. Indeed, one should underscore the point that Jesus' Davidic sonship is a pre-Pauline tradition rather than part of Paul's own characteristic theology. Apart from this traditional formula, Paul never directly mentions Jesus' Davidic sonship in any of the undisputed epistles.[14]

The very early nature of this formula and the fact that Paul cites it when writing to a Christian community that may have had strong ties with the Jerusalem church raise a tantalizing side issue—though I stress that it is not the major point of this presentation. Paul knew personally and had had theological as well as practical dealings with James of Jerusalem, whom Paul refers to deferentially as "the brother of the Lord." James and apparently other members of Jesus' family were prominent members of the Jerusalem church; and, as is clear from the dispute between Peter and Paul at Antioch, James was respected and influential in churches outside Palestine. Indeed, Paul mentions that some of Jesus' brothers (including James?) went on missionary journeys to other churches. Granted the fact that both the pre-Pauline formula and members of Jesus' family circulated and were well known in various parts of the first-generation Christian church, is it likely that James, other members of his family, or other Christians who knew his family, would have acquiesced in the claim of Davidic descent preserved in Rom. 1:3 if they knew it to be false or at least previously unheard of?[15] This train of thought raises the possibility that Jesus' family did claim to be of Davidic descent; but, since the possibility must remain fairly speculative, I prefer not to make it the major focus of this presentation or its main line of argument.

3. That Davidic sonship was enshrined in early creedal formulas rather than in the detailed theological elaboration of the faith developed by Paul or by the later Pauline school is confirmed by a similar formula cited by the author of the Pastoral Epistles (hereafter, the Pastor) toward the end of the first century. As is well known, the Pastoral Epistles are studded with snatches of Christian hymns and creeds. A clear example of the latter is the at-first-glance-puzzling text found in 2 Tim. 2:8:

> *Remember Jesus Christ*   *mnēmoneue Iēsoun Christon*
> *raised from the dead,*   *egēgermenon ek nekrōn*
> *from the seed of David*   *ek spermatos Dauid*

That the Pastor is apparently citing some sort of tradition rather than theologizing on his own is suggested not only by the laconic, balanced, two-line summary of what the Pastor, speaking in the person of Paul, calls "my gospel" but also by the total absence of any mention—let alone theological evaluation—of David elsewhere in the Pastorals.[16] Now it is conceivable that the Pastor simply knew the Epistle to the Romans and recycled the formula he found in Rom. 1:3–4. However, the formulation of 2 Tim. 2:8 is curious if it is simply lifted out of Romans.[17] In 2 Tim. 2:8, the title "Son of God" is absent, no participles are used to describe two distinct events (birth and resurrection) taking place within salvation history, and most strikingly "from the seed of David" is placed after "raised from the dead." In fact, so strange and jarring is the order that some modern English translations presume to correct the Pastor by putting "from the seed of David" first, as in Rom 1:3–4.[18]

Such a solution is mistaken; indeed, it misses an important point. The Greek text of 2 Tim. 2:8 has a specific theological meaning that differentiates it from its not-quite-identical twin in Rom. 1:3–4.[19] "From the seed of David" signifies in both texts that Jesus is the royal Davidic Messiah. But while Romans associates this dignity with Jesus' earthly life, 2 Timothy associates it with his resurrection. For the Pastor, or at least for the tradition he cites, it was the resurrection that constituted Jesus' ascent to the royal throne of Israel; the resurrection installed Jesus in the office of royal Davidic Messiah. Nothing is said about his already possessing this dignity during his earthly life, and no higher designation such as "Son of God" trumps Davidic descent. Consequently, the form of the tradition in 2 Timothy, with its singular focus on the resurrection and with "from the seed of David" as the sole designation of the risen, enthroned Messiah, strikes some critics as more primitive, from the viewpoint of tradition history, than the two-part form found in Romans. Romans 1:3–4 reflects instead a two-stage Christology, in which Jesus' earthly life is already given positive theological value that is messianic but that is nevertheless elevated, surpassed, or transcended by enthronement as the royal Son of God at the resurrection.

I grant that this interpretation of 2 Tim. 2:8 and its origins is not the only way the tradition history might be read, though I think it the more likely reading. To be sure, one might argue that, instead of 2 Tim. 2:8 reflecting an even earlier stage of the pre-Pauline formula than that reflected in Romans, 2 Timothy represents a secondary contraction of the formula's focus to death and resurrection alone, in keeping with Paul's own preferred emphasis. At the very least, though, I think it clear that 2 Tim. 2:8 is not simply a case of a later Pauline author rewriting a text he has read in Romans. More likely, 2 Tim. 2:8 represents an alternate version of the "from the seed of David" formula that circulated in various forms, early and late, in the oral tradition of the first-century church. As I have indicated, my own view is that 2 Tim. 2:8 probably represents, from the tradition-historical perspective, a form of the tradition earlier than the one Paul cites. This very primitive form might well have reached back to the earliest Jewish Christians in Jerusalem—though, admittedly, that is a point I cannot prove.

4. It may not be by accident that we find the same formula, "from the seed of David," in an ambiguous text in John. In John 7:42, the puzzled

crowd wonders about the possible identity of Jesus. Some affirm that he is
the Messiah.[20] Others object with the rhetorical question: "Has not Scripture said that the Messiah comes from the seed of David [*ek tou spermatos
Dauid*] and from Bethlehem, the town where David was?" As often in John,
one is sure that the text is ironic, but one is not entirely sure where the
irony lies. Is the crowd unconsciously speaking the truth about Jesus, or is
it instead right about the unimportant earthly origins of Jesus while missing entirely the all-important truth of his heavenly origins?[21] In any case,
7:42 makes clear that the "from the seed of David" tradition—connected
here with birth in Bethlehem!—is witnessed in a back-handed way even in
John, though whether it is accepted, ignored, or rejected by John remains
uncertain.[22] Indeed, since this close connection between the Messiah of
Davidic descent and birth in Bethlehem is not common in Jewish texts
composed around the turn of the era,[23] John most likely is reacting in one
way or another to a stream of Christian tradition that Matthew and Luke
have also used—though in a very different fashion—in their infancy narratives. At the very least, then, the tradition of Jesus as Son of David was
known in the Johannine tradition or community before the Fourth Evangelist wrote his Gospel.

5. When we move to the Marcan tradition, three pericopes bunched
together in the pre–passion narrative chapters of Mark 10–12, are relevant
to our quest:

(a) In Mark 10:47–48, the blind Bartimaeus cries out repeatedly to
Jesus, "Son of David, have mercy on me." Jesus responds positively to his
cry by healing him of his blindness; indeed, Jesus says explicitly: "Your faith
has healed [or: saved] you." Obviously, by these words as well as by the act
of healing, Jesus is accepting rather than rejecting the designation "Son of
David," with which the blind man expressed his trust (i.e., his faith) in
Jesus. I have argued in volume 2 of *A Marginal Jew* that this story goes back
to an event in the life of the historical Jesus. But, for the moment, suffice it
to say that most commentators would allow that the story is not a pure creation of Mark but reflects a pre-Marcan miracle story.[24]

(b) A fortiori, the story of Jesus' entry into Jerusalem in Mark 11:1-10 is
not a pure Marcan creation, since the basic incident is paralleled in the
somewhat different and independent account in John 12:12-19.[25] However, an acclamation of Jesus that explicitly mentions David is—not surprisingly—lacking in John's version of the event. (In general, John's Gospel
evinces no interest in a Son-of-David Christology.) Nevertheless, the
Johannine crowd does hail Jesus as "King of Israel." In addition, the Johan-

nine Jesus, like the Synoptic one, goes out of his way to ride into Jerusalem on an ass; and John, like Matthew (but not Mark or Luke), seeing here a fulfillment of prophecy, directly cites Zech. 9:9 (with a touch of Zeph. 3:16), a prophecy with Davidic overtones: "Fear not, daughter Zion! Behold, your king comes, seated on the foal of an ass." Hence, in the whole context of John's presentation of Jesus' entry, a royal-Davidic atmosphere is not entirely lacking—a point that is all the more striking, given John's lack of interest in a Son-of-David Christology.

In Mark's and Matthew's versions, there is an explicit reference to David, though the evangelists differ in its formulation. In contrast, Luke pointedly drops the reference to David he found in Mark. Luke instead has the crowd of disciples acclaim Jesus simply as the king who comes in the name of the Lord (Luke 19:38)—though, granted the strong Davidic emphasis in the Lucan infancy narrative and later on in some of the kerygmatic sermons in Acts, Luke probably understands "king" in a Davidic sense. Matthew, in keeping with his interest in Son-of-David Christology, has the crowds shout "Hosanna to the Son of David" (21:9, 15).[26] Matthew and Luke thus react in different ways to the vague reference in Mark 11:10, where the crowd cries out in a surprising formulation, "Blessed be the coming kingdom of our father David." Here Jesus' royal Davidic sonship is implied, but not expressly stated. David is said to be the father of all the Jews who await the restoration of his kingdom—though, doubtless, Mark, in the light of the preceding story about Bartimaeus (10:46–52), understands this to take place through Jesus the Son of David. In sum, granted the multiple attestation of the "triumphal" entry in the Marcan and Johannine traditions, and granted that both streams of the traditional story have an explicit royal theme, with at least implicit Davidic overtones, it seems probable that the idea of a royal entry of Jesus into Jerusalem with some allusion to Davidic descent is not just a Marcan redactional creation but lies farther back in the Marcan tradition.

(c) The third Marcan reference to Davidic sonship, likewise an oblique one, is found in Jesus' rhetorical question about how the Messiah could be the Son of David when David in Psalm 110 calls him "Lord" (12:35–37). In the Marcan context, which evaluates positively Bartimaeus's cry to the Son of David for mercy, Jesus' question probably indicates that the Messiah is not only David's son but also David's Lord.[27] Whether, as an isolated pre-Marcan tradition, Jesus' rhetorical question intended instead to reject Davidic sonship is debatable, though I tend to think that Mark may have preserved the original sense of the pericope.[28] This point, admittedly, is disputed among scholars. Opinions range from the view that Jesus' question is simply an exegetical conundrum meant to reduce his enemies to silence, without any position being taken by Jesus, to the view that Jesus intends a positive answer that, at the same time, corrects a political and military conception of the Son of David, such as we see in *Psalms of Solomon* 17, to the view that Jesus rejects the idea that the Messiah must be the Son of David.[29]

In any event, this pericope, like the other two in Mark, is generally taken to be not a pure Marcan creation but a pre-Marcan tradition. Likewise pointing to the pre-Marcan origin of all three pericopes is the absence of any great interest in the title Son of David in Mark's redactional theology, which focuses instead on the titles Messiah, Son of God, and Son of Man.[30] The upshot of these observations is that most probably some stories presenting Jesus as a Son of David or Davidic Messiah existed in the pre-Marcan gospel tradition in circulation prior to 70 C.E.

6. As for Matthew, apart from his infancy narrative, it is difficult to know whether references to Davidic sonship are anything but redactional expansions on what he has inherited from Mark. This is the most likely explanation of the two blind men crying out, "Have mercy on us, Son of David," in Matt. 9:27. It is simply a doublet of Matt. 20:29–34, which in turn is the Matthean reworking of the Marcan story about Bartimaeus.

Less clear is the case of Matt. 12:22–23. Here, at the beginning of Matthew's version of the Beelzebul dispute, Jesus exorcises and heals a demoniac who is blind and mute. The crowd reacts by wondering, "Could this possibly be the Son of David?" The basic stock of this exorcism story seems to have come from Q, since on the one hand it is paralleled in Luke's version of the beginning of the Beelzebul dispute, while on the other hand it is absent from Mark's version of the same dispute. However, Matthew alone mentions the question of the crowd concerning the Son of David. This question could therefore be simply Matthean redaction, since Matthew clearly shows an interest in Jesus as the "therapeutic" Son of David. Still, as Dennis Duling points out, Jewish tradition around the turn of the era exalted Solomon, the literal Son of David, as a great exorcist.[31] So it is possible that the Son-of-David Christology in Matt. 12:23, connected as it is with exorcism rather than with Davidic dynastic claims, may represent early Jewish-Christian tradition or even the view of some Jews during Jesus' ministry. But the case remains unclear. Consequently, the only clear example of Son-of-David Christology in Matthew that is not derivable from Mark's Gospel or from Matthean redaction is in the infancy narrative. In brief, apart from the infancy narrative, the M tradition, as far as we can distinguish it from Matthean redaction, is surprising in that it offers not a single unambiguous case of Son-of-David Christology.

7. Technically, the special Lucan tradition (L) in the Gospel of Luke does have one case of Son-of-David Christology outside the infancy narrative, but the one instance does not contribute anything really new to the fund of data. In the Third Gospel, unlike the First, the genealogy that traces Jesus' line back to David (though through nonreigning descendants of David) is not located in the infancy narrative. It appears at the end of Luke 3 (vv. 23–38), between the baptism of Jesus and the temptation narrative. Hence, technically it counts as a special L tradition outside the infancy narrative that affirms Jesus' Davidic lineage, but in a very different way from Matthew's genealogy. While Matthew, with an emphasis on Jewish roots and history, traces Jesus' lineage down from Abraham, Luke ascends back from Jesus all the way to Adam, intimating the Lucan theme of universal salvation. Accordingly, in Matthew's genealogy, David is singled out as a pivotal point in the genealogy. He stands at the end of the first group of fourteen generations (1:6a) and at the beginning of the second group (1:6b; cf. 1:17); he is also the only figure specifically called "the King" (1:6). Luke, on the other hand, makes no differentiations as he ascends from Jesus to Adam; David, not adorned with any title, is simply one name among all the rest. Thus, the emphasis on David in the Lucan infancy narrative finds no echo in the Lucan genealogy. In Luke, unlike Matthew, infancy narrative and genealogy most likely reflect different strands of tradition.

In the Acts of the Apostles, we do not find a great deal of explicit Son-of-David Christology.[32] In a number of passages in Acts, David's role seems to be that of a prophet who foretells various events in the life of Jesus. There are, however, a few passages that present Jesus directly in a Davidic light:

(a) In Acts 2:30, in his Pentecost sermon, Peter states that David, being a prophet, knew that God would set one of his descendants on his throne.

(b) Likewise, in Paul's sermon in the synagogue at Pisidian Antioch (Acts 13:16-41), a sermon that in some respects parallels Peter's Pentecost sermon, Paul affirms that from David's seed (*apo tou spermatos* in v. 23, once again the key phrase from the early tradition, as we have seen in Rom. 1:3–4 and 2 Tim. 2:8), God has brought forth to Israel a savior, namely, Jesus. In raising Jesus from the dead, God has fulfilled the promise he made in Isa. 55:3, "I will give you the holy and sure blessings of David."

(c) There may also be a fleeting reference to Davidic sonship in James's speech at the Council of Jerusalem in 15:16. In arguing for the circumcision-free mission to the Gentiles, James uses a citation from LXX Amos 9:11, which speaks of God rebuilding the tent of David, which has fallen. But one would catch a reference to Jesus as Son of David here only from the clearer references in Luke-Acts.

In sum, we can say that a Christology that explicitly connects Jesus with David is not the most prominent type of Christology in Acts. The title Son of David never appears (unlike Lord, Christ, and Son), and there are only two clear references to Davidic descent, one in a sermon by Peter and one in a sermon by Paul. While the present form of these kerygmatic speeches is obviously Luke's work,[33] the very rarity of the references to Davidic sonship in Acts, which is not a pressing theological concern for the book as a whole, may argue for pre-Lucan tradition. This is especially true of the occurrence of the traditional phrase "from the seed" of David in Paul's sermon, echoing as it does Rom. 1:3–4 and 2 Tim. 2:8. Moreover, the thrust of both Paul's sermon in Pisidian Antioch and Peter's Pentecost sermon is the identification of the enthronement of the Davidic Jesus with the event of the resurrection. There is nothing in Acts about the significance of Jesus' status as Son of David from the virginal conception onwards, as inculcated in Luke 1, nor is there any significance given to his Davidic status during his earthly ministry, such as we find in Luke's Gospel in the healing of the blind beggar, which Luke 18:35–43 takes over from Mark.

Yet, despite the connection made by the two kerygmatic speeches in Acts, the passion narrative of Luke's Gospel does not notably connect the theme of Davidic sonship with Jesus' death and resurrection,. The connection Acts makes between Davidic status and the resurrection, especially with the phrase "from the seed of David" used in the very sermon that applies Psalm 2 to the resurrection, is a connection we see not in Luke's Gospel but rather in the primitive pre-Pauline formula preserved in 2 Tim. 2:8. Hence, far from the link between Davidic status and resurrection being the result of Luke's redactional activity in Acts, it seems rather to be an echo of early Jewish-Christian preaching.[34]

8. The Epistle to the Hebrews, not surprisingly, does not explicitly consider the question of Jesus as Son of David, since Hebrews has other theological fish to fry. The basic theological thesis of Hebrews is that Jesus the Son of God (the traditional title known and accepted by the author's community) is also the one true (high) priest of the new covenant (the author's special contribution to New Testament Christology). As he elaborates in ch. 1 the first christological point, namely, that Jesus is the Son of God

enthroned in heaven, the author cites seven Old Testament texts.[35] One of these is the promise God makes to David through the prophet Nathan in 2 Sam. 7:14: "I shall be his father, and he shall be my Son" (Heb. 1:5). Granted the image of Jesus as the Son of God enthroned in power that pervades ch. 1, the use of Nathan's prophecy to David intimates that Jesus, precisely as enthroned king and Son of God, is also the descendant of King David.

This idea receives further support from what the author says almost in passing in 7:14. In ch. 7, the author is arguing at length that Jesus is a priest not in the line of the Levitical priests of the old covenant, but rather in the line of the mysterious priest-king Melchizedek. In the course of his convoluted argument, the author remarks, almost as an aside (7:14), "For it is evident that our Lord has arisen from [the tribe of] Judah, and in reference to this tribe Moses said nothing about priests." When we connect this remark with the presentation of Jesus as the Son and king who fulfills the prophecy of 2 Sam. 7:14, it seems likely that our author presupposes but has no particular interest in articulating the idea that Jesus as Messiah and Son belongs not only to the tribe of Judah but also specifically to the house of David.[36] Since our author does not trace Jesus' priesthood through that house, he does not pursue that avenue of thought.

9. Finally, in a very different stream of New Testament Christology, the book of Revelation refers three times to Jesus as descended from David. Interestingly, though, neither the title Son of David nor the traditional phrase "from the seed of David" is used. Rather, steeped in Old Testament traditions and texts reinterpreted through the prism of early Jewish-Christian apocalyptic, the author of Revelation evokes Jesus' Davidic origins and authority with a series of striking metaphors.[37]

(a) In 3:7, in the letter to the church of Philadelphia, Jesus is said to be the one who holds the key of David, who opens and no one closes, who closes and no one opens. This is apparently an allusion to Isa. 22:22, though what is said in that text of Eliakim, a majordomo of the palace of the Davidic king, is here applied to the eschatological Davidic king himself, now risen from the dead.[38] The reapplication of the image is typical of the author's highly imaginative recycling of Old Testament metaphors and traditions.

(b) In 5:5, with a startling combination of clashing images, the risen Jesus is presented as the lamb who was slain, who is nevertheless described as the victorious lion from the tribe of Judah, the root (i.e., descendant) of David, who can open the heavenly book with its seven seals.[39]

(c) The affirmation of 5:5 is repeated in an expanded form toward the conclusion of the book of Revelation. In 22:16, Jesus speaks directly to the audience in the first person: "I am the root and the stock of David." Interestingly, this is the only time in the New Testament that Jesus—here, obviously, the risen Jesus speaking through the seer John—refers to himself in the first person as a descendant of David.[40] Everywhere else in the New Testament, Davidic descent is attributed to Jesus by the author speaking in his own person, by a traditional formula the author cites or uses, or by a character in a Gospel narrative.

What should be emphasized here is that, within the range of New Testament thought, the book of Revelation represents a notably different stream of theology and Christology. It is the only book in the New Testament canon that, as a whole, belongs to the apocalyptic genre. To be sure, it has theological contacts with parts of other New Testament books, from the eschatological discourse in Mark 13 to the apocalyptic scenarios in 1 and 2 Thessalonians. All the more remarkable, therefore, is the fact that the eschatological passages in other New Testament books that parallel Revelation do not have a Son-of-David Christology. The picture of Jesus as the definitive, eschatological descendant of David in a detailed apocalyptic scenario is proper to the book of Revelation. In this, it represents a different strand of New Testament tradition.

In summary, the multiple attestation of sources for the attribution of Davidic sonship to Jesus is quite striking in its breadth: pre-Pauline formulas contained in both an authentic Pauline and a deutero-Pauline epistle, pre-Marcan narratives taken over by Mark, a special L tradition connected with the public ministry, special M and L traditions that pervade the two different versions of the infancy narrative, two kerygmatic sermons in the Acts of the Apostles, an implicit reference in the Epistle to the Hebrews, and scattered references in the book of Revelation. Not surprisingly, this wide range of sources goes hand in hand with a wide range of literary forms: short creedal formulas, lengthy genealogies, annunciation narratives of Jesus' birth, exorcism and healing narratives from the public ministry, other scattered narratives from the final days of Jesus in Jerusalem, Christian homilies, and revelatory speeches of or about the risen Jesus.

What is likewise striking in this survey is that most of this material is contained in earlier traditions taken over by the authors of the New Testament books. Apart from Matthew, there are few if any instances where the redactor of a New Testament book has created *ex nihilo* a reference to Jesus as Son of David, descended from David, or the Davidic Messiah. Indeed, in some cases, such as Rom. 1:3–4, 2 Tim. 2:8, and the Epistle to the Hebrews, the presence of the motif in the tradition is apparently the major or sole reason why it appears in the New Testament book. In these cases, the author of the book has no particular interest in it and makes nothing of it. In short, we are faced with an astonishing phenomenon. The idea of Jesus' Davidic descent reaches back in many forms to the earliest days of the church and continues to be referred to throughout the first and second Christian generations down to the relatively late books of Acts and Revelation. Yet no New Testament author makes Davidic descent the main focus of his redactional Christology.

An Attempt to Explain the Data

This remarkable phenomenon demands an adequate explanation. Two explanations readily present themselves: (1) The idea that Jesus was of Davidic descent circulated already among some of Jesus' disciples and/or members of his family during the public ministry. The events surrounding his death, the claim of his resurrection, and the development of the early church tended to give this idea new meaning and theological weight, but did not create the idea *ex nihilo.* (2) The opposite view, quite popular in recent decades, is that the tradition of Jesus' Davidic sonship did not exist during the public ministry of the historical Jesus. Rather, it arose from the events surrounding his crucifixion and the subsequent belief in his resurrection. To put it in a provocative way: Jesus was born Son of David not on Christmas Day but on Easter Sunday.[41] Which of these two theories explains more adequately all the data we have just examined?

The second alternative is favored by many scholars today, notably Christoph Burger, but it is vulnerable to a number of objections. Before we accept it, we should consider the following points:

1. It is doubtful that early Christian belief in the resurrection of Jesus, interpreted as his appointment or enthronement as Messiah or Son of God, is a sufficient explanation of his identification as Son of David or, more primitively, "of the seed of David." As is now clear from detailed inventories of the Qumran and intertestamental literature, "Messiah" and "Son of God" were vague and flexible titles. They were not necessarily tied—in fact, they were rarely explicitly tied—to descent from King David. Rather, putting the Qumran and intertestamental literature together, we

can see that "Messiah(s)" or "anointed one(s)" could apply to a priestly Messiah, a royal Messiah, both a royal and a priestly Messiah, some heavenly being, or to the prophets of old. Likewise Son or sons of God remained an elastic term, ranging from angelic beings to some sort of ruler in an apocalyptic context. Nothing demanded that "Messiah" or "Son of God" carry a reference to a son of David. Such a reference is found at times, such as in the *Psalms of Solomon* (see *Psalm* 17), but this connection is more the exception than the rule. In *Psalm* 17, the Son of David is primarily a mighty political and military ruler, who rids Israel of its Roman oppressors and their Herodian puppet. This lies at the antipodes from a Galilean prophet crucified by Roman might.

2. Some but not all Jews around the turn of the era hoped for a future resurrection of the dead (at least a resurrection of the righteous or the martyred dead) at the end of the present age. Nowhere in such apocalyptic hopes do we find articulation of the idea that some key eschatological ruler will die and rise within the ongoing course of human history. *A fortiori,* there is no idea of the death and resurrection of a royal Davidic Messiah occurring within this present age.

3. In the face of these negative observations, some critics turn to the crucifixion of Jesus and the grounds for his crucifixion by the Romans as the ultimate explanation of the application of Davidic sonship to Jesus. The reasoning is straightforward and simple. We have multiple attestation in both the Marcan and Johannine passion narratives that Jesus was condemned by the Romans on the charge of claiming to be King of the Jews. This charge was enshrined in the *titulus crucis* affixed to Jesus' cross. From the historical fact of Jesus' being crucified as King of the Jews *plus* the early Christian belief in Jesus as the risen and enthroned King and Messiah, there naturally arose the belief in Jesus as Son of David.

The fatal flaw in this chain of reasoning is that there was nothing in Jewish experience or recent history around the turn of the era that would have automatically translated the title King of the Jews into Davidic sonship. Jews of the first centuries B.C.E. and C.E. had known a number of types of kings of the Jews. None of them had been Davidic. Hasmonean priestly rulers from Aristobulus I onwards had presented themselves as kings of the Jews, but they were of the tribe of Levi, not Judah, and of the house of Aaron, not David. Herod the Great, technically a Jew but of Idumean ancestry, was hardly Davidic, and he never claimed to be so. The temper of the times is shown by the fact that he tried to gain legitimacy in Jewish eyes by marrying into the Hasmonean dynasty through Mariamme I, and not into any Davidic family. Herod the Great's grandson, Herod Agrippa I, was just as much King of the Jews as his grandfather and just as little a Davidic scion. Some of the insurgents during the First Jewish War apparently assumed royal trappings or claims, but we hear of no claim made by them to be of Davidic descent.

In brief, Jews around the turn of the era experienced many real or would-be kings of the Jews on the stage of Palestinian politics and military action. But not one of them was or claimed to be or was generally thought to be a son of David. To put the point as sharply as possible: in the real political history of the first centuries B.C.E. and C.E. in Palestine, being king of the Jews had nothing to do with being a son of David. There was nothing in the title King of the Jews, applied to a concrete historical Jew of the time, that would automatically make his fellow Jews think that he was of Davidic origin.

Hence the pressing question: In the earliest days of the Christian movement, why would Christian Jews—that is, Palestinian Jews for Jesus—attribute Davidic sonship to a Galilean prophet from the obscure hill town of Nazareth, a prophet who wound up being crucified by the Romans? Neither his crucifixion on the charge of being King of the Jews nor their belief in his being the Messiah risen from the dead would naturally generate the further belief that he was a Son of David.

Consequently, the popular explanation of the genesis of the idea of Jesus' Davidic sonship on the basis of his crucifixion proves, upon testing, to be surprisingly weak. We are faced, then, with two facts: (1) On the one hand, the idea that Jesus was from the seed of David or son of David was widespread in many strata of Christian tradition, both early and late. (2) On the other hand, there was nothing in Jewish experience at the turn of the era, in Jesus' crucifixion as King of the Jews, or in early Christian faith in his resurrection as Messiah that would automatically generate this further Christian belief in his Davidic sonship. Therefore, given the multiple attestation of sources and forms, I think we must conclude that the first explanation I suggested is the more likely one: namely, the crucified and risen Jesus was believed to be Son of David because the historical Jesus was thought to be of Davidic descent by at least some of his followers and/or family during his public ministry.[42]

Please notice my careful formulation of the first explanation: Jesus was thought to be of Davidic descent by some of his followers or family. We are not talking here about verifiable facts of biology, genealogies that can be checked by archivists, or DNA that can be tested in a laboratory. Indeed, the chapters of Matthew and Luke that focus most intensely on Davidic descent, namely, the infancy narratives, make clear that they do not consider Jesus' sonship to be a matter of biological connection. In the faith perspective of the infancy narratives, Jesus is virginally conceived of Mary, who is never said in the New Testament to be of Davidic descent. In fact, Luke apparently thinks that Mary is of the tribe of Levi (Luke 1:5 + 36). Instead, both Matthew and Luke, independently of each other, base Jesus' Davidic descent on Joseph, his legal but not his biological father. For Matthew in particular, Joseph's pivotal role is his acknowledgment of Jesus as his legal son, thus placing Jesus in a Davidic genealogy that Jesus otherwise would not have had. Thus, even the Gospel texts that most emphatically inculcate Jesus' Davidic sonship do not make this sonship a matter of physical descent or biological connection.

QUESTION TWO

How Does the Idea of the Historical Jesus as Son of David Cohere with the Self-Presentation of Jesus as the Elijah-like Eschatological Prophet?

Granted all we have seen thus far, I would suggest we reverse the usual cause-and-effect explanation of the idea of Jesus' Davidic sonship. Far from Jesus' crucifixion as king or belief in his resurrection causing belief in his Davidic sonship, the chain of causality is more likely in the opposite direction. That Jesus was thought to be a son of David during his public ministry was a contributing factor in bringing him to his cross.

Here we touch upon one of the greatest problems—if not the greatest—of historical Jesus research: the cause or causes of Jesus' condemnation and crucifixion as King of the Jews. How does one explain how an itinerant Galilean prophet, faith healer, teacher of the Law, and spiritual guide wound up being crucified by the Romans in Jerusalem on the charge of being King of the Jews? The specific problem of how one gets from an Elijah-like prophet to a crucified king of the Jews simply sharpens and narrows the focus of this much more basic problem.[43] I will probably have to spend the whole of volume 4 working out a full answer. But, for the sake of discussion, permit me to list briefly just some of the elements that must go into a full answer:

1. There is no one cause or reason for Jesus' crucifixion. Like most pivotal events in history that have far-reaching effects, Jesus' crucifixion resulted from the convergence of a number of different factors or causes.

2. Among the many relevant factors we might list the following:

(a) Jesus was an itinerant prophet moving regularly back and forth between Galilee and Judea (and specifically Jerusalem). In these movements, he was usually followed by a band of personally chosen disciples and at times by large and enthusiastic crowds.

(b) This following would have been especially large when, as a pious Jew, he would go up to Jerusalem for the great feasts of pilgrimage. Let me say as an aside that, here, as in a number of other areas touching upon Jerusalem, John's Gospel, rather than the Synoptics, probably gives the more accurate picture.[44] After all, as an eschatological prophet seeking to address and prepare all Israel for the coming kingdom of God, Jesus naturally wished to proclaim his message to as many of his fellow Israelites as possible. What is the use of being a preacher or teacher if you have no audience or class? And during the great pilgrimage feasts, where would Jesus find ready-made crowds to hear him if not in Jerusalem, especially in the temple area?

(c) Jesus' regular activity in Jerusalem and the temple during the feasts would have increasingly annoyed and worried the priestly aristocracy that ran the temple and a great deal of daily Jewish life in Roman-controlled Judea. Their concern would have been shared by their allies among the lay aristocrats as well as by the Roman authorities, who expected the priestly oligarchy to maintain order among their coreligionists. To give them help and incentive, as well as to give them a warning, the Romans stationed soldiers for crowd control in the Fortress Antonia, just north/northwest of and overlooking the temple complex. In addition, during the great feasts, the Roman prefect came up to Jerusalem with his auxiliary troops to help control the massive crowds pouring into the city. We should bear in mind, therefore, that both Pontius Pilate during his ten-year tenure and Jesus of Nazareth during his two- or three-year ministry had the habit, for different reasons, of going up to Jerusalem for the great feasts. Hence Jesus' final stay in the city may not have been the first time Pilate heard about this popular and potentially trouble-making prophet.[45] We should also recall in this connection Josephus's presentation of the death of John the Baptist.[46] The problem that proved fatal for John was not that John actually stirred up his followers to open rebellion. The mere fact that he attracted many enthusiastic followers caused the fearful tetrarch Herod Antipas to decide that a preemptive strike was better than a major crisis down the road.

3. As far as the Jewish authorities in Jerusalem were concerned, the mixture of many religious roles in the one figure called Jesus would have made him seem all the more curious, disturbing, or downright dangerous:

(a) After all, they were faced with an oral prophet, reminiscent of the oral prophets of the Jewish Scriptures, who proclaimed the imminent end of the present order of things.

(b) Worse still, this message of imminent end and new beginnings for Israel was summed up in the explosive phrase and symbol "the *kingdom* of God."

(c) Moreover, Jesus claimed that in some way the coming definitive rule of God over Israel was already present and active in his own ministry, notably in his supposed miracles, which naturally tended to legitimize and accredit him in the eyes of the common people as a true prophet. What with the idea that Solomon, the son of David, was the exorcist par excellence, and what with other ideas circulating about miracles being connected with the time of the Messiah (4Q521; *Psalms of Solomon* 17),[47] the miracles of Jesus the Elijah-like prophet might easily be interpreted as well in terms of the miracles of Jesus the Solomon-like Son of David. Popular religion is not as worried about mixing categories that are theoretically quite distinct as are academic theologians.

(d) In addition to Jesus' claim to authority as prophet and miracle worker, there was also the implicit claim to be a divinely authorized teacher of proper observance of the Mosaic Law. One need only think of Jesus' teachings on divorce (Mark 10:9, 11 parr.), oaths (Matt. 5:33–37), and legal retaliation (Matt. 5:33–37), as well as his willingness to have his followers contravene the sacred duty of honoring and supporting one's parents, especially with decent burial (Matt. 8:21–22 par.).[48]

(e) Other aspects of Jesus' halakic teaching and practice did not revoke commandments or institutions enshrined in the Mosaic Law, but they certainly would have raised eyebrows among the pious. One need only think of his table fellowship with toll collectors and sinners,[49] his clearly nonascetic approach to eating and drinking well (e.g., Matt. 11:18–19), his rejection of voluntary fasting (Mark 2:18–19),[50] his liberal views on Sabbath observance (e.g., Mark 2:27), and in general his personal lifestyle as an itinerant celibate prophet who nevertheless had in his traveling entourage female supporters who accompanied him around Galilee apparently without benefit of husbands or chaperones (e.g., Mark 15:40–41; Luke 8:1–3).

Some of these points, especially in regard to personal behavior, are obviously less important than Jesus' major deeds and message. But all of them flowing together in one public person over two short years tended to create a highly combustible compound. It was the whole *Gestalt* that was so disturbing, and there was something somewhere in this *Gestalt* to disturb just about everyone. The whole was greater than the sum of its parts.

Yet is there enough here to explain Jesus' crucifixion as King of the Jews? Especially when faced with this question, one must grant that some elements of the *Gestalt* were more decisive than others. Perhaps among the most aggravating and fatal elements were (a) proclaiming an imminent new order of things precisely with the set slogan "the *kingdom* of God"; and (b) having as the chief proclaimer of this new kingdom a Jew thought to be a son of David and followed as such by large crowds up to Jerusalem for the great feasts.

Still, we have to ask: Why was Jesus executed at this particular Passover of 30 C.E. rather than at any other feast when Jesus was in Jerusalem? I think the answer can be discerned in the three symbolic, prophetic actions, two public and one private, that Jesus performs during what turns out to be his final stay in Jerusalem. All three actions proclaimed to the public and/or his disciples that he saw himself and was presenting himself to Israel as something more than just another prophet in the long line of prophets.[51]

1. First, there is the so-called triumphal entry into Jerusalem. One need not think of the entry in terms of some Hollywood-style spectacle or a political rally on the Mall in Washington. Indeed, such a huge mob action would have occasioned immediate intervention by the authorities. One need only think of Jesus arranging a formal entry into the Davidic capital amid acclamation by his followers. If we may take as historical the detail that Jesus chose to ride into the capital on a donkey—a detail attested by both the Marcan and the Johannine passion traditions (Mark 11:1-7; John 12:14)—then Jesus may have been consciously acting out the prophecy of Zech. 9:9: "Shout for joy, O daughter of Jerusalem, behold your king shall come to you . . . meek and riding on an ass."[52] While the Gospel accounts differ, they all speak of references to kingdom or kingship. However restricted to Jesus' disciples this prophetic demonstration may have been, we should remember that the Roman imperial system made abundant use of spies, especially under the ever-suspicious Tiberius.[53] I doubt that Jesus was unaware of that danger. It may be that he intended his action to be deliberately provocative. More than that, to a Jew imbued with a prophetic mind-set, the symbolic act of a prophet did not simply foretell future events; it actually unleashed the course of such future events.[54] This point may not have been lost on the temple establishment.

2. Even more openly provocative, and more aimed directly at the temple establishment, was the second prophetic-symbolic act of Jesus, the so-called cleansing of the temple, which seems to have followed close upon his triumphal entry.[55] Combined with various sayings about the destruction of the temple and/or Jerusalem (e.g., Mark 13:2; 14:58; John 2:19; Matt. 23:38 || Luke 13:35a; Luke 19:41–44), this so-called cleansing is to be seen most likely as another prophecy-in-action. Whether or not it contained a call for reform of the present temple, it was more than just that.[56] It foretold and, in Jesus' eyes, unleashed the coming destruction of the Second Temple, rebuilt by Herod the Great.

Once again, as with the triumphal entry, we should think not of a mass demonstration but rather of a symbolic action of Jesus carefully staged in the presence of his followers. A biblical comparison might be Jeremiah's breaking of the potter's flask, which acted out his prophecies of woe against the temple (Jer. 19:1–15) and brought him swift punishment from the temple authorities (Jer. 20:1–6). The very choice of the temple as the venue for his prophetic action signals that Jesus was consciously seeking to confront the temple authorities, in a final, definitive fashion, with his eschatological message of the coming kingdom. Not only had the Son of David taken symbolic possession of his capital city; he had proceeded to express symbolically his control over the temple whose prototype had been built by the Solomon, the Son of David. As long as any son of David had reigned in Jerusalem, he had effectively controlled the temple, and now a son of David was reasserting his claim in the face of the priestly aristocracy and in the name of the coming kingdom that would spell an end to the present system of temple worship.

The royal-yet-prophetic act of cleansing the temple thus ties in perfectly with the royal-yet-prophetic act of the triumphal entry. Both were consciously provocative street theater. By both actions, Jesus was seeking a final confrontation with the Jerusalem authorities. Taken together, they were historically the proximate causes of Jesus' arrest.[57] The eschatological prophet clothed in the mantle of Elijah had finally decided to clothe himself as well, by metaphorical actions, in the royal robes of the Son of David. And he decided to do so right at the gates and in the temple of Jerusalem, as he proclaimed the end of the present order embodied in the temple and its worship. This was probably the straw that broke the camel's back. This was why this Passover feast would turn out to be the last one for Jesus. And this was why the final accusation would be claiming to be King of the Jews. In a sense, Jesus had no one to blame but himself for what happened. Having already stressed the theme of the *kingdom* of God in his preaching, he now chose to push into public view the idea of his royal, Davidic status, precisely in the volatile context of Passover in Jerusalem.

3. That Jesus sensed the dangerous nature of his provocation and the mortal danger in which it placed him seems likely from the third and final symbolic-prophetic act he performed in those last days of his life, namely, his words and gestures over bread and wine at his last meal with his disciples (Mark 14:22–24 parr.; 1 Cor. 11:23–25). Whatever the exact wording and meaning of his statements over the bread and wine that he shared with his disciples at that meal, his gestures and interpretive words seem to indicate that he sensed his coming death and saw it as somehow part of his prophetic, eschatological mission to Israel.[58] How precisely he saw it integrated into his ministry is hard to say, if indeed he himself thought about such a question. Perhaps he saw himself as the last in the line of Israel's rejected and martyred prophets. Such an idea would have been more than theological theory for Jesus. His mentor, John the Baptist, had embodied the fatal destiny of prophetic ministry in his own violent death at the hands of a fearful and suspicious ruler.[59]

Still, whatever the exact meaning of his statements over the bread and wine, Jesus went on to proclaim his faith that, in spite of or because of his death, God would bring his kingdom to Israel and would bring Jesus, even beyond death, to the banquet of that kingdom (Mark 14:25).[60] To the end, Jesus the parable-speaker and symbol-maker, spoke in enigmatic symbols and gestures. What precise scenario he envisioned, how exactly he thought his rejection and death tied in with his Elijah-like and Davidic roles remains unclear. Perhaps it remained unclear to him. If we may accept some reference to the covenant in the cup-word as coming from the historical Jesus (and such a reference is present in both the Pauline and Marcan eucharistic traditions),[61] then somehow he saw the shedding of his blood, the blood of the martyred eschatological prophet and Son of David, as restoring God's covenant with his people Israel (cf. Exod. 24:8), broken at Sinai and broken many times since. In any event, with this prophetic-symbolic action, as with the other two actions, Jesus intimated that he was making a conscious choice in provoking the denouement of the drama he had set in motion.

CONCLUSION

Admittedly, the ultimate, internal coherence between the eschatological miracle-working prophet like Elijah and the royal Son of David (or

Davidic King or Davidic Messiah) remains elusive if not insoluble. Perhaps there is no internal, theoretical coherence. Perhaps the Western academic is simply venting his frustration at an ancient Semitic prophet who had no concern about the inner coherence of his message or actions. Or perhaps the connection and coherence are purely personal and existential, dependent on the particular person, message, vision, and final choices of this enigmatic Jew called Jesus. Perhaps we must fall back on Eduard Schwiezer's bon mot: "Jesus the man who fits no formula."

I hasten to add, though, that I quote this bon mot as an empirical-historical judgment, not a crypto-theological claim. Simply as a matter of fact, no other identifiable Jewish individual living in Palestine around the turn of the era embodied in himself, indeed, in a career spanning only a few years, the varied roles of itinerant preacher, eschatological prophet, herald of the kingdom of God, supposed miracle worker, teacher and interpreter of the Mosaic Law, wisdom teacher and spinner of parables and aphorisms, personal guru and leader of an itinerant band of male and female disciples, Jewish prophet from Galilee who wound up being crucified in Jerusalem by the Roman prefect on grounds of claiming to be King of the Jews. Simply on the historical level, apart from any vision of faith or theological claims, the combination of so many different C.V.s is astounding. Need we be surprised that a Son-of-David type of messianic claim is another ingredient Jesus added to this confusing mix? And need we be surprised that this ingredient, like some of the others, resists academic attempts to discern theoretical coherence?

Since this presentation has involved so many hypotheses strung together, permit me to hazard one final surmise about why in particular there is no neat coherence or fit between Jesus as Elijah-like prophet and Jesus as royal Son of David. From volume 1 of *A Marginal Jew* onwards, I have stressed that in historical Jesus research there is no temporal before-and-after between Jesus' baptism by John and his last days in Jerusalem.[62] One need not rehearse here what Karl Ludwig Schmidt[63] and the other form critics—as well as many redaction critics—have shown at length: the temporal order and plot lines of all the evangelists are their own creations, their artificial frameworks for holding together the many individual traditions that go to make up the story of Jesus. Without the framework, there is no chronological before-and-after in the public ministry. And so all developmental theories that try to trace a step-by-step unfolding of Jesus' eschatology or his messianic consciousness are untenable from the start.

However, at the end of my musings on Jesus as Elijah and Jesus as Son of David, I am tempted to make one exception. (After all, Roman Catholics are addicted to creating iron-clad laws from which they then graciously grant dispensations.) It may be—one can say no more than that—it may be that, from the beginning of his ministry, Jesus was thought at least by some people to be of Davidic lineage. If the family of his putative father Joseph enjoyed such a reputation in Galilean peasant society around Nazareth, the family would naturally have been proud of it and hardly reticent about it.

This could be one reason why, throughout most of his ministry, Jesus purposely, consciously, chose to play up the role of the prophet-like-Elijah, almost as a way of countering or refusing to countenance hopes harbored by followers that he was the prophesied royal Messiah of the house of David—a Messiah understood by them in this-worldly, political, and even military terms. If it be true that Jesus did not openly make claims for himself as the Davidic Messiah during the public ministry, if indeed he purposely suppressed such ideas with his self-chosen role as the Elijah-like prophet, then the triumphal entry and the temple demonstration constitute a notable break by Jesus with his own reticence and mode of self-presentation. Why he makes this break when he does, we do not know. Possibly he was increasingly frustrated by his fruitless past encounters with the temple authorities in Jerusalem, and so he quite literally decided to "go for broke," to provoke the authorities with public actions that intimated a royal Davidic claim.

Yoked with his constant speaking about the kingdom of God, imminent and yet somehow already present in his ministry, his new demarche *was* indeed understood by the authorities—at least in the sense that Jesus was claiming to be the royal Davidic Messiah coming to his capital and symbolically claiming control over the capital's temple. This would explain what galvanized the authorities to act decisively at this particular visit of Jesus. Jesus' public symbolic actions made the difference by precipitating his arrest and crucifixion on the charge of claiming to be King of the Jews, which was simply the Roman-Gentile way of understanding a royal Davidic Messiah.

Was then, as some would claim, Jesus' crucifixion all a sad mistake arising from a misunderstanding? Yes and no. Caiaphas and Pilate cannot be accused of entirely misunderstanding what Jesus was doing. In the midst of enthusiastic crowds at the pilgrimage feast of Passover in Jerusalem, Jesus, a popular prophet, was claiming to be the royal Son of David foretold by the prophets. At the same time, Jesus did not understand his claim in the same realpolitik way that Caiaphas and Pilate probably did, with the possible threat of a political coup achieved by armed rebellion.

One might say, then, that, on the question of how Elijah-like prophet and Son of David cohered, Caiaphas and Pilate stood on one side of a fateful hermeneutical divide, and Jesus on the other. Priest and prefect understood the coherence in terms of a popular prophet and leader of the masses now revealing that he was also a rebel messianic pretender preparing to seize power, possibly by armed revolt. Jesus understood the coherence in terms of the coming kingdom of God somehow already present. As the Elijah-like prophet, he announced the coming kingdom with his words while proleptically realizing it with his powerful, startling deeds, including the symbolic actions that would help unleash the full coming of the kingdom in which he would reign as Son of David, God's vicegerent. In Jesus' view, it was not armed rebels but God alone, coming to Israel in the endtime with his transcendent power, who would bring this new state of affairs, the final kingdom of God, to full realization.

In the end, this first-century hermeneutical divide places researchers today before another hermeneutical divide, one that moves beyond what historical research can adjudicate, namely, the divide between belief and unbelief. In the last analysis, *either* Jesus was a hopelessly deluded, though perhaps sincere and naive, Israelite prophet. *Or* God did what Jesus had prophesied—though in the totally unexpected way of death, resurrection, the sending of the Spirit, and the mission of the church. But then the God of the Jewish Scriptures has a long track record of fulfilling prophecies in ways undreamed of even by his prophets.

NOTES

1. I am constantly reminded of the appropriateness of the title of one of the early books of John Dominic Crossan on the historical Jesus: *In Fragments: The Aphorisms of Jesus* (San Francisco: Harper & Row, 1983).

2. See, e.g., the summary statement in *A Marginal Jew: Rethinking the Historical Jesus*, Anchor Bible Reference Library, 2 vols. (New York: Doubleday, 1991, 1994), 2:1039–49.

3. On this point, see Christoph Burger, *Jesus als Davidssohn,* Forschungen zur Religion und Literatur des Alten und Neuen Testaments 98; Göttingen: Vandenhoeck & Ruprecht, 1970), 9–15. It is telling that, as Raymond E. Brown (*The Birth of the Messiah,* new updated ed., Anchor Bible Reference Library [New York: Doubleday, 1993]) begins his treatment of the problem in "Appendix II: Davidic Descent" (pp. 505–12), he poses the question in terms of an either-or: either Jesus was in historical fact a descendant of David or Davidic sonship is simply a theolo-

goumenon created by the early church. Actually, as Brown pursues the question in appendix 2, he gradually refines the way the question is posed.

4. John J. Collins, *The Scepter and the Star: The Messiahs of the Dead Sea Scrolls and Other Ancient Literature,* Anchor Bible Reference Library (New York: Doubleday, 1995). See also Burger, *Jesus,* 24.

5. Collins, *Scepter and the Star,* 213–14 (n. 68).

6. For an exhaustive study of all the exegetical and historical questions connected with the infancy narratives, see Brown, *Birth of the Messiah.*

7. Any attempt to reconstruct the infancy traditions prior to the evangelists' redaction must remain highly speculative. For such an attempt in regard to the Matthean infancy narrative, see George M. Soares Prabhu, *The Formula Quotations in the Infancy Narrative of Matthew,* Analecta Biblica 63 (Rome: Biblical Institute Press, 1976), esp. 294–300.

8. Burger, *Jesus,* 91–106, 127–37.

9. As can be seen by my reconstruction (which follows the lead of critics like Eduard Schweizer and Christoph Burger), I consider "in power" and "Jesus Christ our Lord" to be additions by Paul. That Rom. 1:3–4 is indeed a pre-Pauline formula rather than a creation by Paul himself is disputed by a few critics, but the vast majority of the authors named in the following note agree that the convergence of indications from structure, vocabulary, and theological content argue for a pre-Pauline formula. For brief summaries of the arguments in favor of a pre-Pauline formula, see the articles by Paul Beasley-Murray and Robert Jewett; for the arguments in favor of composition by Paul, see the article by Vern S. Poythress cited below.

10. For commentary and bibliography on this formula, see the standard commentaries on Romans, notably James D. G. Dunn, *Romans,* Word Biblical Commentary 38A, 38B, 2 vols. (Dallas: Word, 1988), 1:3–26; Joseph A. Fitzmyer, *Romans,* Anchor Bible 33 (New York: Doubleday, 1993), 227–42. Among significant essays and monographs, note in particular Nils A. Dahl, "Die Messianität Jesu bei Paulus," in *Studia Paulina* (Haarlem: Bohn, 1953), 83–95, esp. 90–91; M.-E. Boismard, "Constitué Fils de Dieu (Rom. I,4)," *Revue Biblique* 60 (1953): 5–17; Oscar Cullmann, *Christology of the New Testament* (Philadelphia: Westminster, 1959), 235, 291–92; David M. Stanley, *Christ's Resurrection in Pauline Soteriology* (Rome: Biblical Institute Press, 1961), 160–66; Klaus Wegenast, *Das Verständnis der Tradition bei Paulus und in den Deuteropaulinen,* Wissenschaftliche Monographien zum Alten und Neuen Testament 8 (Neukirchen: Neukirchener-Verlag, 1962), 70–76; Eduard Schweizer, "Röm 1,3f und der Gegensatz von Fleisch und Geist vor und bei Paulus," in *Neotestamentica* (Zurich/Stuttgart: Zwingli, 1963), 180–89; Rudolf Bultmann, *Theology of the New Testament* (London: SCM, 1965), 49–50; Reginald Fuller, *The Foundations of New Testament Christology* (New York: Scribner's, 1965), 165–67, 187; Werner Kramer, *Christ, Lord, Son of God,* Studies in Biblical Theology 1/50 (London: SCM, 1966), 108–11; Peter Stuhlmacher, "Theologische Probleme des Römerbriefpräskripts," *Evangelische Theologie* 27 (1967):

374–89; Hans-Werner Bartsch, "Zur vorpaulinischen Bekenntnisformel im Eingang des Römerbriefes," *Theologische Zeitschrift* 23 (1967): 329–39; Giuseppe Ruggieri, *Il figlio di Dio davidico,* Analecta Gregoriana 166; Rome: Gregorian University, 1968); Ferdinand Hahn, *The Titles of Jesus in Christology* (London: Lutterworth, 1969), 246–51; Heinrich Zimmermann, *Neutestamentliche Methodenlehre,* 3rd ed. (Stuttgart: KBW, 1970), 192–202; Burger, *Jesus,* 25–41; Richard Longenecker, *The Christology of Early Jewish Christianity,* Studies in Biblical Theology 2/17 (London: SCM, 1970), 80, 96–98, 111; Eta Linnemann, "Tradition und Interpretation in Röm 1,3f.," *Evangelische Theologie* 31 (1971): 264–75 (with a response by Eduard Schweizer on pp. 275–76); Heinrich Schlier, "Zu Röm 1,3f," in *Neues Testament und Geschichte: Historisches Geschehen and Deutung im Neuen Testament,* Oscar Cullmann Festschrift, ed. H. Baltensweiler and B. Reicke (Zurich: Theologischer Verlag; Tübingen: Mohr [Siebeck], 1972), 207–18; Klaus Wengst, *Christologische Formeln und Lieder des Urchristentum,* Studien zum Neuen Testament 7; Gütersloh: Mohn, 1972), 112–17; James D. G. Dunn, "Jesus—Flesh and Spirit: An Exposition of Romans i. 3–4," *Journal of Theological Studies* 24 (1973): 40–68; Dennis C. Duling, "The Promises to David and Their Entrance into Christianity—Nailing Down a Likely Hypothesis," *New Testament Studies* 20 (1973–74): 55–77; Vern S. Poythress, V.S., "Is Romans 1 3–4 a Pauline Confession after All?" *Expository Times* 87 (1975–76): 180–83; Paul Beasley-Murray, "Romans 1:3f: An Early Confession of Faith in the Lordship of Jesus," *Tyndale Bulletin* 31 (1980): 147–54; Michael Theobald, "'Dem Juden zuerst und auch dem Heiden': Die paulinische Auslegung der Glaubensformel Röm 1,3f.," in *Kontinuität und Einheit: Für Franz Mussner,* ed. P.-G. Müller and W. Stenger (Freiburg: Herder, 1981), 376–92; Robert Jewett, "The Redaction and Use of an Early Christian Confession in Romans 1:3–4," in *The Living Text: Essays in Honor of Ernest W. Saunders,* ed. D. Groh and R. Jewett (Lanham, Md.: University Press of America, 1985), 99–122; Marinus de Jonge, "Jesus, Son of David and Son of God," in *Intertextuality in Biblical Writings: Essays in Honour of Bas van Iersel,* ed. S. Draisma (Kampen: Kok, 1989), 95–104.

11. On the question of the origins and makeup of the Christian community (or communities) in Rome, see Peter Lampe, *Die stadtrömischen Christen in den ersten beiden Jahrhunderten,* Wissenschaftliche Untersuchungen zum Neuen Testament 2/18; Tübingen: Mohr [Siebeck], 1987; 2nd ed. 1989); and the various essays in *The Romans Debate,* revised and expanded ed., ed. Karl Paul Donfried (Peabody, Mass.: Hendrickson, 1991), notably Wolfgang Wiefel, "The Jewish Community in Ancient Rome and the Origins of Roman Christianity" (pp. 85–101); Peter Stuhlmacher, "The Purpose of Romans" (pp. 231–42); and Fitzmyer, *Romans,* 25–36.

12. This is not to claim that the authentication of his gospel and apostleship is the only reason Paul cites the formula; its content also leads into the major theological themes of the epistle. On this, see Theobald, " 'Dem Juden zuerst und auch dem Heiden,' " 376–92; and Jewett, "The Redaction," 99–122.

13. The knowledge of this creedal formula early on in Rome is readily understandable if, as many critics suggest, the Christian community in Rome had strong ties from the beginning with the Christian church in Jerusalem; see, e.g., Fitzmyer, *Romans*, 29–33; also Raymond E. Brown and John P. Meier, *Antioch and Rome: New Testament Cradles of Catholic Christianity* (New York/Ramsey, N.J.: Paulist, 1983), 89–127. See, in particular, Brown's comments on pp. 104, 119–24. Burger denies that this formula could come from the Jerusalem church or from Palestinian Jewish Christianity in general (*Jesus*, 25–31). Unfortunately, Burger works with a Bultmannian dichotomy between Palestinian Judaism and Hellenism that many would consider passé today; he likewise extends the dichotomy to Palestinian and Hellenistic Jewish Christianity.

14. The two other references to David in Romans (4:6; 11:9, which are the only other passages in which David is mentioned by name in the whole of the undisputed Paulines) simply use David's name to introduce quotations from the Psalms. For Paul, Abraham rather than David is the pivotal Jewish ancestor of Jesus.

In addition to the sole direct reference to Jesus as born of the seed of David in Rom. 1:3, Paul cites in Rom. 15:12 the prophecy of Isa. 11:10, which speaks of "the root of Jesse." As Burger correctly notes (*Jesus*, 31 n. 33), the indirect allusion to Christ in this passage has an ecclesiological (the salvation of the Gentiles and their inclusion in the church alongside the Jews) rather than a christological (Jesus as Son of David) thrust. The Isaiah quotation in Rom. 15:12 is the only verse in all of the Pauline letters where Jesse is mentioned.

15. It is also interesting to note that, when, in the second and subsequent centuries, pagan and Jewish polemical writings attacked Jesus' birth as illegitimate, there was no attempt to dispute his Davidic descent. On this, see Brown, *Birth of the Messiah*, 507.

16. As a matter of fact, in all the Paulines, disputed as well as undisputed, the name David occurs only in the three Romans passages mentioned above and this once in 2 Tim. 2:8. Likewise unusual for the Pastor is the order "Jesus Christ" rather than his customary "Christ Jesus."

17. I. Howard Marshall (*The Pastoral Epistles*, International Critical Commentary [Edinburgh: Clark, 1999], 734) rightly rejects the attempt by some commentators to see the Pastor as directly dependent on the text of Romans here; so too Philip H. Towner, *The Goal of Our Instruction*, Journal for the Study of the New Testament, Supplement 34 (Sheffield: JSOT Press, 1989), 101, 287 n. 152.

18. For example, this is the translation in the original form of the New American Bible (NAB); the order of the Greek has been restored in the revised NAB NT. The inversion of the Greek order is found also in J. B. Phillips's *New Testament in Modern English*.

19. This insight is missed by the all-too-brief treatment of 2 Tim. 2:8 in Burger, *Jesus*, 33–35.

20. For standard treatments of the text, see Raymond E. Brown, *The Gospel*

According to John, Anchor Bible 29, 29A, 2 vols. (Garden City, N.Y.: Doubleday, 1966, 1970), 1:330 (Brown prefers the view that the evangelist knew and accepted the Davidic and Bethlehem traditions); Rudolf Schnackenburg, *Das Johannes-evangelium, II Teil,* Herders theologischer Kommentar zum Neuen Testament 4/2 (Freiburg: Herder, 1971), 218 (Schnackenburg sees Christian apologetic stressing that the Jewish contemporaries of Jesus could have recognized the awaited savior).

21. For the view that the evangelist accepts the Davidic and Bethlehem traditions but considers them a trivial matter in comparison with his heavenly origin from God, see C. K. Barrett, *The Gospel According to St John* (London: SPCK, 1965), 273; in a similar vein, D. Moody Smith, *John,* Abingdon NT Commentaries (Nashville: Abingdon, 1999), 175–76. In contrast, Burger concludes that John did not consider Jesus a descendant of David (*Jesus,* 153–58). Burger allows that the ambiguous formulation of John 7:42 might mean that John knew of the tradition of Jesus' Davidic descent but rejected it.

22. I should note here that, as a methodological principle (defended at length by such respected Johannine scholars as C. H. Dodd, Raymond E. Brown, and D. Moody Smith), I hold that John's Gospel represents a tradition similar to but independent of that in the Synoptic Gospels. Hence, whatever the source of John's knowledge of the David-and-Bethlehem tradition, it is not directly Matthew or Luke.

23. A point made by Burger, *Jesus,* 155–56.

24. See my treatment in *A Marginal Jew,* 2:686–90. Burger's treatment of the Bartimaeus story (*Jesus,* 42–46) is unsatisfying on a number of grounds. Most notably, Burger moves too quickly to identify supposed tensions in the text that then allow him to distinguish pre-Marcan tradition from Marcan redaction. Suffice it to say that many of the tensions he discerns are questionable or even highly dubious. To take one striking example: Burger claims that the title "Son of David" and miracle-working activity stand in tension; this betrays a surprising ignorance of research done on the figure of Solomon as exorcist and miracle worker in recent decades.

25. It is telling that Burger never discusses John's version of the story when he evaluates the historicity of Mark 11:1–11.

26. The philological problem of "Hosanna" (literally, "Save us, please") construed with prepositional phrases like "to the Son of David" or "in the highest" is a perennial conundrum that does not, thankfully, affect the basic argument here. A major part of the problem is that "Hosanna" must be understood in this Gospel story not as a prayer of petition (as we find in the Old Testament) but as an acclamation of praise—for which there is no evidence in either Old Testament or postbiblical Judaism. For the intriguing suggestion that the dative phrases in the Gospel story of the triumphal entry are actually mistranslations of the proclitic Hebrew *lĕ-* used to introduce a vocative phrase, see Marvin H. Pope, "Hosanna," *Anchor Bible Dictionary,* 6 vols., ed. David Noel Freedman (New York: Doubleday, 1992), 3:290–91. Accordingly, Pope reconstructs the Hebrew cries behind

Matthew's text as *hôšaʿnnā lĕ-ben dāwîd* ("Save, please, O Son of David!") and *hôšaʿnnā lĕ-ʿelyôn* ("Save, please, O Highest [God]!"). While intriguing, the suggestion suffers from a number of difficulties: (1) It demands that an ordinary Jewish crowd use Hebrew rather than Aramaic as it shouts its sentiments in a noncultic and nonacademic context. (2) It takes Matthew's redaction of Mark as reflecting historical events. (3) It presumes rather than proves that this vocative *lĕ-* existed in popular, spoken Hebrew (or Aramaic) in Palestine in the first century C.E.

27. Even Burger admits this point in *Jesus,* 64–65.

28. Vincent Taylor takes the conservative view that the basic event in the pericope goes back to the historical Jesus and that Jesus denied neither the Messiah's Davidic descent nor his own (*The Gospel According to St. Mark,* 2nd ed. [London: Macmillan,1966], 490–93). A similar view is held by Rudolf Pesch, *Das Markusevangelium,* Herders theologischer Kommentar zum Neuen Testament 2, 2 vols. (Freiburg: Herder, 1976, 1977), 2:249–57. In contrast, Morna D. Hooker thinks that the pericope comes not from Jesus but from the early church (*The Gospel According to Saint Mark,* Black's NT Commentary [Peabody, Mass.: Hendrickson, 1991], 290–94); however, she holds that at least Mark understood the story as not denying Jesus' Davidic sonship. While Rudolf Bultmann firmly denies the origin of the pericope in the historical Jesus, he is uncertain about its actual origin (*Die Geschichte der synoptischen Tradition,* Forschungen zur Religion und Literatur des Alten und Neuen Testaments 29, 8th ed. [Göttingen: Vandenhoeck & Ruprecht, 1921, 1970], 144–46). Either it comes from a group within the primitive community (apparently Palestinian Jewish Christianity is meant) that upholds belief in the Son of Man in opposition to an expectation of a Son of David; or it comes from "the Hellenistic community" and intends to prove that Jesus is more than Son of David, namely, Son of God.

29. See the treatment in Burger, *Jesus,* 52–59. Burger all too easily decides that an unbiased view of the pre-Marcan pericope must adopt the third opinion. While it is true that a form critic must prescind from the redactional sense that the pericope acquires from the Marcan context, form criticism must also take seriously the context that the pericope most likely would have had in the oral tradition of the early church—an oral tradition that early and late views Jesus as Davidic. The idea that early in the first Christian generation some Christians disputed Jesus' Davidic origins is unsubstantiated by the evidence. The relatively late evidence gleaned from the *Epistle of Barnabas* is itself ambiguous. For a less skeptical evaluation of the pericope, see de Jonge, "Jesus, Son of David and Son of God," 95–101.

30. Culling from his tradition these three pericopes that sounded the Son of David theme, Mark may have clustered them right before his passion narrative as an introduction to his own emphasis on Jesus as Messiah, King of the Jews, and King of Israel in chs. 14–15. That Mark has not simply created these three pericopes for his redactional purpose is suggested by the fact that the first of the three voices the Son of David theme most clearly, while the next two are more indirect

in their statements. A purely redactional creation, especially by Mark, who delights in the theme of secrecy and lack of understanding, would most likely have moved in the opposite direction—a point that Burger fails to see in his treatment in *Jesus*, 42–71.

31. See Dennis C. Duling, "The Eleazar Miracle and Solomon's Magical Wisdom in Flavius Josephus's *Antiquitates Judaicae* 8.42–49," *Harvard Theological Review* 78 (1985): 1–25. On the title "Son of David," the Christology connected with it, and the pericopes in which it appears, see in particular Burger, *Jesus;* see also Loren R. Fisher, "'Can This Be the Son of David?'" in *Jesus and the Historian,* Ernest Cadman Colwell Festschrift, ed. F. Thomas Trotter (Philadelphia: Westminster, 1968), 82–97; Joseph A. Fitzmyer, "The Son of David Tradition and Mt 22:41–46 and Parallels," in *Essays on the Semitic Background of the New Testament* (Missoula, Mont.: Scholars Press, 1971), 113–26; Vernon K. Robbins, "The Healing of Blind Bartimaeus (10:46–52) in the Marcan Theology," *Journal of Biblical Literature* 92 (1973): 224–43; Klaus Berger, "Die königlichen Messiastraditionen des Neuen Testaments," *New Testament Studies* 20 (1974): 1–44; Dennis C. Duling, "The Promises to David and Their Entrance into Christianity—Nailing Down a Likely Hypothesis," *New Testament Studies* 20 (1974): 55–77; idem, "Solomon, Exorcism, and the Son of David," *Harvard Theological Review* 68 (1975): 235–52; idem, "The Therapeutic Son of David: An Element in Matthew's Christological Apologetic," *New Testament Studies* 24 (1978): 392–410; idem, "Matthew's Plurisignificant 'Son of David' in Social Science Perspective: Kinship, Kingship, Magic, and Miracle," *Biblical Theology Bulletin* 22 (1992): 99–116; Evald Lövestam, "Jésus Fils de David chez les Synoptiques," *Studia theologica* 28 (1974): 97–109; Dietrich-Alex Koch, *Die Bedeutung der Wundererzählungen für die Christologie des Markusevangeliums,* Beihefte zur Zeitschrift für die neutestamentliche Wissenschaft 42 (Berlin/New York: de Gruyter, 1975), 126–32; Jack Dean Kingsbury, "The Title 'Son of David' in Matthew's Gospel," *Journal of Biblical Literature* 95 (1976): 591–602; W. Michaelis, "Die Davidssohnschaft Jesu als historisches und kerygmatisches Problem," in *Der historische Jesus und der kerygmatische Christus* (Berlin: Evangelische Verlag, 1962), 317–30; F. Neugebauer, "Die Davidssohn Frage," *New Testament Studies* 21 (1974–75): 81–108; Pesch, *Das Markusevangelium,* 2:167–75; Paul J. Achtemeier, "'And He Followed Him': Miracles and Discipleship in Mark 10:46–52," in *Early Christian Miracle Stories,* Semeia 11, ed. Robert W. Funk (Missoula, Mont.: Scholars Press, 1978), 115–45; W. R. G. Loader, "Son of David, Blindness, Possession, and Duality in Matthew," *Catholic Biblical Quarterly* 44 (1982): 570–85; Michael G. Steinhauser, "Part of a 'Call Story'?" *Expository Times* 94 (1982–83): 204–6; idem, "The Form of the Bartimaeus Narrative (Mark 10.46–52)," *New Testament Studies* 32 (1986): 583–95.

32. One should, however, take into account a number of implicit allusions. For example, in Acts 4:25 + 27, David is said to be "your [God's] servant [*paidos sou*]" and then practically in the same breath Jesus is called "your holy servant . . . whom you anointed [*ton hagion paida sou . . . hon echrisas*]." The juxtaposition of David

and Jesus in salvation history as two servants of God, one prophesying the other, with the second expressly referred to as anointed, intimates—but only intimates—a Son-of-David Christology. One should also note, as Burger does (*Jesus*, 138), that it is hardly by accident that Luke introduces a reference to Davidic descent at three key turning points in the history of the early church (the Pentecost sermon, the major synagogue sermon during Paul's first missionary journey, and the decision of the Council of Jerusalem to allow Gentiles to become Christians without circumcision) and places the three references in the mouths of the three great leaders: Peter, Paul, and James.

33. This has become a truism as a result of the work of such critics as Martin Dibelius, Ernst Haenchen, Eduard Schweizer, and Ulrich Wilckens.

34. Here once again I differ with Burger (*Jesus*, 137–52), who spends a good part of his book trying to limit the number of independent attestations of Jesus' Davidic descent in the New Testament.

35. For a detailed study of these texts, see John P. Meier, "Symmetry and Theology in the Old Testament Citations of Hebrews 1:5–14," in *The Mission of Christ and His Church*, Good News Studies 30 (Wilmington, Del.: Glazier, 1990), 92–122.

36. On this, see Harold W. Attridge, *The Epistle to the Hebrews*, Hermeneia (Philadelphia: Fortress, 1989), 201: "Our author no doubt refers to the widely accepted Davidic descent of Jesus. He does not, however, explicitly cite David as the Judahite from whom Christ descended, nor does he develop any of his christological reflections on the basis of a Davidic relationship." See also Otto Michel, *Der Brief an die Hebräer*, Meyer Kommentar 13, 12th ed. (Göttingen: Vandenhoeck & Ruprecht, 1966), 271.

37. For a general survey of the three passages, see Burger, *Jesus*, 159–64.

38. David E. Aune explains *Dauid* here as an objective genitive: that is, Jesus holds the key to the Davidic or messianic kingdom (*Revelation*, Word Biblical Commentary 52, 52B, 52C, 3 vols. [Dallas: Word, 1997–98], 1:235).

39. As Aune points out (*Revelation*, 1:350), "lion of the tribe of Judah" alludes to Gen. 49:9, while "the root of David" alludes to Isa. 11:1, 10. The use of "root" to mean descendant reflects the Hebrew *šōreš*, which can mean not only "root" but also "what springs from the root"—"shoot," "sprout," and hence metaphorically "descendant." One sees this metaphorical usage applied to descendants of David in Sir. 47:22 and in Paul's use of Isa. 11:10 in Rom. 15:12.

40. Aune (*Revelation*, 3:1226) observes that this is one of the five *egō eimi* sayings in Revelation (1:8, 17; 2:23; 21:6; 22:16). Burger (*Jesus*, 161–62) thinks that the author of Revelation uses *to genos Dauid* ("the race" or "stock" of David) instead of *ek genous Dauid* ("from the stock of David") to indicate that Christ is not simply one among many descendants of David but rather represents the entire Davidic line since he is the fulfillment of the promise made to the house of David.

41. As noted above, Burger thinks that an early countertradition (Jesus was not the Son of David) can be seen in the original meaning of the pre-Marcan pericope on the question of the Messiah as Son of David (Mark 12:35–37) and a reference

to Jesus' Davidic descent in the *Epistle of Barnabas* 12:10–11 (*Jesus*, 165–78) . But both passages are ambiguous (the pre-Marcan pericope is hardly the clear rejection of Jesus' Davidic sonship that Burger claims it to be), and the *Epistle of Barnabas* is too late to be a witness to a first-generation Christian rejection of Davidic sonship.

42. By a different line of reasoning, Paula Fredriksen comes to the conclusion that, at least shortly before his death, Jesus was thought by some people to be the royal Messiah (*Jesus of Nazareth, King of the Jews* [New York: Knopf, 1999], 154, 215). For a similar view, see Bart D. Ehrman, *Jesus: Apocalyptic Prophet of the New Millennium* (Oxford: Oxford University Press, 1999), 218.

43. Fredriksen puts the points slightly differently in her *Jesus of Nazareth, King of the Jews*, 8: "This problem of linking Jesus' Jewish career with his Roman death challenges many. . . ."

44. Fredriksen rightly emphasizes the importance and historical likelihood of the Fourth Gospel's presentation of Jesus' activity in Judea and Jerusalem throughout his ministry; see, e.g., *Jesus of Nazareth, King of the Jews*, 235–41. As Fredriksen notes, Jesus felt himself called to proclaim the kingdom to all Israel, not just to Galilee. For the view that Jesus spent most, if not all, of his adult life in the rural towns and villages of Galilee, see Ehrman, *Jesus: Apocalyptic Prophet*, 209.

45. I think Fredriksen is quite right to stress this, though I doubt her views that (1) Pilate had detailed knowledge about Jesus' teaching and that (2) consequently Pilate knew that Jesus was harmless (see *Jesus of Nazareth, King of the Jews*, 241–44). Some sort of new kingdom was being proclaimed by a person thought by some Jews to be a son of King David, and this proclamation was being done before swelling and volatile Jewish crowds at the great pilgrim feasts in Jerusalem. All this would not persuade Pilate that Jesus was harmless; there was potential for great harm here, and Pilate was hardly privy to Jesus' private intentions. In the end, Pilate's (and Caiaphas's) reason for acting was probably not too different from that of Herod Antipas in regard to the Baptist: preventive action before a potential crisis is better than reaction to an actual crisis.

46. See John P. Meier, "John the Baptist in Josephus: Philology and Exegesis," *Journal of Biblical Literature* 111 (1992): 225–37.

47. For the Hebrew text and translation of 4Q521, see *The Dead Sea Scrolls Study Edition*, 2 vols. (Leiden: Brill; Grand Rapids: Eerdmans, 1997, 1998), 2: 1044–47. It should be noted that this fragmentary text does not state that the Messiah will work the miracles that recall the eschatological prophecies of the book of Isaiah. Rather, the Lord (God) "will perform marvelous acts" (healing the wounded, making the dead live, proclaiming good news to the poor) at a time when, according to the beginning of fragment 2, col. 2, "the heavens and the earth will listen to his [God's] anointed one [or: his Messiah, *lmšyw*]." Yet, since it is difficult to think of the Lord God proclaiming good news to the poor without some human spokesperson, it may well be that the text understands that all these marvelous deeds will be performed through the mediation of the Lord's anointed one.

As for "their king, the Son of David . . . the Lord Messiah" in *Psalms of Solomon* 17, while it is true that the portrait is largely of a political and military leader reigning in Jerusalem after having destroyed the Gentile oppressors, this messianic figure is endowed with certain superhuman powers. He is said to destroy the law-breaking Gentiles simply "by the word of his mouth" (v. 24). Taught by God, he will make the whole people of Israel holy (vv. 31–32). This Messiah is thus something more than a powerful warrior and a skillful politician.

48. Space does not allow detailed arguments about the authenticity of each of these sayings. Suffice it to say here that at least the prohibition of divorce and the peremptory command "Let the dead bury their dead" are commonly accepted by scholars as coming from Jesus (multiple attestation in the first case, discontinuity or embarrassment in both cases).

49. On the historicity of this practice of Jesus, see *A Marginal Jew*, 2:1035–37 n. 317.

50. On the authenticity of this saying and practice, see *A Marginal Jew*, 2:439–50.

51. It is interesting to note here the difference in approach between Fredriksen in her *Jesus of Nazareth, King of the Jews* and Ehrman in his *Jesus: Apocalyptic Prophet*. While Fredriksen emphasizes the pivotal role of Jesus' entry into Jerusalem (it excited the populace with hopes that he was the coming royal Messiah), she largely dismisses the impact of Jesus' cleansing of the temple (a stray tradition of dubious value that cannot be definitely connected with Jesus' final days in Jerusalem). Ehrman (pp. 210–14) does basically the opposite, playing down the impact of Jesus' entry but stressing Jesus' temple action (which could have been both predictive of the temple's destruction and critical of present priestly practice). My own view is that both the entry and the cleansing enjoy multiple attestation (Mark and John) and help explain why Jesus was arrested and executed at this particular Passover. While enthusiasm about Jesus as a possible royal Messiah may have spread among the festal crowd in general, its more precise source and locus would have been the immediate followers of Jesus. In this connection, Ehrman (pp. 216–18) raises the intriguing possibility that Judas Iscariot "betrayed" not so much the place where Jesus could easily be arrested out of the sight of the festal crowds as rather Jesus' private teaching, addressed to his inner circle of disciples, that he would play a kingly role in the coming kingdom.

52. John's account of Jesus riding into Jerusalem on a donkey is hardly dependent on Mark's. It is Mark who gives us a short story stressing Jesus' prophetic foreknowledge and authority in sending two of his disciples to find and bring the donkey to him. Such control and supernatural knowledge of events before they happen would fit in perfectly with John's passion narrative and overall Christology. Yet this Marcan story is lacking in John's version. We instead are told with surprising banality that "Jesus found a young donkey and sat on it" (John 12:14). For extensive treatment of and bibliographies on the pericope of the triumphal entry, see Brent Kinman, *Jesus' Entry into Jerusalem*, Arbeiten zur Geschichte des antiken

Judentums und des Urchristentums 28 (Leiden: Brill, 1995); Jacques Nieuviarts, *L'entrée de Jésus à Jérusalem,* Lectio Divina 176 (Paris: Cerf, 1999). The former monograph focuses on the Lucan narrative, the latter on the Matthean.

53. See, e.g., the presentation of Tiberius's life in book 3 of Suetonius's *Lives of the Caesars.* For modern critical presentations, see Barbara Levick, *Tiberius the Politician,* rev. ed. (London/New York: Routledge, 1999), 180–200; David Shotter, *Tiberius Caesar* (London/New York: Routledge, 1992), 29–33, 73; and, in a psychologizing mode, Gregorio Marañón, *Tiberius the Resentful Caesar* (New York: Duell, Sloan & Pierce, 1956), 201–3. Needless to say, we must bear in mind the bias that both Suetonius and Tacitus show against Tiberius. For evaluations of the ancient sources, see Manfred Baar, *Das Bild des Kaisers Tiberius bei Tacitus, Sueton und Cassius Dio,* Beiträge zur Altertumskunde 7 (Stuttgart: Teubner, 1990); also Levick, *Tiberius the Politician,* 222–25; Shotter, *Tiberius Caesar,* 74–81. Tiberius was determined to maintain *quies* throughout the empire, and one notable tool was the *lex de majestate. Majestas minuta* (the diminution of the "majesty" of the Roman people or the princeps) meant, in effect, treason; but it was such a malleable term that almost anything could be brought under it if the authorities so wished. The ancient sources tell lurid tales of the multiplication of accusers and spies that Tiberius's policy fostered.

54. On the dynamic nature of the symbolic actions of prophets, see the concise comments by Bruce Vawter, "Introduction to Prophetic Literature," in *New Jerome Biblical Commentary,* ed. Raymond E. Brown et al. (Englewood Cliffs, N.J.: Prentice-Hall, 1990), 199 (11:23). For fuller treatment, see, e.g., Gerhard von Rad, *Old Testament Theology,* 2 vols. (Edinburgh/London: Oliver & Boyd, 1962, 1965), 2:95–98: "For antiquity, the sign, like the solemn word . . . , could not only signify a datum but actually embody it as well; this means that it could act creatively, and in early cultures it probably had an even greater power to do so than the word. . . . Jahweh himself acts in the symbol, through the instrument of his prophet. The symbol was a creative prefiguration of the future which would be speedily and inevitably realised. When the prophet, by means of a symbolic act, projects a detail of the future into the present, this begins the process of realisation. . . . This way of regarding symbolic actions, which was only opened up by the study of comparative religion, is therefore basic for exegesis." See also J. Lindblom, *Prophecy in Ancient Israel* (Philadelphia: Fortress, 1962), 165–73; Georg Fohrer, *Die symbolischen Handlungen der Propheten,* Abhandlungen zur Theologie des Alten und Neuen Testaments 54, 2nd ed. (Zurich/Stuttgart: Zwingli, 1968). On the symbolic actions of Jesus in particular, see Maria Trautmann, *Zeichenhafte Handlungen Jesu: Ein Beitrag zur Frage nach dem geschichtlichen Jesus,* Forschung zur Bibel 37 (Würzburg: Echter, 1980); Jacques Schlosser, *Jésus de Nazareth* (Paris: Noesis, 1999), 272–74 (with reference to Jesus' temple action).

55. I presuppose here the general view that Mark has preserved the original time frame for the cleansing of the temple and that John has purposely placed it

at the beginning of Jesus' ministry for his own theological purposes. See *A Marginal Jew*, 1:381–82; 2:892–94.

56. For various opinions on the historicity of Jesus' temple action and its meaning, see, e.g., E. P. Sanders, *Jesus and Judaism* (Philadelphia: Fortress, 1985), 61–76; M. D. Hooker, "Traditions about the Temple in the Sayings of Jesus," *Bulletin of the John Rylands Library* 70, no. 1 (1988): 7–19; Craig A. Evans, "Jesus' Action in the Temple: Cleansing or Portent of Destruction?" *Catholic Biblical Quarterly* 51 (1989): 237–70; David Seeley, "Jesus' Temple Act," *Catholic Biblical Quarterly* 55 (1993): 263–83; Kinman, *Jesus' Entry*, 145–58; Schlosser, *Jésus de Nazareth*, 263–80. Fredriksen downplays the cleansing of the temple in favor of the triumphal entry as a catalyst of Jesus' arrest (*Jesus of Nazareth, King of the Jews*, 207–14, 235–59). I think instead that both played a role as Jesus pressed for a final confrontation.

57. This is not to deny that further debates within the temple precincts and additional threatening prophecies spoken by Jesus may have added impetus to the authorities' decision.

58. For a survey of the historical and theological issues, see John P. Meier, "The Eucharist at the Last Supper: Did It Happen?" *Theology Digest* 42 (1995): 335–51. For further treatments and extensive bibliography, see Joachim Jeremias, *The Eucharistic Words of Jesus* (London: SCM, 1966); H. Merklein, "Erwägungen zur Überlieferungsgeschichte der neutestamentlichen Abendmahlstraditionen," *Biblische Zeitschrift* 21 (1977): 88–101, 235–44; Rudolf Pesch, *Das Abendmahl und Jesu Todesverständnis*, Quaestiones disputatae 80 (Freiburg: Herder, 1978); José Luis Espinel Marcos, *La eucaristía del Nuevo Testamento* (Salamanca: San Esteban, 1980), 43–115; Xavier Léon-Dufour, *Sharing the Eucharistic Bread: The Witness of the New Testament* (New York/Mahwah, N.J.: Paulist, 1987); Joachim Gnilka, *Jesus von Nazaret: Botschaft und Geschichte*, Herders theologischer Kommentar zum Neuen Testament, Supplement 3 (Freiburg: Herder, 1990), 280–89; Jean-Marie van Cangh, "Le déroulement primitif de la Cène (Mc 14, 18-26 et par.)," *Revue Biblique* 102 (1995): 193–225; Andrew Brian McGowan, "'Is There a Liturgical Text in This Gospel?' The Institution Narratives and Their Early Interpretive Communities," *Journal of Biblical Literature* 118 (1999): 73–87; Enrico Mazza, *The Celebration of the Eucharist* (Collegeville, Minn.: Liturgical Press, 1999), 19–28; Schlosser, *Jésus de Nazareth*, 281–301.

59. See *A Marginal Jew*, 2:175–76.

60. On this text, see *A Marginal Jew*, 2:302–9.

61. See 1 Cor. 11:25; Mark 14:24; as I indicate in my article "The Eucharist at the Last Supper," I think that Mark's simple "covenant" is more primitive than Paul's "new covenant."

62. See *A Marginal Jew*, 1:408–9.

63. Karl Ludwig Schmidt, *Der Rahmen der Geschichte Jesu* (1919; Darmstadt: Wissenschaftliche Buchgesellschaft, 1969).

4

Jesus in Oral Memory

The Initial Stages of the Jesus Tradition

JAMES D. G. DUNN

ORAL TRADITION

*A*NYONE WHO WISHES TO TAKE PART in what has become familiarly known as "the quest of the historical Jesus" can only hope to do so with any effect through the Jesus tradition. "Jesus tradition" is shorthand for the material used by the Gospel writers, particularly (for reasons we don't need to go into here) the Synoptic Gospels—that is, stories about Jesus, teachings attributed to Jesus. Does that tradition give us access to the "historical Jesus"?[1] Immediate access, or only at some remove? Does it tell us what Jesus actually did and said, or only what pious reverence attributed to him? In the attempt to answer such questions, all agree, the evidence of the Jesus tradition itself has to be decisive. The history of the quest has been the history of the investigation of the character and value of the Jesus tradition, its sources, its forms, its redaction—in a word, its tradition history.

It soon becomes apparent, however, that there has been a huge and persisting gap in the analysis of that evidence. I refer to the repeated failure to take seriously the fact that in the initial stages of the traditioning process the tradition must have been *oral* tradition. In conseequence there has also been the failure to investigate the character of the tradition in its oral phase, and to ask what its orality must have meant for the transmission of that material. I do not say that the subject has not been raised during the period covered by the various quests of the "historical Jesus." But unfortunately, when it has been raised, the issue has usually been sidetracked into other questions and its significance for our understanding of the tradition history of the Jesus tradition lost to sight.

J. G. Herder

Within the history of the quest J. G. Herder (1744–1803) is usually given the credit for first raising the issue. Herder was unhappy with Lessing's idea that behind the Synoptic Gospels lay an original Aramaic Gospel of the Nazarenes: "Neither apostolic nor church history knows of any such Primal Gospel." What did lie behind them was indeed a "common Gospel," but it was an *oral* gospel.[2] Herder's description of this material foreshadows later treatments, not least his description of the orally transmitted material as "an oral saga."

> In the case of a free, oral narrative, not everything is equally untrammeled. Sentences, long sayings, parables are more likely to retain the same form of expression than minor details of the narrative; transitional material and connecting formulae the narrator himself supplies.... The common Gospel consisted of individual units, narratives, parables, sayings, pericopes. This is evident from the very appearance of the Gospels and from the different order of this or that parable or saga....
>
> The fact that it consists of such parts vouches for the truth of the Gospel, for people such as most of the apostles were, more easily recall a saying, a parable, an apothegm that they had found striking than connected discourses.[3]

Unfortunately these potentially fruitful insights were absorbed into and lost to sight in the quest for sources of the Synoptic Gospels, which became the dominant concern of nineteenth-century Gospels research.[4]

Rudolf Bultmann

It was not until the rise of form criticism early in the twentieth century that the question of the earliest Jesus tradition's oral character reemerged. In his preface to the 1962 publication of one of his essays on form criticism, Bultmann began with a summary definition: "The purpose of Form Criticism is to study the history of the oral tradition behind the gospels."[5] And in his summary description of how oral tradition was transmitted, he made an observation similar to that of Herder: "Whenever narratives pass from mouth to mouth the central point of the narrative and general structure are well preserved; but in the incidental details change takes place. . . ."[6] Unfortunately, once again, the possibilities of working fruitfully with a realistic conceptualization of oral tradition and how it functioned were more or less strangled at birth by several assumptions that distorted Bultmann's reconstruction of the oral traditioning processes.

Two in particular are worth noting. (1) Bultmann focused on the forms and assumed that certain "laws of style" determined the transmission of the forms. These laws, apparently drawn from some acquaintance with studies in folklore elsewhere,[7] included the further assumptions of a "pure" form,[8] of a natural progression in the course of transmission from purity and simplicity toward greater complexity,[9] and of a development in the tradition determined by form rather than content.[10] (2) More significant was Bultmann's assumption of a *literary* model to explain the process of transmission. This becomes most evident in his conceptualization of the whole tradition about Jesus as "composed of a series of layers."[11] The imagined process is one where each layer is laid or builds upon another. Bultmann made such play with it because, apart from anything else, he was confident that he could strip off later (Hellenistic) layers to expose the earlier (Palestinian) layers.[12] The image itself, however, is drawn from the literary process of editing, where each successive edition (layer) is an edited version (for Bultmann, an elaborated and expanded version) of the previous edition (layer). But is such a conceptualization really appropriate to a process of oral retellings of traditional material? Bultmann never really addressed the question, despite its obvious relevance.

Here then, we have to speak of form criticism's missed opportunity. The main body of discussion following Bultmann stayed with the literary model, and the focus shifted more to the communities that shaped the tradition or to the easier question of its later shaping in redaction criticism.[13] There were two main exceptions. One is the too little regarded attempt by C. F. D. Moule to highlight the vitality of the form history process in the life of the churches, "to place in their setting in life and thought the processes which led up to the writing of early Christian books."[14] His concern, however, was primarily to explain the genesis of Christian literature, and not with the character and processes of oral tradition, though some of his observations are entirely relevant to our inquiry.[15]

Birger Gerhardsson

The other was the protest by Harald Riesenfeld and his pupil Birger Ger-hardsson that Bultmann had indeed ignored the most obvious precedents for the transmission of tradition in Palestine. Riesenfeld noted that the technical terms used for transmission of rabbinic tradition underlie the Greek terms used in the New Testament for the same process (*paralam-banein* and *paradidonai*) and deduced that the early Christian traditioning process, like the rabbinic, was a "rigidly controlled transmission" of words and deeds of Jesus, "memorized and recited as holy word." The idea of a community-shaped tradition was too inaccurate. Rather we must think of tradition derived directly from Jesus and transmitted by authorized teach-ers "in a far more rigid and fixed form."[16]

Gerhardsson developed Riesenfeld's central claim by a careful study of rabbinic tradition transmission, as the nearest parallel for the Palestinian Jesus tradition, and reinforced his teacher's main claim.[17] Unlike the form critics, Gerhardsson recognized the need to investigate the actual tech-niques of oral transmission. The key word, he confirmed, is "memoriza-tion,"[18] memorization by means of constant repetition, the basic technique of all education then and since (in fact, until only recently in the West).[19] In rabbinic Judaism the pupil had the duty "to maintain his teacher's exact words," as the basis for any subsequent comment(ary) of his own.[20] Prin-cipally on the basis of the importance of "the word of the Lord" in earliest Christianity, as attested by Luke and Paul, Gerhardsson went on to deduce that Jesus "must have made his disciples learn certain sayings off by heart; if he taught, he must have required his disciples to memorize"; "his sayings must have been accorded even greater authority and sanctity than that accorded by the Rabbis' disciples to the words of their teachers." Conse-quently, when the evangelists edited their Gospels they were able to work "on a basis of a fixed, distinct tradition from, and about, Jesus."[21]

Unfortunately these contributions were largely dismissed, in large part because the appeal to rabbinic precedent was deemed (unfairly) to be anachronistic.[22] More to the point, unlike the rabbinic tradition, the Gos-pel tradition does not depict Jesus teaching by repetition.[23] More impor-tant for present purposes, the claims of both Riesenfeld and Gerhardsson seem to envisage a far more rigid and fixed tradition than could explain the obvious disparities between the same tradition as used by the evangelists.[24] Even allowing for the importance of teachers and tradition in the earliest churches,[25] the process envisaged is evidently too controlled and formal to explain the divergences in the tradition as it has come down to us.[26] The possibility of finding the key to the tradition history from Jesus to the Synoptics in the processes of oral transmission had once again eluded scholarship.

Werner Kelber

To Werner Kelber is due the credit for being the first New Testament scholar to take seriously the distinctive character of oral tradition as illuminated by a sequence of studies from classicists, folklorists, and social anthropologists.[27] Characteristics include "mnemonic patterns, shaped for ready oral recurrence," "heavily rhythmic, balanced patterns, in repetitions or antitheses, in alliterations and assonances, in epithetic and other formulary expressions, in thematic settings, . . . in proverbs." Typical of oral performances were variations on what nevertheless were recognizable versions of the same story, with some more or less word-for-word repetition in places, both fixed and flexible formulaic elements, and so on.[28] Kelber drew attention to similar features that had already been observed in the Jesus tradition: "the extraordinary degree to which sayings of Jesus have kept faith with heavily patterned speech forms, abounding in alliteration, paronomasia, appositional equivalence, proverbial and aphoristic diction, contrasts and antitheses, synonymous, antithetical, synthetic, and tautologic parallelism and the like," miracle stories "typecast in a fashion that lends itself to habitual, not verbatim, memorization."[29] And in his description of oral transmission he fully acknowledges his indebtedness to earlier studies. "Oral thinking consists in formal patterns from the start"; "formulaic stability" and "compositional variability" go hand in hand—"'this mid-state between fixed and free.'"[30] Oral transmission "exhibits 'an insistent, conservative urge for preservation' of essential information, while it borders on carelessness in its predisposition to abandon features that are not met with social approval."[31] "Variability and stability, conservatism and creativity, evanescence and unpredictability all mark the pattern of oral transmission"—the "oral principle of 'variation within the same.'"[32]

The chief thrust of Kelber's book, however, is to build on the distinction between oral and written, between oral performance and literary transmission, which he draws from Walter Ong in particular. The distinction is important, not least since it requires modern literary scholars to make a conscious effort to extricate their historical envisaging of the oral transmission of tradition from the mind-set and assumptions of long-term literacy.[33] Equally important is the immediacy of an oral communication in contrast to written, the direct and personal engagement of speaker and auditor not possible in writing—what Kelber call(s) the "oral synthesis."[34] This is partly what I have in mind when I talk of the "impact" made by Jesus on his disciples. The contrast can be overplayed: for example, the recognition that in the ancient world documents were written to be *heard*, that is, read out and listened to rather than read, is commonplace in all these disciplines;[35] the fact that letters can be a fairly effective substitute for personal absence has become important in recent study of Paul's letters;[36] and the encounter with its written version can be as creative as a hearing of the original speech—indeed, in reader-response criticism each reading of a text is like a fresh performance of it.[37] Even so, for anyone who has experienced a (for them) first performance a great musical work, like Beethoven's *Ninth* or Verdi's *Requiem,* the difference between hearing in the electric atmosphere of the live performance and hearing the recorded version played later at home (let alone simply reading the score) is unmistakable.[38]

There are other important observations made by Kelber. He takes up the key observation of Albert Lord in warning against the ideal of "original form";[39] "each oral performance is an irreducibly unique creation"; if Jesus said something more than once there is no "original."[40] This is true, although the impact made by each retelling by Jesus on those who heard and retained the teaching should be distinguished from the effect of their own reteaching on others. Kelber also rightly notes that oral retelling of Jesus' words will already have begun during Jesus' lifetime; the Bultmannian thesis of a tradition that began to be transmitted only after Easter is highly questionable.[41] Moreover, in Kelber's work, very noticeably, *narratives,* the retold stories about Jesus, reemerge into prominence from the marginalization imposed on them by the almost exclusive focus of scholarly interest on the sayings of Jesus.[42] Not least of importance, given Kelber's developed thesis, is his recognition that Mark (his main focus in the Gospels) retains many of the indices of orality—for example, its "activist syntax" and colloquial Greek, its use of the storyteller's three, and its many redundancies and repetitions; "Mark may be treating an oral story in order for it to remain functional for the ear more than for the eye."[43] Mark's Gospel may be *frozen* orality,[44] but it is frozen *orality.*[45]

Unfortunately, Kelber pushes his thesis about Mark marking a major transition from oral to written far too hard and seriously diminishes its overall value. The first step in his thesis development is that the written Gospel disrupts the "oral synthesis"; it "arises not from orality *per se,* but out of the debris of deconstructed orality"; it indicates "alienation from

the oral apparatus"; it "accomplishes the death of living words for the purpose of inaugurating the life of textuality."[46] The transition is overdrama-
tized: it is widely recognized that in a predominantly oral culture, oral
versions of a tradition would continue after it had been transcribed and
that knowledge of the written version would usually be in an oral
medium.[47] At the same time, it is true that only with a written text can we
begin to speak of an editing process, such as Bultmann envisaged; prior to
that, in repeated oral performances the dynamics are different, more of the
order of "theme and variations" than Gerhardsson's "memorization."[48]
This is why talk of sources, appropriate in considering the origin of a written text, can be inappropriate with oral tradition. It is also why, I may add,
even talk of oral transmission can mislead such discussions, since it envisages oral performance as intended primarily to transmit (transfer) rather
than, say, to celebrate tradition.[49]

However, Kelber pushes on to argue that Mark's textualizing of the tradition amounts to an "indictment of oral process and authorities," an
"emancipation from oral norms," an objection to "the oral metaphysics of
presence." Thus Mark repudiates the first disciples, Jesus' family and ongoing prophetic activity, as oral authorities to be discredited; the first disciples are "effectively eliminated as apostolic representatives of the risen
Lord."[50] Paul is called in as apostle of orality and set over against Mark's
Gospel as written text, with the classic gospel/law antithesis reworked as an
antithesis between oral gospel and written law, spirit and (written) letter,
"under the law" as under textuality.[51] In all this a different Christology is at
stake: the passion narrative as a literary phenomenon implies a distancia-
tion from an oral Christology; Q, with its "fundamentally oral disposition"
and inclusion of prophetic utterances, maintains the living voice of Jesus,
whereas Mark elevates "the earthly Jesus at the price of silencing the living
Lord" by "relegating all sayings to the former while silencing the voice of
the latter."[52]

Here is a thesis too quickly gone to seed. To find Paul as apostle of orality lumped with Q is a refreshing change. But Paul himself would almost
certainly have been baffled by the thrust of such an argument. As one who
in his preaching vividly and openly portrayed Christ as crucified (Gal. 3:1),
and who both preached the kerygma of the first witnesses (1 Cor. 15:1–11)
and depended on the Spirit's inspiration for the effect of his preaching of
the crucified Christ (1 Cor. 2:4–5), Paul would certainly not have recognized such distinctions. Not only does Kelber forget the continuity
between oral and first writing (as initially written orality), which he had
earlier acknowledged, but he ignores the points made above, that in an age

of high illiteracy documents were written to be *heard* and that a reading can also be likened to a performance. In claiming that, in contrast to Mark's Gospel, "Q effects a direct address to present hearers"[53] he ignores the fact that Q is generally regarded as a *written* source. He also forgets the living character of tradition, that written as well as oral tradition can effect a re-presentation (making present again) of ancient teaching and events,[54] particularly in liturgy, as in Paul's recollection of Jesus' words in regard to the Lord's Supper (1 Cor. 11:23–26). Regrettably then, once again, the potential significance of recognizing the distinct character of the oral traditioning process in the case of the Jesus tradition has been subverted by another agenda and lost to sight.

Kenneth Bailey

What has been missing in all this has been a sufficiently close parallel to the oral traditioning that presumably was the initial mode of and vehicle for the Jesus tradition. As Kelber himself noted, however helpful the lessons learned from the study of Homeric epics and Yugoslavian sagas, we cannot simply assume that they provide the pattern for oral transmission of Jesus tradition within the thirty or so years between Jesus and the first written Gospel.[55] The nearest we have to fill the gap is the essay by Kenneth Bailey in which he has reflected on more than thirty years experience of Middle East village life.[56] These villages have retained their identity over many generations, so that, arguably, their oral culture is as close as we will ever be able to get to the village culture of first-century Galilee. Bailey puts forward the idea of "*informal controlled tradition*," to distinguish it from the models used by both Bultmann ("informal, uncontrolled tradition") and Gerhardsson ("formal controlled tradition"). In informal controlled tradition the story can be retold in the setting of a gathering of the village by any member of the village present, but usually the elders, and the community itself exercises the control.[57]

Bailey characterizes the types of material thus preserved under various headings. (1) Pithy proverbs: he describes "a community that can create (over the centuries) and sustain in current usage up to 6,000 wisdom sayings." (2) Story riddles: "in the story the hero is presented with an unsolvable problem and comes up with a *wise* answer." (3) Poetry, both classical and popular. (4) Parable or story: "Once there was a rich man who . . . , or a priest who . . ." and so on. (5) Well-told accounts of the important figures in the history of the village or community: "if there is a central figure critical to the history of the village, stories of this central figure will abound."[58]

Particularly valuable are Bailey's notes on how the community controlled its tradition. He distinguishes different levels of control. (1) No flexibility: poems and proverbs. (2) Some flexibility: parables and recollections of people and events important to the identity of the community. "Here there is flexibility *and* control. The central threads of the story cannot be changed, but flexibility in detail is allowed." (3) Total flexibility—jokes and casual news: "The material is irrelevant to the identity of the community and is not judged wise or valuable."[59]

He illustrates more recent tradition by retelling stories about John Hogg, the primary founder of the new Egyptian Evangelical community in the nineteenth century. These were orally transmitted and sustained stories that had been drawn on for Dr. Hogg's biography (published in 1914) and which were still being retold in almost the same way when Bailey dipped into the tradition in 1955–65.[60]

He also tells two stories from his own experience.[61] One concerns a fatal accident that took place at a village wedding, at which it was customary to fire hundreds of rifle rounds into the air in celebration. On his way (back) to the village Bailey heard the story from several people, including the boatman taking him across the Nile, a boy on the far bank, and other villagers including the village mayor. Each retelling included different details, but the climax of the story was almost word for word:

> Hanna [the bridegroom's friend] fired the gun. The gun did not go off. He lowered the gun. The gun fired [passive form]. The bullet passed through the stomach of Butrus [the bridegroom]. He died. He did not cry out, "O my father," nor "O my mother" [meaning he died instantly without crying out]. When the police came we told them, "A camel stepped on him."

The point was that the community had quickly determined that the death was an accident and the story had been crystallized to make this clear ("The gun fired," not "He fired the gun").[62] By the time Bailey heard it (a week after the event) the story had been given its definitive shape.[63] His other story is of his own experience of preaching. Often he would tell a story new to the community. As soon as the story was finished the congregation would enact "a form of oral shorthand."

> The elder on the front row would shout across the church to a friend in a loud voice, "Did you hear what the preacher said? He said . . ." and then would come a line or two of the story including the punch-line. People all across the church instinctively turned to their neighbours and repeated the central thrust of the story twice or thrice to each other. They wanted to retell the story that week across the village and they had to learn it on the spot.

The hypothesis that Bailey offers on the basis of his reflections on these experiences is that informal controlled oral tradition is the best explanation for the oral transmission of the Jesus tradition. Up until the upheaval of the First Jewish Revolt (66–73 C.E.) informal controlled oral tradition would have been able to function in the villages of Palestine. But even then, anyone twenty years and older in the sixties could have been "an authentic reciter of that tradition."[64]

All this confirms that the previous paradigms offered by Bultmann and Gerhardsson are inadequate for our own understanding of the oral transmission of the Jesus tradition. In particular, the paradigm of literary editing is confirmed as wholly inappropriate: one telling of a story is in no sense an editing of a previous telling; rather, each telling starts with the same subject and theme, but the retellings are different; each telling is a performance of the tradition itself, not of the first, or third, or twenty-third "edition" of the tradition. Our expectation, accordingly, should be of the oral transmission of Jesus tradition as a sequence of retellings, each starting from the same storehouse of communally remembered events and teaching, and each weaving the common stock together in different patterns for different contexts.

Of special interest is the degree to which Bailey's thesis both informs and refines the general recognition among students of the subject that oral tradition is typically flexible, with constant themes, recognizable versions of the same story, some word-for-word repetition, and both fixed and variable formulaic elements depending on the context of the performance. What he adds is significant; in particular the recognition of the likelihood that (1) a community would be concerned enough to exercise some control over its traditions; (2) the degree of control exercised would vary both in regard to form and in regard to the relative importance of the tradition for its own identity; and (3) the element in the story regarded as its core or key to its meaning would be its most firmly fixed element.[65]

The key question, of course, is whether we can find the marks of such "informal controlled oral tradition" in the Synoptic tradition itself.

THE SYNOPTIC TRADITION AS ORAL TRADITION: NARRATIVES

We certainly do not know enough about oral traditioning in the ancient world to draw from that knowledge clear guidelines for our understanding of how the Jesus tradition was passed down in its oral stage. Any inquiry on this subject is bound to turn to the Jesus tradition itself to ask whether there is sufficient evidence of oral transmission and what the tradition itself tells us about the traditioning process. We need to bear in mind, of course, that the only evidence we have is already literary (the Synoptic Gospels) and therefore also the possibility that the mode of transmission has been altered. On the other hand, Kelber readily acknowledges the oral character of much of Mark's material, and the boundaries between oral Q and written Q seem to be rather fluid, as we shall see. We shall therefore focus on Mark and Q material in the next two sections.

For convenience we will look first at the narrative traditions. Here at least we do not have the problem of deciding whether such traditions came from Jesus (as we inevitably ask in respect of sayings attributed to Jesus). At best such traditions derive from those who were with Jesus and who witnessed things he did and said.

The Conversion of Saul

The first example comes not from the Synoptics themselves but from Luke's second volume, Acts. All that is necessary for the example to be relevant for an inquiry into Jesus tradition is the assumption that Luke handled such a tradition in Acts in the same way he handled traditions in his Gospel.[66] The value of the example is threefold. (1) The three accounts (Acts 9:1–22; 22:1–21; 26:9–23) all come from a single author (Luke), so we avoid some of the unknowns operative when two or three different authors deal with the same episode; there is no need to hypothesize different sources. (2) They are manifestly all accounts of the same event (Saul's conversion), so the harmonizer's hypothesis of different episodes to explain differences between parallel accounts is not open to us. (3) Yet they are strikingly different in their detail, so if the *same* author can tell the *same* story in such *different* ways, it must tell us much about his own attitude to retelling traditional material, and possibly about the early Christian traditioning process more generally.[67]

When we examine the three accounts more closely there quickly becomes evident a striking parallel to the patterns of oral tradition observed above (see pp. 88–93 above). There are several constants: the chief character—Saul; the setting—a journey to Damascus to persecute followers of Jesus; the circumstances—a (bright) light from heaven, Saul fallen to the ground, Saul's companions; the heavenly voice. But beyond that the details vary considerably. Did Saul's companions all fall to the ground (26:14), or only Saul himself (9:4, 7)? Did they hear the voice of

Jesus (9:7), or not (22:9)? Saul's blindness, so prominent in chs. 9 and 22, is not mentioned in ch. 26. Likewise, Ananias has considerable prominence in chs. 9 and 22, but is nowhere mentioned in ch. 26. The other constant, the commission to go to the Gentiles, comes once to Saul directly on the road (26:16–18), once through Ananias (9:15–17), and once later in Jerusalem (22:16–18). Most striking of all is the fact that what was evidently accounted the core of the story, the exchange between Saul and the exalted Jesus, is *word for word*, after which each telling of the story goes its own distinctive way:

9:3 As he was traveling and approaching Damascus,	22:6 "While I was traveling and approaching Damascus,	26:12 "I was traveling to to Damascus with the authority and commission of the chief priests,
	about noon	13 when at midday along the road, your Excellency,
suddenly a light from heaven flashed around him. 4 He fell to the earth	a great light from heaven suddenly shone about me. 7 I fell to the ground	I saw a light from heaven, brighter than the sun, shining around me and my companions. 14 When we had fallen to the earth, I
and *heard a voice saying* to him, "*Saul, Saul, why are you persecuting me?*"	and *heard a voice saying* to me, "*Saul, Saul, why are you persecuting me?*"	*heard a voice saying* to me in the Hebrew language, "*Saul, Saul, why are you persecuting me?*" It hurts you to kick against the the goads." 15 I asked,
5 He asked, "*Who are you, Lord?*" The reply came, "*I am Jesus, whom you are persecuting.*	8 I answered, "*Who are you, Lord?*" Then he said to me, "*I am Jesus* of Nazareth *whom you are persecuting.*" Now those who were with me saw the light but did not hear the voice of the one who was speaking to me. 10 I asked, "What am I to do, Lord?" The Lord said to me, "*Get up and* go to Damascus; there you will be told everything that has been assigned to you to do."	"*Who are you, Lord?*" The Lord said, "*I am Jesus whom you are persecuting.*
6 But *get up and* enter the city, and you will be told what you are to do."		16 But *get up and* stand on your feet; . . . ."

Here, then, we have an excellent example of the oral principle of "variation within the same," and specifically of Bailey's finding that the key point in the story will be held constant, while the supporting details can vary according to the circumstances. In this case in particular, the second account is clearly angled to bring out Saul's Jewish identity (22:3, 17; also Ananias—22:12) and the account of the heavenly commission delayed for dramatic effect (22:17–21), whereas the third account functions as part of Paul's defense by implying that Paul's commission was part of Israel's commission (26:18, 23 with echoes of Isa. 42:6, 17 and 49:6). In short, what becomes evident here is the fact that Luke was himself a good storyteller and that his retelling the story of Paul's conversion is a good example not simply of the use of oral tradition in a written work but of the oral traditioning process itself.

The Centurion's Servant

Within the Gospel tradition itself, one of the most intriguing episodes is the one recorded in Matt. 8:5–13 and Luke 7:1–10 (with a likely parallel in John 4:46b–54). The first point of interest is that the pericope is usually credited to Q, despite its being a narrative and despite there being no parallel to such an episode within other sayings Gospels.[68] But why should a pericope be attributed to the document Q[69] simply because it belongs to the non-Marcan material common to Matthew and Luke (q)?[70] Did Matthew and Luke have no common (oral) tradition other than Q? That hardly seems likely as an a priori. In fact, the logic behind the Q hypothesis is that the degree of *closeness* between Matthew and Luke (q) can be explained only by postulating a common written source (Q), whereas the divergence between Matthew and Luke in the first half of the story is substantial, to put it no more strongly. Of course, it is possible to argue, as most do, that Matthew or Luke, or both, have heavily edited the Q version; but when q properly speaking covers only part of the pericope, the argument for the existence of Q at this point becomes very slippery.

Is common oral tradition a more plausible hypothesis? Let us not assume that Matthew's and Luke's only source for such non-Marcan Jesus tradition was a written document (Q). When we then examine the matter more closely, the oral tradition hypothesis does indeed seem to make better sense.

Matthew 8	Luke 7
5 When *he entered* Capernaum, *a centurion* came to him appealing to him 6 and saying, "Lord my servant is lying at home paralyzed in terrible distress." 7 And he said to him "I will come and cure him."	1 After Jesus had finished all his sayings in the hearing of the people, *he entered* Capernaum. 2 *A centurion* there had a slave whom he valued highly, and who was ill and close to death. 3 When he heard about Jesus, he sent some Jewish elders to him, asking him to come and heal his slave. 4 When they came to Jesus, they appealed to him earnestly, saying, "He is worthy of having you do this for him, 5 for he loves our people, and it is he who built our synagogue for us." 6 And Jesus went with them, but when he was not far from the house, the centurion sent friends to say to him, "Lord, do not trouble your-
8 The centurion answered, "*Lord,* *I am not fit to have you come* under *my roof;*	self, for *I am not fit to have you come* under *my roof;* 7 therefore I did not con- sider myself worthy to come to you.
but only *speak the word, and my* servant will *be healed.* 9 *For I also am* *a man under authority, with soldiers* *under me; and I say to one, 'Go,' and he* *goes, and to another, 'Come,' and he* *comes, and to my slave, 'Do this,' and* *the slave does it.*" 10 *When Jesus heard* him, *he was amazed and* *said* to those who *followed him,* "Truly *I tell you,* in *no* one *in Israel have I found* *such faith.* 11 I tell you, many will come from east and west and will eat with Abraham and Isaac and Jacob in the kingdom of heaven, 12 while the heirs of the kingdom will be thrown into the	*But* *speak the word, and let my* servant *be healed.* 8 *For I also am* *a man* set *under authority, with soldiers* *under me; and I say to one, 'Go,' and he* *goes, and to another, 'Come,' and he* *comes, and to my slave, 'Do this,' and* *the slave does it.*" 9 *When Jesus heard* this *he was amazed* at him, and turning to the crowd that *followed him,* he *said,* "*I tell you, not* even *in Israel have I found* *such faith.*"
outer darkness, where there will be weeping and gnashing of teeth." 13 And	Luke 13:28–29
to the centurion Jesus said, "Go; let it be done for you according to your faith." And the servant was healed in that hour.	10 When those who had been sent returned to the house, they found the slave in good health.

The episode is clearly the same: it is the story of the healing at a distance of the seriously ill servant of a centurion who lived in Capernaum. Within that framework we find the same striking features: (1) a core of the story where the agreement is almost word for word (Matt. 8:8–10/Luke 7.6–9); (2) details that vary on either side of the core, to such an extent that the two versions seem to contradict each other (in Matthew the centurion comes to plead with Jesus personally; in Luke he makes a point of not coming).

Evidently the exchange between Jesus and the centurion made a considerable impression on the disciples of Jesus: the combination of humility and confidence in Jesus on the part of such a figure, and Jesus' surprise at its strength would have been striking enough.[71] Equally noticeable is the way in which Matthew and Luke have both taken the story in their own way: Matthew emphasizes the theme of the centurion's *faith*, by inserting the saying (Matt. 8:11–12) that Luke records in Luke 13:28–29 (the centurion as precedent for Gentile faith),[72] and by rounding off his telling with a further commendation by Jesus of the centurion's faith (Matt. 8:13); Luke emphasizes the theme of the centurion's *worthiness*, by having the elders testify to his worthiness (*axios*) (7:4–5) in counterpoise to the centurion's expression of unworthiness (*ēxiōsa*) (7:7a). Nor should we ignore the fact that both Matthew and Luke draw their different emphases from the same core—faith (Matt. 8:10), worthiness/fitness (*hikanos*) (Luke 7:6).

Here I would suggest is a fine example of oral traditioning, or, if it is preferred, of evangelists writing the story in oral mode.[73] The story was no doubt one that belonged to several communities' store of Jesus tradition. The story's point hangs entirely on the central exchange between Jesus and the centurion; that is maintained with care and accuracy. We may deduce that the story was important for these communities' identity, not least for their own sense of respect for and openness to Gentiles.

What, however, about John 4:46–54?

46 Then he came again to Cana in Galilee where he had changed the water into wine. Now there was a royal official whose son lay ill in Capernaum. 47 When he heard that Jesus had come from Judea to Galilee, he went and begged him to come down and heal his son, for he was at the point of death. 48 Then Jesus said to him, "Unless you see signs and wonders you will not believe." 49 The official said to him, "Sir, come down before my little boy dies." 50 Jesus said to him, "Go; your son will live." The man believed the word that Jesus spoke to him and started on his way. 51 As he was going down, his slaves met him and told him that his child was alive. 52 So he asked them the hour when he began to recover, and they said to him, "Yesterday at one in the afternoon the fever left him." 53 The father realized that

this was the hour when Jesus had said to him, "Your son will live." So he himself believed, along with his whole household.

Agreement in no fewer than eleven points of detail is probably enough to substantiate the conclusion that this story of the healing at a distance of the seriously ill servant of a person of rank in Capernaum is another version (more distant echo?) of the same episode that we find in Matthew 8/Luke 7.[74] Particularly noticeable, however, are the facts that the official is not (no longer) identified as a Gentile and that the Matthean/Lucan core is not (no longer) there. On the other hand, the key emphasis on the person's faith is present, and Jesus' response to that faith (despite some initial hesitation); John strengthens the theme and uses it to develop his own warning against a faith based merely on miracle (John 4:48).[75]

What to make of this in terms of early Christian oral transmission? The simplest answer is that two versions of the same episode diverged in the course of various retellings. It could be that the idea of the official as a *Gentile* centurion was introduced in the course of the retelling.[76] Alternatively, and if anything more probable, it could be that in the second (Johannine) stream of tradition the identity of the official as a Gentile was seen as a subsidiary detail to the main emphasis on his faith, and so was neglected in the retellings. Either way, the differences are so great that the hypothesis of literary dependence becomes highly improbable;[77] on the contrary, the two versions (Matt/Luke and John) provide good evidence of stories of Jesus being kept alive in oral tradition.[78] And either way we can see something of both the retentiveness of the oral traditioning process and its flexibility in allowing traditions to be adapted to bring out differing emphases.

Marcan Narratives

There is no need to rerun the standard arguments for Marcan priority (Mark as the earliest of the Synoptic Gospels)[79] or to give examples of where Synoptic analysis points to the firm conclusion of Matthean and Lucan dependence on Mark. In other cases, however, the variation in detail is such that the straightforward hypothesis of literary dependence on Mark becomes very strained. Consider the following narratives: the stilling of the storm (Mark 4:35–41/Matt. 8:23–27/Luke 8:22–25); the Syrophoenician woman (Mark 7:24–30/Matt. 15:21–28); the dispute about greatness (Mark 9:33–37/Matt. 18:1–5/Luke 9:46–48); and the widow's mite (Mark 12:41–44/Luke 21:1–4).

The Stilling of the Storm

Matthew 8	Mark 4	Luke 8
23 And when he got into the boat, his disciples followed him.	35 On that day, when evening had come, he said to them, "Let us go across to the other side." 36 And leaving the crowd behind, they took him with them in the boat, just as he was. Other boats were with him.	22 One day he got into a boat with his disciples, and he said to them, "Let us go across to the other side of the lake." So they put out,
24 A great storm arose on the sea, so great that the boat was being swamped by the waves;	37 A great stormwind arose, and the waves beat into the boat, so that the boat was already being filled. 38 But he was in the stern, asleep on the cushion; and *they woke him up* and said to him, "Teacher, do you not care that *we are perishing*?"	23 and while they were sailing he fell asleep. A stormwind swept down on the lake, and the boat was filling up, and they were in danger. 24 They went to him and *woke him up*, shouting, "Master, Master, *we are perishing!*"
but he was asleep. 25 And they went and *woke him up*, saying, "Lord, save us! *We are perishing!*" 26 And he said to them, "Why are you *afraid*, you of little *faith*?" Then *he got up and rebuked the winds and the sea*;		
and there was a dead calm.	39 *He got up and rebuked the wind,* and said to the sea, "Be quiet! Silence!" Then the wind ceased, *and there was a dead calm.* 40 He said to them, "Why are you *afraid*? Have you still no *faith*?" 41 And they were filled with great awe and said to one another,	And *he got up and rebuked the wind* and the raging waves; they ceased, *and there was a calm.* 25 He said to them, "Where is your *faith*?" They were *afraid* and amazed, and said to one another,
27 The men were amazed, saying, "What sort of man *is this, that even the winds and the sea obey him?*"	"Who then *is this, that even the wind and the* sea *obey him?*"	"Who then *is this, that* he commands *even the winds and the* water, and they *obey him?*"

Here again we have the characteristic features of different retellings of a single story about Jesus. The key points remain constant: Jesus with his disciples in a boat (on the lake); a great storm and Jesus asleep (differently described); the disciples rouse Jesus, he rebukes the wind and sea, and a calm results; Jesus questions the disciples' lack of faith and they express wonder. The key lines are clearly: "he got up and rebuked the wind(s), and there was a calm"; "who is this that even the wind(s) obey him?"[80] Around this core the story could be told and retold, with the details varying in accordance with the context of retelling and with any particular angle the storyteller wished to bring out.[81]

Once again it is quite possible to argue for a purely literary connection —Matthew and Luke drawing upon and editing Mark's (for them) original. The problem with the purely literary hypothesis is that most of the differences are so inconsequential. Why, for example, as literary editors would it be necessary for them to vary the description of the storm and the danger of the boat being swamped (each uses different verbs)? It is surely more plausible to deduce that Matthew and Luke knew their own (oral) versions of the story and drew on them primarily or as well. Alternatively, it could be that they followed Mark in oral mode, as we might say; that is, they did not slavishly copy Mark (as they did elsewhere), but, having taken the point of Mark's story, they retold it as a storyteller would, retaining the constant points which gave the story its identity and building around the core to bring out their own distinctive emphases.

The Syrophoenician Woman

The picture here is very similar. The story is again clearly the same: an event that took place in the district of Tyre; a non-Israelite woman with a demon-possessed daughter; healing at a distance. Most striking is the fact that the two versions share almost no word in common apart from the core section (italicized). The core of the story is manifestly the exchange between Jesus and the woman, held constant, more or less verbatim (Mark 7:27–28/Matt. 15:26–27). Apart from that, the retelling is completely variable: in particular, Mark emphasizes the woman's Gentile identity, while Matthew plays up both the resulting tension and the woman's faith. As with the story of the centurion's servant above, the fact that the healing was successful is almost an afterthought in every telling.

Matthew 15	Mark 7
21 Jesus left that place and went off to the district of Tyre and Sidon. 22 Just then a Canaanite woman from that region came out and started shouting, "Have mercy on me, lord, son of David; my daughter is tormented by a demon." 23 But he did not answer her at all. And his disciples came and urged him, saying, "Send her away, for she keeps shouting after us." 24 He answered, "I was sent only to the lost sheep of the house of Israel." 25 But she came and knelt before him, saying, "Lord, help me." 26 He answered, "*It is not fair to take the children's food and throw it to the dogs.*" 　　27 She said, "*Certainly, lord, for also the dogs eat from the crumbs* that fall from their masters' table." 28 Then Jesus answered her, "Woman, great is your faith! Let it be done for you as you wish." And her daughter was healed from that hour.	24 From there he set out and went away to the region of Tyre. He entered a house and did not want anyone to know he was there. Yet he could not escape notice, 25 but a woman whose little daughter had an unclean spirit immediately heard about him, and she came and bowed down at his feet. 26 Now the woman was a Gentile, of Syrophoenician origin. She begged him to cast the demon out of her daughter. 　　27 He said to her, "Let the children be fed first, for *it is not fair to take the children's food and throw it to the dogs.*" 28 But she answered him, "*Certainly, lord, and the dogs* under the table *eat from the crumbs* of the children." 29 So he said to her, "For saying that, you may go, the demon has left your daughter." 30 So she went to her home, and found the child lying on the bed, and the demon gone.

Here too the same feature is evident as in the stilling of the storm: the variation between the two versions is such that the hypothesis of literary dependence becomes very implausible. A connection at the level of oral retelling is much more probable. Either Matthew knew the story through oral tradition and drew directly from that tradition, or he himself retold Mark's story as a storyteller would. It would be misleading to say that Matthew knew a different *version* of the story.[82] For that would be to slip back into the idiom of literary editions, as though each retelling of the story was a fresh "edition" of the story, whereas the reality with which we are confronted is more like spontaneously different variations (retellings) on a theme (the identifiable theme and core).

The Dispute about Greatness

Matthew 18	Mark 9	Luke 9
1 At that time the disciples came to Jesus and asked, "*Who* is *greater* in the kingdom of heaven?"	33 Then they came to Capernaum; and when he was in the house he asked them, "What were you arguing about on the way?" 34 But they were silent, for on the way they had argued with one another about *who* was *greater*. 35 He sat down, called the twelve, and said to them, "Whoever wants to be first must be last of all and servant of all." 36 Then he took *a little child and put it* among them; and taking it in his arms, he said to them,	46 An argument arose among them as to *who* of them was *greater*. 47 But Jesus, aware of their inner thoughts, took *a little child and put it* by his side, 48 and said to them,
2 He called *a little child, and put it* among them, 3 and said, "Truly I tell you, unless you turn and become like little children, you will never enter the kingdom of heaven. 4 Whoever humbles himself like this little child is greater in the kingdom of heaven. 5 And *whoever welcomes one such little child in my name welcomes me.*"	37 "*Whoever welcomes one of such little children in my name welcomes me,* and whoever welcomes me welcomes not me but the one who sent me."	"*Whoever welcomes this little child in my name welcomes me,* and whoever welcomes me welcomes the one who sent me; for he who is lesser among all of you, that one is great."

The basic picture is the same as before. The constants are clear: the disciples' dispute about who is greater; Jesus' rebuke by drawing a little child into the company; and the core saying that climaxes the story. Each retelling elaborates the basic outline in the evanglist's own way (Mark 9:35; Matt. 18:3–4; Luke 9:48c). Matthew and Luke were able also to use the fuller tradition of Jesus' speaking about "the one who sent me" (Matt. 18:37b/Luke 9:48b). And here again the degree of verbal interdependence tells against literary interdependence, whereas the mix of constancy and flexibility indicates an oral mode of performance.[83]

The Widow's Pence

Mark 12	Luke 21
41 He sat down opposite the treasury, and watched how the crowd *put* money *into the treasury.* Many *rich people* put in large sums. 42 A poor *widow* came and *put in two small copper coins,* which are worth a penny. 43 Then he called his disciples and said to them, "Truly *I tell you, this poor widow has put in more than all those* who are contributing to the treasury. 44 *For all have contributed out of their abundance; but she out of her poverty has put in all she had,* her entire *life.*"	1 He looked up and saw *rich people putting into the treasury* their gifts; 2 he also saw a needy *widow putting in two small copper coins.* 3 He said, "Of a truth *I tell you, this poor widow has put in more than all of them;* 4 *for all* those *have contributed out of their abundance* for the gifts, *but she out of her poverty has put in all the life she had.*"

The episode is brief, being almost entirely taken up with the identifying details (the contrast between the rich people's giving and the two small copper coins of the poor widow) and Jesus' observation, which evidently made the episode so memorable (and therefore was retained close to word for word). With such a brief pericope the scope for explanation in terms of Luke's editing of Mark is stronger. But even so, the flexibility of detail in the buildup to the climactic saying bespeaks more of oral than literary tradition.

Results

Other examples could be offered.[84] None of this is intended to deny that Matthew and Luke knew Mark as such and were able to draw on his version of the tradition at a literary level and often did so; in terms of written sources, the case for Marcan priority remains overwhelmingly the most probable. Nor have I any wish to deny that Matthew and Luke regularly edited their Marcan *Vorlage*—sometimes by substantial abbreviation,[85] sometimes by adding material to make a better[86] or a further point,[87] and sometimes to clarify or avoid misunderstandings.[88] At the same time, however, it would be improper to ignore the fact that in a good number of cases, illustrated above, the more natural explanation for the evidence is *not* Matthew's or Luke's literary dependence on Mark, but rather their own knowledge of oral retellings of the same stories (or, alternatively, their own oral retelling of the Marcan stories). We really must free ourselves from the assumption that variations between parallel accounts can be explained only in terms of literary redaction. After all, it can hardly be assumed that the first time Matthew and Luke heard many of these stories was when they first came across Mark's Gospel. The claim that there were churches in the mainstream(s) represented by Matthew and Luke who did not know any Jesus tradition until they received Mark (or Q) as documents simply beggars belief and merely exemplifies the blinkered perspective imposed by the literary paradigm. To repeat: the assumption, almost innate to those trained within Western culture, that the Synoptic traditions have to be analyzed in terms of a linear sequence of literary editions, where each successive version is an editing of its predecessor, simply distorts critical perception and skews the resultant analysis. The transmission of the narrative tradition has too many oral features to be ignored.

The more appropriate conclusions are twofold. (1) The variations between the different versions of same story in the tradition do not indicate a cavalier attitude to or lack of historical interest in the events narrated. In almost every case examined or cited above it is clearly the same story that is being retold. Rather, the variations exemplify the character of oral retelling.[89] In such oral transmission the concern to remember Jesus is clear from the key elements that give the tradition its stable identity, and the vitality of the tradition is indicated by the performance variants. These were not traditions carried around in a casket like some sacred relic of the increasingly distant past, their elements long rigid by textual rigor mortis; but neither were they the free creation of teachers or prophets with some theological axe to grind. Rather they were the lifeblood of the communities in which they were told and retold. What Jesus did was important to these communities for their own continuing identity.[90]

(2) In the material documented above the differences introduced by the evangelists, whether as oral diversity or as literary editing, are consistently

in the character of abbreviation and omission, clarification and explanation, elaboration and extension of motif. The developments often reflect the deeper faith and insight of Easter; that is true—but they do not appear to constitute any radical change in substance or character or thrust of the story told.[91] Of course, we have only sampled the Jesus tradition to a limited extent, and further checks are necessary. But at least we can say that thus far developments in the Jesus tradition were consistent with the earliest traditions of the remembered Jesus.

THE SYNOPTIC TRADITION AS ORAL TRADITION: TEACHINGS

I choose the term "teachings" rather than "sayings" because the latter is too casual. It allows, possibly even fosters, the impression of serendipity—sayings of Jesus casually overheard and casually recalled, as one today might recall impressions of one's school or college days in a class reunion thirty years later. But we should not forget that Jesus was known as a teacher[92] and was so regarded by his disciples,[93] and that the disciples understood themselves as just that, "disciples" = "learners" (*mathētai*). Even that reminder should be sufficient to indicate that the recollection of Jesus' teaching would have been altogether a more serious enterprise from the start. Moreover, if I am right, the earliest communities of Jesus' disciples would have wanted to retain such teaching, as part of their own foundation tradition and self-identification, a fact that Paul and other early letter writers were able to exploit when they incorporated allusions to Jesus' teaching in their own parenesis.[94] We need not assume a formal process of memorization, such as Gerhardsson envisaged. But a concern to learn what the master had taught and to exercise some control over the degree of variations acceptable in the passing on of that teaching can both be assumed on a priori grounds and find at least some confirmation in the oral traditioning processes envisaged by Bailey.

Aramaic Tradition

We may start by recalling that the tradition as it has come down to us has already been translated once, from Aramaic to Greek. Here is another curious blind spot in most work on Jesus' teaching, in all phases of the "quest for the historical Jesus." I refer to the repeated failure to ask about the Aramaic form that Jesus' teaching presumably took.[95] Without such inquiry any assertions about earliest forms of the teaching tradition are bound to be suspect in some measure. Not that such a criterion (Can this saying be retrojected back into Aramaic?) should be applied woodenly; translation aimed to achieve dynamic equivalence could easily produce a Greek idiom quite different from the nearest Aramaic equivalent.[96] What is of more immediate importance for us here are the important observations by Aramaic experts with regard to the character of the teaching tradition. All have noted that the tradition, even in its Greek state, bears several marks of oral transmission in Aramaic. Already in 1925 C. F. Burney had drawn attention to the various kinds of parallelism (synonymous, antithetic, synthetic)[97] and rhythm (four-beat, three-beat, *qina* meter) characteristic of Hebrew poetry.[98] Matthew Black noted many examples of alliteration, assonance, and paronomasia.[99] This is all the stuff of oral tradition, as we noted above (see pp. 88–91 above). Joachim Jeremias climaxed a lifetime's scholarship by summarizing the indications that many of the words appearing in Jesus' teaching had an Aramaic origin, and that the speech involved had many characteristic features, including "divine passive," as well as the features already noted by Burney and Black.[100]

Such evidence should be given more weight than has usually been the case. Of course, an Aramaic phase may only be evidence of an early (post-Easter) stage of transmission when the tradition was still circulating in Aramaic. But if the tradition is consistently marked by particular stylistic features, as the Aramaic specialists conclude, then it has to be judged more likely that these are the characteristics of one person rather than that the multitude of Aramaic oral tradents had the same characteristics. The possibility that we can still hear what Jeremias called "the *ipsissima vox*" (as distinct from the *ipsissima verba*) of Jesus coming through the tradition should be brought back into play more seriously than it has in the thirty years since Jeremias last wrote on the subject.[101]

As with the narrative tradition, so with the teaching tradition, various examples are readily forthcoming. We begin with two examples from within earliest Christianity's liturgical tradition. In this case the studies in orality have confirmed what might anyway have been guessed: that tradition functioning as "sacred words" within a cult or liturgy is generally more conservative in character; the transmission (if that is the best term) is in the nature of sacred repetition in celebration and affirmation of a community's identity-forming tradition. Within the Jesus tradition two passages immediately call for attention.

The Lord's Prayer (Matt. 6.7–15/Luke 11.1–4)

Matthew 6	Luke 11
7 "When you are praying, do not heap up empty phrases as the Gentiles do; for they think that they will be heard because of their many words. 8 Do not be like them, for your Father knows what you need before you ask him.	
	1 He was praying in a certain place, and after he had finished, one of his disciples said to him, "Lord, teach us to pray, as John taught his disciples."
9 Pray then in this way: Our *Father* who are in heaven, *hallowed be your name.* 10 *Your king-dom come.* Your will be done, on earth as it is in heaven. 11 *Give us* to*day our daily bread.* 12 *And forgive us our* debts, as *we* also have *forgiven* our *deb*tors.　　13 *And do not bring us to the time of trial,* but rescue us from the evil one. 14 For if you forgive others their trespasses, your heavenly Father will also forgive you; 15 but if you do not forgive others, neither will your Father forgive your trespasses."	2 He said to them, "When you pray, say: *Father,* *hallowed be your name. Your kingdom come.* 　　　　　3 *Give us* each *day our daily bread.* 4 *And forgive us our* sins, for *we* ourselves *forgive* everyone in*deb*ted to us. *And do not bring us to the time of trial.*"

What is the explanation for such variation? It would be odd indeed if Matthew and Luke derived this tradition from a common written source (Q).[102] Why then the variation, particularly within the prayer itself? Here again the curse of the literary paradigm lies heavy on discussion at this point. To think that this tradition was known only because it appeared in writing in a Q document! Whereas, much the more obvious explanation is that this was a tradition maintained in the living liturgy of community worship (as the first person plural suggests). Almost certainly, the early

Christian disciples did not know this tradition only because they had heard it in some reading from a written document. They knew it because they prayed it, possibly on a daily basis.[103] In this case, in addition to the curse of the literary paradigm, the fact that so many academic discussions on material like this take place in isolation from a living tradition of regular worship, probably highlights another blind spot for many questers.

The point is that liturgical usage both conserves and adapts (slowly).[104] As Jeremias argued, the most likely explanation for the two versions of the Lord's Prayer is two slightly diverging patterns of liturgical prayer, both versions showing signs of liturgical adaptation: in Matthew the more reverential address and an opening phrase more readily said in congregational unison, and the additions at the end of each half of the prayer to elaborate the brevity and possibly clarify the petition to which the addition has been made; in Luke particularly the modification for daily prayer ("each day").[105] That the liturgical development/modification continued is indicated by the later addition of the final doxology ("for yours is the kingdom and the power and the glory for ever, Amen") to Matthew's version.[106] It is not without relevance to note that such liturgical variation within what is manifestly the same prayer continues to this day. In Scotland pray-ers tend to say "debts," in England "trespasses." And contemporary versions jostle with traditional versions in most modern service books. Since liturgy is in effect the most like to oral tradition in modern Western communities (regular worshipers rarely need to "follow the order" in the book), the parallel has some force.

One other point worth noting is that both introductions (Matt. 6:9a; Luke 11:1–2a) confirm what was again likely anyway: that this prayer functioned as an identity marker for the first disciples.[107] Christians were recognizable among themselves, as well as to others, as those who said "Father" or "Our Father" to God,[108] whereas the typical prayer of Jewish worship had more liturgical gravitas.[109] Moreover, both versions of the tradition attribute the prayer explicitly to Jesus, and report the prayer as explicitly given to his disciples by Jesus.[110] That no doubt was why the prayer was so cherished and repeated. It would be unjustifiably skeptical to conclude despite all this that the prayer was compiled from individual petitions used by Jesus[111] and/or emerged only later from some unknown disciple.[112] Its place in the early tradition indicates rather the influence of some widely and highly regarded person, among whom Jesus himself is the most obvious candidate for the speculator.

The Last Supper

The obvious second example is the record of Jesus' last supper with his disciples, which evidently became a matter of regular liturgical celebration (1 Cor. 11:23–26). The tradition here is fourfold.

Matthew 26	Mark 14
26 *While they were eating,* Jesus *took a loaf of bread, and after blessing it he broke it,* giving it to the disciples, *and said, "Take,* eat; *this is my body."* 27 *Then he took a cup, and after giving thanks he gave it to them,* saying, "Drink *from it, all of you;* 28 for *this is my blood of the covenant, which is poured out* for *many* for the forgiveness of sins. 29 *I tell you,* from now on *I will not drink of this fruit of the vine until that day when I drink it new* with you *in the kingdom* of my Father."	22 *While they were eating,* he *took a loaf of bread, and after blessing it he broke it,* gave it to them, *and said, "Take; this is my body."* 23 *Then he took a cup, and after giving thanks he gave it to them,* and *all* of them drank *from it.* 24 He said to them, "*This is my blood of the covenant, which is poured out* on behalf of *many.* 25 Truly *I tell you,* no more will *I drink of the fruit of the vine until that day when I drink it new in the kingdom* of God."

Luke 22	1 Corinthians 11
17 Then he took a cup, and after giving thanks he said, "Take this and divide it among yourselves; 18 for I tell you that from now on I will not drink of the fruit of the vine until the kingdom of God comes." 19 Then *he took a loaf of bread, and when he had given thanks, he broke it and* gave it to them, saying, "*This is my body, which is* given *for you. Do this in remembrance of me."* 20 *Also the cup likewise after supper, saying, "This cup is the new covenant in my blood* which is poured out for you.	23 For I received from the Lord what I also handed on to you, that the Lord Jesus on the night when he was betrayed *took a loaf of bread,* 24 *and when he had given thanks, he broke it and* *said, "This is my body which is* *for you. Do this in remembrance of me." 25 Likewise also the cup after supper, saying, "This cup is the new covenant in my blood.* Do this, as often as you drink it, in remembrance of me." 26 For as often as you eat this bread and drink the cup, you proclaim the Lord's death until he comes.

The tradition has been preserved in two clearly distinct forms, one in Mark and Matthew (A), the other in Luke and Paul (B). In A, Jesus "blesses" the bread; in B, he "gives thanks." B adds to the word over the bread, "which is (given) for you. Do this in remembrance of me." Over the cup, A has "This is my blood of the covenant which is poured out (for) many"; whereas B has "This cup is the new covenant in my blood." This variation is most obviously to be explained in terms neither of literary dependence, nor of one or other more easily retrojected into Aramaic,[113] but in terms of two slightly variant liturgical practices. For example, the fact that in the A version the words over the bread and the wine are set in parallel ("This is my body; this is my blood") probably indicates a liturgical shaping to bring out the parallelism. Whereas the B version maintains the framework of a meal, with the bread word presumably said at the beginning (in accordance with the normal pattern of the Jewish meal) and the cup bringing the meal to a close ("after supper"). In A the modification puts the focus more directly on the wine/blood, whereas in B the focus is more on the cup.[114]

Here again it would be somewhat farcical to assume that this tradition was known to the various writers only as written tradition and only by hearing it read occasionally from some written source. The more obvious explanation, once again, is that these words were familiar within many/most early Christian communities because believers used them in their regular celebrations of the Lord's Supper: this was living oral tradition before and after it was ever written down in semiformal or formal documentation. Here too it was a matter of fundamental tradition, the sort of tradition Paul took care to pass on to his newly formed churches (1 Cor. 11:23),[115] the sort of tradition that gave these churches their identity and by the performance of which they affirmed their identity (cf. again 1 Cor. 10:21). It was tradition remembered as begun by Jesus himself, and remembered thus from as early as we can tell.[116]

It is, of course, a fair question as to whether in the earliest form Jesus was remembered as celebrating a Passover meal or instituting a ritual to be repeated. On the latter issue, the A version does not in fact say so, and the call for or assumption of repetition is a distinctive feature both of B and of the elaboration in 1 Cor. 11:25b–26. Moreover the evidence of redaction is apparent elsewhere.[117] Nevertheless the characteristics of oral tradition remain clear: a concern to maintain the key elements of the words used by Jesus as carefully as necessary, with a flexibility (including elaboration) which in this case no doubt reflects the developing liturgical practices of different churches.

Sermon on the Mount/Plain

A curious feature of the Sermon on the Mount tradition is the variableness in the closeness between the Matthean and Lucan versions. In what we might call (for the sake of convenience) the third quarter of Matthew's Sermon, the degree of closeness is such that the passages qualify as good evidence for the existence of a Q document.[118] But in the other three-quarters the verbal parallel is much less close, so as to leave a considerable question as to whether there is evidence of any literary dependence.[119] In most cases much the more plausible explanation is of two orally varied versions of the same tradition. As before, the evidence does not determine whether one or other (or both) has simply drawn directly from the living oral tradition known to them, or whether one or other has borrowed in oral mode from the Q document. Either way the evidence is more of oral dependence than of literary dependence. Consider the following examples.

Matthew 5:13	Luke 14:34–35
13 You are the salt of the earth; *but if salt has lost its taste, how can it be* restored? It is no longer good for anything, but is *thrown out* to be trampled under foot	34 Salt is good; *but if* even *salt has lost its taste, how can it be* seasoned? 35 It is fit neither for the earth nor for the manure heap; they *throw* it *out.*

Matthew 5:25–26	Luke 12:57–59
25 Come to terms quickly *with your accuser* while you are on *the way* (to court) with him, *lest* your accuser hand you over to *the judge, and the judge* to the guard, and you will be *thrown in prison.* 26 Truly *I tell you, you will never get out from there until you have paid back the last* penny.	57 And why do you not judge for yourselves what is right? 58 Thus, when you go *with your accuser* before a magistrate, *on the way* (to court) make an effort to settle with him, *lest* you be dragged before *the judge, and the judge* hand you over to the officer, and the officer *throw* you *in prison.* 59 *I tell you, you will never get out from there until you have paid back the* very *last* halfpenny.

Matthew 5:25–26	Luke 12:57–59
25 Come to terms quickly *with your accuser* while you are *on the way* (to court) with him, *lest* your accuser hand you over to *the judge, and the judge* to the guard, and you will be *thrown in prison.* 26 Truly *I tell you, you will never get out from there until you have paid back the last* penny.	57 And why do you not judge for yourselves what is right? 58 Thus, when you go *with your accuser* before a magistrate, *on the way* (to court) make an effort to settle with him, *lest* you be dragged before *the judge, and the judge* hand you over to the officer, and the officer *throw* you *in prison.* 59 *I tell you, you will never get out from there until you have paid back the* very *last* halfpenny.

Matthew 5:25–26	Luke 12:57–59
25 Come to terms quickly *with your accuser* while you are *on the way* (to court) with him, *lest* your accuser hand you over to *the judge, and the judge* to the guard, and you will be *thrown in prison.* 26 Truly *I tell you, you will never get out from there until you have paid back the last* penny.	57 And why do you not judge for yourselves what is right? 58 Thus, when you go *with your accuser* before a magistrate, *on the way* (to court) make an effort to settle with him, *lest* you be dragged before *the judge, and the judge* hand you over to the officer, and the officer *throw* you *in prison.* 59 *I tell you, you will never get out from there until you have paid back the* very *last* halfpenny.

Matthew 5:39b–42	Luke 6:29–30
But whoever hits you on your right *cheek,* turn to him *the other also;* 40 and to the one who wants to sue you and take your *tunic,* let him have your *cloak also;* 41 and whoever forces you to go one mile, go with him a second. 42 *Give to* the one *who asks you,* and do not turn away the one who wants to borrow from you.	29 To the one who strikes you on the *cheek,* offer *the other also;* and from the one who takes away your *cloak* do not withhold your *tunic also.* 30 *Give to* everyone *who asks you;* and from the one who takes what is yours, do not ask for them back.

Matthew 7:13–14	Luke 13:24
13 *Enter through the narrow gate;* for the gate is wide and the road is easy that leads to destruction, and there are *many* who *enter* through it. 14 For the gate is narrow and the road is hard that leads to life, and there are few who find it.	24 Strive to *enter through the narrow door;* for *many,* I tell you, will try to *enter* and will not be able.

In each case two features are evident: the teaching is the same in substance; the main emphases are carried by key words or phrases (salt, lost its taste, thrown out; accuser, [danger of being] thrown in prison, "I tell you, you will never get out until you have paid back the last [half]penny";[120] cheek, other, cloak/tunic also, "Give to him who asks you";[121] "Enter through the narrow gate"); otherwise the detail is quite diverse. It is hard to imagine such sayings being simply copied from the same document. The alternative suggestion that there were several editions of Q (Matthew copying from one, Luke from another) smacks of desperation, since the suggestion undermines the arguments for the existence of a Q document in the first place. Similarly with the suggestion that Matthew was free in his editing of Q (= Luke) or vice versa.[122] Here once again the literary paradigm will simply not serve. These are all teachings remembered as teachings of Jesus in the way that oral tradition preserves such teaching, with the character and emphasis of the saying retained through stable words and phrases, but the point elaborated in ways the re-teller judged appropriate to the occasion.

Other Q/q tradition

The picture is little different for traditions shared by Matthew and Luke elsewhere in the record of Jesus' teaching. Once again there are passages where the wording is so close that a literary dependence is the most obvious explanation.[123] But once again, too, there are parallel passages which simply cry out to be explained in terms of the flexibility of oral tradition.

Matthew 10:34–38	Luke 12:51–53; 14:26–27
34 Do not think that I came to bring *peace* to *the earth;* I came not to bring peace, *but* a sword.	12.51 Do you consider that I am here to give *peace* on *the earth?* No, I tell you, *but* rather division! 52 From now on five in one household will be divided; three against two and two against three 53 they will be divided, father against son and son against *father,* mother against daughter and *daughter* against *mother,* mother-in-law against her daughter-in-law and *daughter-in-law* against *mother-in-law.*
35 For I came to set a man against his *father,* and a *daughter* against her *mother,* and a *daughter-in-law* against her *mother-in-law;* 36 and a man's foes will be members of his own household. 37 Whoever loves *father* or *mother* more than me is not worthy of me; and whoever loves son or daughter more than me is not worthy of me; 38 and he *who does not* take up *his cross* and follow *after me* is not worthy *of me.*	14.26 Whoever comes to me and does not hate his *father* and *mother,* and wife and children, and brothers and sisters, yes, and even his own life, cannot be my disciple. 27 *Whoever does not carry his* own *cross and* come *after me* cannot be *my* disciple.

Matthew 18:15, 21–22	Luke 17:3–4
15 *"If your brother sins* against you, go and point out the fault when you and he are alone. If he listens to you, you have regained your brother." 21 Then Peter came and said to him, "Lord, if my brother sins against me, how often should I *forgive him?* As many as *seven times?"* 22 Jesus said to him, "I tell you, not *seven times,* but seventy-seven times."	3 Be on your guard! *If your brother sins,* rebuke him, and if he repents, forgive him. 4 And if someone sins against you *seven times* a day, and turns back to you *seven times* and says, "I repent," you must *forgive him.*

Matthew 22:1–14	Luke 14:16–24
1 Once more Jesus spoke to them in parables, saying: 2 "*The kingdom of* heaven may be compared to a king who *gave* a wedding banquet for his son.	15 One of the dinner guests, on hearing this, said to him, "Blessed is anyone who will eat bread in *the kingdom of* God!" 16 Then Jesus said to him, "A certain person *gave* a great dinner and invited many. 17 At the time for the dinner *he sent his slave* to say to those who had been invited, 'Come; for it is now ready.' 18 But they all alike began to make excuses.
3 *He sent his slave*s to call those who had been invited to the wedding banquet, but they would not come. 4 Again he sent other slaves, saying, 'Tell those who have been invited: Look, I have prepared my dinner, my oxen and my fat calves have been slaughtered, and everything is ready; come to the wedding banquet.' 5 But they made light of it and went away, one to his *farm,*	
another to his business,	The first said to him, 'I have bought a *farm,* and I must go out and see it; please accept my regrets.' 19 Another said, 'I have bought five yoke of oxen, and I am going to try them out; please accept my regrets.' 20 Another said, 'I have married a wife, and therefore I cannot come.' 21 So the slave returned and reported this to his master. Then the owner of the house became *angry*
6 while the rest seized his slaves, mistreated them, and killed them.	
7 The king was *angered.* He sent his troops, destroyed those murderers, and burned their city. 8 Then he *said to his slave*s, 'The wedding is ready, but those invited were not worthy. 9 Go therefore into the streets, and invite everyone you find to the wedding banquet.'	and *said to his slave,* 'Go out at once into the roads and lanes of the town and bring in the poor, the crippled, the blind, and the lame.' 22 And the slave said, 'Sir, what you *ordered* has been done, and there is still room.' 23 Then the master said to the slave, 'Go out into the roads and lanes, and compel them to come in, so that my house may be full. 24 For I tell you, none of those who were invited will taste my dinner.'"
10 Those slaves went out into the streets and gathered all whom they found, both good and bad;	
so the wedding hall was filled with guests.	
11 But when the king came in to see the guests, he noticed a man there who was not wearing a wedding robe, 12 and he said to him, 'Friend, how did you get in here without a wedding robe?' And he was speechless. 13 Then the king said to the attendants, 'Bind him hand and foot, and throw him into the outer darkness, where there will be weeping and gnashing of teeth.' 14 For many are called, but few are chosen."	

In each of the above cases we clearly have the same theme. But the agreement and overlap in wording between the Matthean/Lucan parallels are so modest, even minimal, that it becomes implausible to argue that the one was derived from the other or from a single common source at the literary level. The hypothesis that Matthew and Luke drew directly from Q (= Luke?)[124] simply does not make enough sense of the data. Whereas the similarity of theme and point being made fits well with the flexibility and adaptability of oral retelling.[125] In each case the evangelist seems to have expressed and/or elaborated the common theme in his own way:

Matt. 10:37–38 (worthiness), Luke 14:26–27 (discipleship);

Matt. 18:15, 21–22 (church discipline);

Matt. 22:7, 11–14 (destruction of Jerusalem; lack of wedding robe),
   Luke 14:21–22, 23 (church's twofold mission).

But such retellings are well within the parameters of orally passed on teaching.[126] We can conclude without strain that Jesus was remembered as warning about the challenge of discipleship and the family divisions that would likely ensue, as encouraging generous and uncalculating forgiveness, and as telling a story (or several stories) about a feast whose guests refused to come (the variation in reasons given is typical of storytelling) and who were replaced by people from the streets.[127]

Results

To sum up, our findings in regard to the traditions of Jesus' teaching accord well with those regarding the narrative traditions. I have no wish to deny the existence of a Q document, any more than to deny the priority of Mark. But again and again in the case of Q/q material we are confronted with traditions within different Synoptics that are clearly related (the same basic teaching) and were evidently remembered and valued as teaching of Jesus. At the same time, in the cases examined above the relation is not obviously literary, each version derived by editing some literary predecessor. The relation is more obviously to be conceived of as happening at the oral level. That could mean that these traditions were known to the evangelists not in a literary form but in the living tradition of liturgy or communal celebration of the remembered Jesus. Or it could mean that they knew the tradition from Q, but regarded Q as a form of oral retelling, so that their own retelling retained the oral characteristics of the traditioning process. The two alternatives are not mutually exclusive, of course, but it can hardly be denied that the consequences for the definition of the scope and content of the Q document are considerable. It is important that future Q research should take such considerations on board.

As with the narrative tradition, the sample of teaching tradition examined above seems to confirm the implications drawn from the oral character of its formulation. (1) There was teaching of Jesus that had made such an impact on his first hearers that it was recalled, its key emphases crystallized in the overall theme and/or in particular words and phrases, which remained constant in the process of rehearsing and passing on that teaching in disciple gatherings and churches. All of the teaching reviewed would have been important to their identity as disciples and communities of disciples and for the character of their shared life. Such teaching would no doubt have been treasured and meditated upon in the communal gatherings, much as Bailey suggested.

(2) The variations in the reteaching indicate a readiness to group material differently, to adapt or develop it, and to draw further lessons from it, consistent with the tradition of initial impact made by Jesus himself and in the light of the developing circumstances of the churches which treasured the teaching. Once again the point is that the tradition was living tradition, celebrated in the communal gatherings of the earliest churches. There was no concern to recall all the precise words of Jesus; in many cases the precise circumstances in which the teaching was given were irrelevant to its continuing value. But neither is there any indication in the material reviewed that these were sayings interjected into the tradition by prophets or free (literary) creation, or that the development of particular teachings subverted their original impact.[128] These were remembered as teaching given by Jesus while he was still with them, and treasured both as such and because of its continuing importance for their own community life and witness.

ORAL TRANSMISSION

In the light of the above we can begin to sketch in the likely process of traditioning in the case of the Jesus tradition.[129]

The Beginning

Already during Jesus' own ministry, as soon as disciples began to gather around him, we can envisage initial impressions and memories being

shared among the group. "Do you remember how/what he said when he
...?" must have been a question often asked as the embryonic community
began to feel and express its distinctiveness. No doubt in similar ways their
village communities had celebrated their identity and history in regular,
even nightly gatherings. And as soon as the disciples of Jesus began to per-
ceive themselves as (a) distinctive group(s), we may assume that the same
impulse characteristic of oral and village culture would have asserted itself.
As Jesus' immediate group moved around Galilee, encountering potential
and then resident groups of disciples or sympathizers in various villages,
the natural impulse would be the same. We should assume, of course, that
Jesus was giving fresh teaching (as well as repeat teaching) all the while. But
in more reflective gatherings, or when Jesus was absent, the impulse to tell
again what had made the greatest impact on them would presumably
reassert itself.

Three features of this initial stage of the process are worth noting. First,
if Bailey's anecdotal accounts bring us closer than any other to the oral culture of Galilee in the second quarter of the first century C.E., then we may
assume that the traditioning process *began* with the initiating word and/or
act of Jesus. That is to say, the impact made by Jesus would not be something that was put into traditional form only (days, months, or years) later.
The impact would include the formation of the tradition to recall what
had made that impact; in making its impact the impacting word or event
became the tradition of that word or event. The stimulus of some
word/story, the excitement (wonder, surprise) of some event would be
expressed in the initial shared reaction; the structure, the identifying elements and the key words (core or climax) would be put into oral form in
the immediate recognition of the significance of what had been said or
happened. Thus established more or less immediately, these features
would then be the constants, the stable themes that successive retellings
could elaborate, around which different performances could build their
variations, as judged appropriate in the different circumstances. Subse-
quently we may imagine a group of disciples meeting and requesting, for
example, to hear again about the centurion of Capernaum, or about the
widow and the treasury, or what it was that Jesus said about the tunic and
the cloak, or about who is greater, or about the brother who sins. In
response to which a senior disciple would tell again the appropriate story
or teaching in whatever variant words and detail he judged appropriate for
the occasion, with sufficient corporate memory ready to protest if one of
the key elements was missed out or varied too much. All this is wholly consistent with the character of the data reviewed above.

It also follows, second, that those accustomed to the prevalent individualism of contemporary culture (and faith) need to make a conscious effort to appreciate that the impact made by Jesus in the beginning was not a series of disparate reactions of independent individuals.[130] Were that so, we might well wonder how any commonality of tradition could emerge as individuals began to share their memories, perhaps only after a lengthy period; postmodern pluralism would have been rampant from the first! But tradition-forming is a communal process, not least because such tradition is often constitutive of the community as community. As it was a shared experience of the impact made by Jesus which first drew individuals into discipleship, so it was the formulation of these impacts in shared words that no doubt helped bond them together as a community of disciples.

At the same time, we should not ignore an important corollary. The character of the tradition as shared memory means that in many instances we do not know precisely what it was that Jesus did or said. What we have in the Jesus tradition are the consistent and coherent features of the shared impact made by his deeds and words, not the objective deeds and words of Jesus as such. What we have are examples of oral retelling of that shared tradition, retellings that evince the flexibility and elaboration of oral performances. There is surely a Jesus who made such impact, the remembered Jesus, but not an original pure form, not a single original impact to which the historian has to reach back in each case. The remembered Jesus may be a synthesis of the several impacts made on and disciple responses made by Jesus' earliest witnesses, but the synthesis was already firm in the first flowering of the tradition.

Third, it follows also and is perhaps worth repeating that the traditioning process should not be conceived of as initially casual and only taken seriously by the first disciples in the post-Easter situation. As just implied, community formation was already at an embryonic stage from the first call of Jesus' immediate circle of disciples; "formative tradition" would have had an indispensable part in that process.[131] In addition, if indeed Jesus did send out his disciples as an extension of his own mission (Mark 6:7–13 pars.),[132] what would they have said when they preached? The implication of the text is clear, and the inference from the fact of a shared mission hard to avoid, that their preaching would have at least included teaching that Jesus had given them. Also that Jesus would have taught them what to say—not in a verbatim mode, but in a mode that would convey the disciple-effecting impact that they themselves had experienced. One way or another, we may be confident that a good deal at least of the retellings of Jesus tradition now in the Synoptic Gospels were already beginning to take shape in any early pre-Easter preaching of the first disciples.[133]

Did Easter and the transition from Galilean village to Hellenistic city, from Aramaic to Greek not make any difference, then? Yes, of course. Easter shaped the perspective within which this first tradition was remembered. The transition from village to city shaped the tradition for changing circumstances. The transition from Aramaic to Greek (already implied by the description of "Hellenists" = "Greek-speakers" in Acts 6:1) would introduce the shifts in nuance which any translation involves.[134] But the oral Jesus tradition itself provided the continuity, the living link back to the ministry of Jesus, and it was no doubt treasured for that very reason; the very character of the tradition, retaining as it does so many of its Galilean village[135] and pre-Easter themes,[136] not to mention its Aramaic resonances (see above, pp. 106–7), makes that point clear enough. Here we may learn from postmodernism's emphasis on both the reader and the tradition. If it is indeed the case that the hearer fills in the "gaps in signification" from the tradition, that an audience interprets a particular performance from their shared knowledge,[137] then we can be fairly confident that the Jesus tradition was an essential part of that shared knowledge, enabling the hearers in church gatherings to "plug in" to particular performances of the oral tradition and to exercise some control over its development.

Tradition Sequences

Another questionable assumption that has dominated the discussion since the early form critics is that in the initial stage of the traditioning process the tradition consisted of individual units.[138] That may indeed have been the case for the very beginning of the process, and the *Gospel of Thomas* gives it some credibility for the continuing tradition. But there is also good evidence of sayings being grouped and stories linked from what may have been a very early stage of the transmission process—even, in some cases, that Jesus may have taught in connected sequences that have been preserved. To group similar teachings and episodes would be an obvious mnemonic and didactic device for both teachers and taught, storytellers and regular hearers, more or less from the beginning. We may think, for example, of the sequence of beatitudes brought together in oral tradition or Q (Matt. 5:3, 4, 6, 11, 12/Luke 6:20b, 21b, 21a, 22, 23), and elaborated differently by Matthew and Luke (Matt. 5:3–12, Luke 6:20b–26). Or the sequence of mini-parables (the wedding guests, new and old cloth, new and old wineskins) in Mark 2:18–22 (followed by Matt. 9:14–17 and Luke 5:33–39). Or Jesus' responses to would-be disciples (Matt. 8:18–22/Luke 9:57–62). Or the sequence of teaching on the cost of discipleship and danger of loss (Mark 8:34–38; again followed by Matt. 16:24–27 and Luke 9:23–26), where Q/oral tradition has also preserved the sayings separately.[139] Similarly with the sequence of sayings about light and judgment in Mark 4:21–25 (followed by Luke 8:16–18), with equivalents scattered in Q and the *Gospel of Thomas*.[140]

A particularly interesting example of traditional material being grouped because of the inner connectedness of the traditions is the sequences of Jesus' teaching related to his exorcisms.

Mark	Theme	Q	
3:22–26	Beelzebul	Matt. 12:24–26	Luke 11:15–18
	Finger/Spirit of God	Matt. 12:27–28	Luke 11:19–20
3:27	Strong man	Matt. 12:29	Luke 11:21–22
	He who has ears	Matt. 12:30	Luke 11:23
3:28–29	Unforgivable sin	Matt. 12:31–32	Luke 12:10
	Return of unclean spirit	Matt. 12:43–45	Luke 11:24–26

Here are two sets of sayings, one with three sayings (Mark), the other with five sayings (Q/Luke), of which only two overlap in that sequence. Both the groupings and their diversity typify the process of oral transmission.[141]

Even more fascinating, but almost impossible to set out in tabular form, is the tradition of the sending out of the disciples on mission, where it is evident from Mark 6:7–13 and the parallels in Matt. 9:37–10:1, 7–16, Luke 9:1–6 and Luke 10:1–12 that there were at least two variations, one used by Mark and another oral (Q?) version. The variations make it probable that the material was used and reused, probably beginning with Jesus' own instructions for mission, but developed and elaborated in terms of subsequent experience of early Christian mission.[142]

As for Q itself, the current growth in Q studies shows amazing confidence in handling a text whose scope and content will always be a matter of argument and hypothesis. How in particular is one to distinguish redaction from (initial) composition?[143] If a redactor was not troubled by the presence of aporiae and tensions in his final text, would an initial compositor of Q have felt any different?[144] How can one both argue for the coherence and unity of Q (as proof of its existence), and at the same time argue that internal tensions indicate disunity, without the one argument throwing the other into question? Textual tensions are no proof of redactional layers (what author ever succeeded in removing all tensions from his/her final product, or attempted to do so?). The point can be pushed further by arguing that Q was itself composed as a sequence of discourses,[145] and the composition of Mark itself can be understood as setting in appropriate sequence a number of groupings already familiar in the oral traditioning process:[146]

24 hours in the ministry of Jesus	Mark 1:21–38
Jesus in controversy (in Galilee)	Mark 2:1–3:6
Parables of Jesus	Mark 4:2–33
Miracles of Jesus around the lake	Mark 4:35–5:43; 6:32–52
Marriage, children, and discipleship	Mark 10:2–31
Jesus in controversy (in Jerusalem)	Mark 12:13–37
The little apocalypse	Mark 13:1–32
The passion narrative	Mark 14:1–15:47

Of course most of this is unavoidably speculative; even more so if we were to guess at whether and how passages such as Mark 4:2–33 (parables of Jesus) and Mark 13:1–32 (the little apocalypse) grew by a process of aggregation from earlier, smaller groupings. The point is that we should not assume that such compositional procedures came into the process only at a later stage of the process or only when the tradition was written down.

Not Layers but Performances

One of the most important conclusions to emerge from this review of the oral character of so much of the Jesus tradition, and of the likely processes of oral transmission, is that the perspective that has dominated the study of the history of Synoptic tradition is simply wrong-headed. Bultmann set out the playing field by conceiving of the Jesus tradition as "composed of a series of layers."[147] The consequence of this literary paradigm was that each retelling of episodes or parts of the Jesus tradition was bound to be conceived of on the analogy of an editor editing a literary text. Each retelling was like a new (edited) edition. And so the impression of each retelling as another layer superimposed upon earlier layers became almost inescapable, especially when the literary imagery was integrated with the archaeological image of the ancient tell, where research proceeds by digging down through the historical layers.[148] The consequence has been widespread disillusion at the prospect of ever being able successfully to strip off the successive layers of editing to leave some primary layer exposed clearly to view. Equally inevitable from such a perspective were the suspicion and skepticism met by any bold enough to claim that they had been successful in their literary archaeology and had actually uncovered a large area of Jesus' bedrock teaching.

But the imagery is simply inappropriate. An oral retelling of a tradition is not at all like a new literary edition. It has not worked on or from a previous retelling. How could it? The previous retelling was not "there" as a text to be consulted. And in the retelling in turn the retold tradition did not come into existence as a kind of artifact, to be examined as by an editor and reedited for the next retelling. In oral transmission a tradition is performed, not edited. And as we have seen, performance includes both elements of stability and elements of variability—stability of subject and theme, of key details or core exchanges; variability in the supporting details and the particular emphases to be drawn out. That is a very different perspective. It allows, indeed requires, rather different conclusions, including the likelihood that the stabilities of the tradition were sufficiently maintained and the variabilities of the retellings subject to sufficient control for the substance of the tradition, and often actual words of Jesus that made the first tradition-forming impact, to continue as integral parts of the living tradition, for at least as long as it took for the Synoptic tradition to be written down. In other words, whereas the concept of literary layers implies increasing remoteness from an "original," "pure," or "authentic" layer, the concept of performance allows a directness, even an immediacy of interaction with a living theme and core even when variously embroidered in various retellings.[149]

The concept of oral transmission, as illustrated from the Synoptic tradition itself, therefore, does not encourage either the skepticism that has come to afflict the "quest of the historical Jesus" or the lopsided findings of the neo-Liberal questers. Rather it points a clear middle way between a model of parrotlike memorization on the one hand and any impression of oral transmission as a series of evanescent reminiscences of some or several retellings on the other. It encourages neither those who are content with nothing short of the historicity of every detail and word of the text, nor those who can see and hear nothing other than the faith of the early churches. It encourages us rather to see and hear the Synoptic tradition as the repertoire of the early churches when they recalled the Jesus who had called their first leaders and predecessors to discipleship and celebrated again the powerful impact of his life and teaching.

Oral Tradition to Written Gospel

We need not follow the course of oral transmission beyond the transition from oral tradition to written Gospel. The significance of that transition can be exaggerated, as we noted above in reviewing the work of Werner Kelber: Jesus tradition did not cease to circulate in oral form simply because it had been written down, and hearings of a Gospel being read would be part of the oral/aural transmission, to be retold in further circles of orality.[150] But there are two other aspects, misleading impressions, or unexamined assumptions that have encouraged false perspectives on the subject and should be highlighted here.

One is the impression that the oral Jesus tradition was like two (or several) narrow streams that were wholly absorbed into the written Gospels through their sources. So much of the focus in Gospel research has been on the question of sources for the Gospels that it has been natural, I suppose, for oral tradition to be conceived simply as source material for the Gospels, without any real attempt being made to conceptualize what oral communities were like and how the oral tradition functioned prior to and independently of written collections and Gospels. As already noted, some narrative criticism and some discussions of Synoptic pericopes at times almost seem to assume that when a copy of Mark or Matthew or Luke was initially received by any church, that was the first time the church had heard the Jesus tradition contained therein. But this is to ignore, or forget, one of the key insights of form criticism in the beginning—that is, the recognition that the tradition took various forms because the forms reflected the way the tradition was used in the first churches. In fact, it is almost self-evident that the Synoptists proceeded by gathering and ordering Jesus tradition that had already been in circulation, that is, had already been well enough known to various churches, for at least some years if not decades. Where else did the evangelists find the tradition? Stored up, unused, in an old box at the back of some teacher's house? Stored up, unrehearsed, in the failing memory of an old apostle? Hardly! On the contrary, it is much more likely that when the Synoptics were first received by various churches, these churches *already* possessed (in communal oral memory or in written form) their own versions of much of the material. They would be able to compare the evangelist's version of much of the tradition with their own versions. As we have seen above, the divergences between different versions of the Synoptic tradition imply a lively and flexible oral tradition known to the evangelists and presumably also to the churches with which they were associated.

This line of thought links in to the other assumption that has become debilitatingly pervasive: that each document belongs to and represents the views of only one community, and that the tensions within and between documents indicate rival camps and already different Christianities. The assumption derives again from the first insights of form criticism: that the forms of the tradition reflect the interests of the churches that used them. This was reinforced by the sociological perspective of the final quarter of the twentieth century: literature as the expression not so much of a single mind as of a social context. But these insights have been narrowed (and distorted) in a quite extraordinary way, to claim in effect that each text was written by and for a particular community—a Q community, a Mark community, a Matthean community, and so on.[151] The assumption is that Q, for example, somehow *defines* its community: it is a "Q community" in the sense that the Q material is its *only* Jesus tradition; it holds to this material in distinction from (defiance of?) other communities who are similarly defined by their document (the logic would be to suppose a passion-narrative community, a miracles-source community, and then a Mark community, and so on).[152] But the assumption must cover also the streams of tradition that entered into the Gospels. The implication, in other words, is of differing and conflicting streams of tradition more or less from the first, celebrating in effect different Jesuses—a prophetic and/or apocalyptic Jesus, Jesus the wisdom teacher, the Jesus of aretalogies (divine man), and so on.[153]

Richard Bauckham has recently challenged this assumption with regard to the written Gospels. His counterthesis is that "the Gospels were written for general circulation around the churches and so envisaged a very general Christian audience. Their implied readership is not specific but indefinite: any and every Christian community in the late-first-century Roman

Empire."[154] The claim may be too exaggerated (for *all* Christians?), though we should not discount the likelihood that evangelists wrote out of their more local experience primarily with a view to a much larger circle of churches, in Syria-Cilicia, for example. Bauckham needs to give more weight to the likelihood that particular communities were the evangelists' *source* for Jesus tradition, as distinct from communities as the evangelists' *target* in writing their Gospels. But he is justified in dismissing the idea that the evangelist would have written his Gospel for the community in which he lived.[155]

The point here, however, is that Bauckham is certainly correct to highlight the evidence that the first churches were by no means as isolated from one another and at odds with one another as has been so often assumed. If Paul's letters (and Acts) are any guide, the first churches consisted rather of "a network of communities in constant communication," linked by messengers, letters, and visits by leading figures in the new movement.[156] This ties in with what we would anyway have expected: that church founding included the initial communication of foundation tradition; and that Paul could assume common tradition, including knowledge of Jesus tradition, even in a church that he had never previously visited (Rome). And though there were indeed severe tensions between Paul and the Jerusalem leadership, Paul still regarded the lines of continuity between the churches in Judea and those of the Gentile mission as a matter of first importance (Gal. 1:22; 1 Thess. 2:14; 2 Cor. 1:16). In short, the suggestion that there were churches who knew only one stream of tradition—Jesus only as a miracle worker, or only as a wisdom teacher, etc.—has been given far too much uncritical credence in scholarly discussions on the Gospels and ought to have been dismissed a lot sooner.

IN SUMMARY

We began by noting the widespread recognition among specialists in orality of the character of oral transmission, as a mix of constant themes and flexibility, of fixed and variable elements in oral retelling. But we also noted that such insights had hardly begun to be exploited adequately in the treatment of Jesus tradition as oral tradition. However, Bailey's observations, drawn from his experience of oral traditioning processes in Middle Eastern village life, have highlighted points of potential importance, particularly on the rationale which, in the cases in point, determined the distinction between the more fixed elements and constant themes on the one hand, and the flexible and variable elements on the other. Where stories or teaching was important for the community's identity and life there would be a concern to maintain the core or key features, however varied other details (less important to the story's or teaching's point) in successive retellings.

Our own examination of the Jesus tradition itself confirmed the relevance of the oral paradigm and the danger of assuming (consciously or otherwise) the literary paradigm. The findings did not call into serious question the priority of Mark or the existence of a document Q. But in each of the examples marshaled the degree of variation between clearly parallel traditions, and the inconsequential character of so much of the variations, should hardly have encouraged an explanation in terms of literary dependence (on Mark or Q) or of literary editing. But the combination of stability and flexibility positively cried out to be recognized as typically oral in character. That probably implies in at least some cases that the variation was due to knowledge and use of the same tradition in oral mode, as part of the community tradition familiar to Matthew and Luke. And even if a pericope was derived from Mark or Q, the retelling by Matthew or Luke is itself better described as in oral mode, maintaining the character of an oral retelling more than of a literary editing.

In both cases (narratives and teachings) we also noted (1) a concern to remember the things Jesus had done and said. The discipleship and embryonic communities that had been formed and shaped by the impact of Jesus' life and message would naturally have celebrated that tradition as central to their own identity as disciples and churches. We noted also (2) that the memories consisted in stories and teachings whose own identity was focused in particular themes and/or particular words and phrases —usually those said by Jesus himself. And (3) that the variations and developments were not linear or cumulative in character, but the variations of oral performance. The material examined indicated neither concern to preserve some kind of literalistic historicity of detail, nor any readiness to flood the tradition with Jewish wisdom or prophetic utterance.

Finally, we have observed that the pattern of the oral traditioning process was probably established more or less from the beginning (before the first Easter) and was probably maintained in character through to (and beyond) the writing of the tradition down. The first impact (sequence of impacts) made by Jesus resulted in the formation of tradition, which was itself formative and constitutive of community/church through Easter and beyond Galilee, and which was preserved and celebrated through regular performance (whether in communal or specifically liturgical gatherings), or reviewed for apologetic or catechetical purposes. In other words, what we today are confronted with in the Gospels is not the top layer (last edition) of a series of increasingly impenetrable layers, but the living tradition of Christian celebration which takes us with surprising immediacy to the heart of the first memories of Jesus.

On the basis of all this we can begin to build a portrayal of the remembered Jesus, of the impact made by his words and deeds on the first disciples as that impact was "translated" into oral tradition and as it was passed down in oral performance within the earliest circles of disciples and the churches, to be enshrined in due course in the written Synoptic tradition.

NOTES

1. I use the term "historical Jesus," mindful of the fact that it can be misleading, since it properly denotes the historians' Jesus, Jesus as "reconstructed" (!) by the methods of historical research, but is regularly used to denote the man himself who walked and talked in the hills and villages of Galilee in the late twenties and/or early thirties of the common era.

2. I draw on W. G. Kümmel's abstract, despite his somewhat misleading decription (*The New Testament: The History of the Investigation of Its Problems* [1970; Nashville: Abingdon, 1972; London: SCM, 1973], 79–82).

3. Extracts from J. G. Herder, *Collected Works* (ed. B. Suphan), Vol. XIX, in Kümmel, *New Testament*, 81–82. B. Reicke (*The Roots of the Synoptic Gospels* [Philadelphia: Fortress, 1986], 11–12) makes special mention of J. C. L. Gieseler, *Historisch-kritischer Versuch über die Entstehung und die frühesten Schicksale der schriftlichen Evangelien* (Leipzig: Englemann, 1818).

4. Kümmel's own treatment represents the same priorities.

5. Rudolf Bultmann, "The Study of the Synoptic Gospels," in *Form Criticism,* with K. Kundsin (1934; New York: Harper Torchbook, 1962), 1.

6. Rudolf Bultmann, "The New Approach to the Synoptic Problem" (1926), in *Existence and Faith* (London: Collins, Fontana, 1964), 39–62, here 47.

7. Rudolf Bultmann, *The History of the Synoptic Tradition* (1921; 2nd ed., 1931; Eng. trans. Oxford: Blackwell, 1963), 6–7; though note the criticism of E. P. Sanders, *The Tendencies of the Synoptic Tradition,* Society for New Testament Studies Monograph Series 9 (Cambridge: Cambridge University Press, 1969), 18 n. 4.

8. "The 'pure form' (*reinen Gattung*) represents a mixture of linguistic and history of language categories, which is to be assigned to an out of date conception of language development" (eine Vermischung linguistischer und sprachhistorischer Kategorien . . . die einer heute überholten Auffassung der Sprachen-

twicklung zuzuweisen ist) (J. Schröter, *Erinnerung an Jesu Worte: Studien zur Rezeption der Logienüberlieferung in Markus, Q und Thomas,* Wissenschaftliche Monographien zum Alten und Neuen Testament 76 (Neukirchen-Vluyn: Neukirchener Verlag, 1997], 59, also 141–42).

9. But see Sanders's critique in *Tendencies,* in summary: "There are no hard and fast laws of the development of the Synoptic tradition. On all counts the tradition developed in opposite directions. It became both longer and shorter, both more and less detailed, and both more and less Semitic . . ." (p. 272).

10. See, e.g., his assertions in "New Approach," 45–47, and "Study," 29, and the fuller analysis of *History* and critique of the assumption by W. H. Kelber, *The Oral and the Written Gospel* (Philadelphia: Fortress, 1983), 2–8.

11. Rudolf Bultmann, *Jesus and the Word* (New York: Scribners, 1935), 12–13.

12. Ibid.

13. The most successful and influential was H. Conzelmann, *Die Mitte der Zeit* (Tübingen: Mohr-Siebeck, 1953; 2nd ed., 1957; 5th ed., 1964; Eng. trans. *The Theology of St. Luke* [London: Faber & Faber, 1961]).

14. C. F. D. Moule, *The Birth of the New Testament* (London: A. & C. Black, 1962; 3rd ed., 1981), 3.

15. See particularly his recognition that Papias (Eusebius, *HE* 3.39.15) conceived of Peter retelling the teaching of Jesus "'*pros tas chreias,* with reference to the needs' (i.e., as occasion demanded, as need arose)" (*Birth,* 108, 120–21); his observation on "the more fluid interchange of forms (in worship), such that snatches of prayer and hymnody flow in and out of the texture of pastoral exhortation" (p. 270) also parallels the recognition among folklorists on the fluidity of oral performances (see pp. 88–91 on Werner Kelber).

16. H. Riesenfeld, "The Gospel Tradition and Its Beginning" (1957), in *The Gospel Tradition* (Philadelphia: Fortress, 1970), 1–29, here 16, 26, 24.

17. B. Gerhardsson, *Memory and Manuscript: Oral Tradition and Written Transmission in Rabbinic Judaism and Early Christianity* (Lund: Gleerup, 1961); refined in a succession of further publications: *Tradition and Transmission in Early Christianity* (Lund: Gleerup, 1964); *The Origins of the Gospel Traditions* (Philadelphia: Fortress, 1979); *The Gospel Tradition* (Lund: Gleerup, 1986); "Illuminating the Kingdom: Narrative Meshalim in the Synoptic Gospels," in *Jesus and the Oral Gospel Tradition,* ed. H. Wansbrough, Journal for the Study of the New Testament Supplement 64 (Sheffield: Sheffield Academic Press, 1991), 266–309.

18. E.g., "The general attitude was that words and items of knowledge must be memorized: *tantum scimus, quantum memoria tenemus*" [we only know as much as we retain in our memory] (Gerhardsson, *Memory,* 124).

19. "Cicero's saying was applied to its fullest extent in Rabbinic Judaism: *repetitio est mater studiorum.* Knowledge is gained by repetition, passed on by repetition, kept alive by repetition. A Rabbi's life is one continual repetition" (Gerhardsson, *Memory,* 168).

20. Gerhardsson, *Memory,* 130–36, here 133; also chs. 9–10.

21. Ibid., 328, 332, 335; similarly *Origins,* 19–20, 72–73; *Gospel,* 39–42. R. Riesner also emphasizes the role of learning by heart (*Auswendiglernen*) in Jesus' teaching (*Jesus als Lehrer,* Wissenschaftliche Untersuchung zum Neuen Testament 2.7 [Tübingen: Mohr-Siebeck, 1981], 365–67, 440-53; idem, "Jesus as Preacher and Teacher," in *Jesus,* ed. Wansbrough, 185–210, here 203–4).

22. See J. Neusner's apology for his earlier review in his Foreword to the recent reprint of Gerhardsson's *Memory* and *Tradition* (Grand Rapids: Eerdmans, 1998).

23. Kelber, *Oral,* 14.

24. Schröter, *Erinnerung,* 29–30. Gerhardsson did not examine the Synoptic tradition itself in *Memory,* though he went a considerable way toward filling the gap twenty-five years later in his *Gospel.*

25. See, e.g., my "Can the Third Quest Hope to Succeed?" in *Authenticating the Activities of Jesus,* ed. B. Chilton and C. A. Evans (Leiden: Brill, 1999), 31-48, here 37–38.

26. Gerhardsson can speak of "a logos fixed by the college of Apostles," with reference to the tradition of 1 Cor. 15:3ff. (*Memory,* 297).

27. The earlier contribution by the Seminar on "Oral Traditional Literature and the Gospels" passed largely unnoticed, mainly, I suppose, because it functioned in service of the theme for the overall Colloquy on *The Relationships Among the Gospels,* ed. W. O. Walker (San Antonio, Tex.: Trinity University Press, 1978), 31–122. L. E. Keck reviews earlier work and summarizes the Seminar's discussion ("Oral Traditional Literature and the Gospels: The Seminar," in *Relationships,* 103–22).

28. W. J. Ong, *Orality and Literacy: The Technologizing of the Word* (1982; London: Routledge, 1988), 33–36, 57–68. The work of A. B. Lord, *The Singer of Tales* (Cambridge, Mass.: Harvard University Press, 1978) has been seminal (here especially ch. 5). Note also R. Finnegan, *Oral Poetry: Its Nature, Significance and Social Context* (Cambridge: Cambridge University Press, 1977), ch. 3, esp. 73–87, also 90–109. See also A. B. Lord, "The Gospels as Oral Traditional Literature," in *Relationships,* ed. Walker, 33–91, here 37–38, 63–64, 87–89; and the overview by D. E. Aune, "Prolegomena to the Study of Oral Tradition in the Hellenistic World," in *Jesus,* ed. Wansbrough, 59–106, with bibliography.

29. Kelber, *Oral,* 27; see also 50–51.

30. Ibid., 27–28, quoting B. Peabody, *The Winged Word: A Study in the Technique of Ancient Greek Oral Composition as Seen Principally through Hesiod's Works and Days* (Albany: State University of New York Press, 1975), 96.

31. Kelber, *Oral,* 29–30; quoting Lord, *Singer,* 120. Lord also characterizes the change from oral to literary composition as the change "from stability of essential story, which is the goal of oral tradition, to stability of text, of the exact words of the story" (*Singer,* 138).

32. Kelber, *Oral,* 33, 54; quoting E. A. Havelock, *Preface to Plato* (Cambridge, Mass.: Harvard University Press, 1963), 92, 147, 184, passim.

33. Ong begins by noting: "We—readers of books such as this—are so literate

that it is very difficult for us to conceive of an oral universe of communication or thought *except as a variation of a literate universe*" (*Orality*, 2, my emphasis). As noted above, Bultmann did not avoid this mistake.

34. Kelber, *Oral*, 19, referring to W. J. Ong, *The Presence of the Word: Some Prolegomena for Cultural and Religious History* (New Haven: Yale University Press, 1967; paperback Minneapolis: University of Minnesota, 1981), 111–38.

35. See further P. J. Achtemeier, "*Omne verbum sonat*: The New Testament and the Oral Environment of Late Western Antiquity," *JBL* 109 (1990): 3–27; R. A. Horsley and J. A. Draper, *Whoever Hears You Hears Me: Prophets, Performance, and Tradition in Q* (Harrisburg, Pa.: Trinity Press International, 1999), 132–34, 144–45, in dependence on R. Thomas, *Literacy and Orality in Ancient Greece* (Cambridge: Cambridge University Press, 1992).

36. Influential here has been R. W. Funk, "The Apostolic Parousia: Form and Significance," in *Christian History and Interpretation*, Festschrift J. Knox, ed. W. R. Farmer et al. (Cambridge: Cambridge University Press, 1967), 249–68.

37. The idea is developed by Frances Young, *The Art of Performance: Towards a Theology of Holy Scripture* (London: Darton, Longman & Todd, 1990).

38. "The reader is absent from the writing of the book, the writer is absent from its reading" (Kelber, *Oral*, 92, quoting P. Ricoeur, *Interpretation Theory: Discourse and the Surplus of Meaning* [Fort Worth: Texas Christian University Press, 1976], 35).

39. Lord, *Singer*, 100–101: "In a sense each performance is 'an' original, if not 'the' original. The truth of the matter is that our concept of 'the original,' of 'the song,' simply makes no sense in oral tradition."

40. Kelber, *Oral*, 29, also 59, 62. Finnegan also glosses Lord: "There is no correct text, no idea that one version is more 'authentic' than another: each performance is a unique and original creation with its own validity" (*Oral Poetry*, 65). She credits Lord with bringing this point home most convincingly (p. 79), though by way of critique she points out that memorization also plays a part (pp. 79, 86).

41. Kelber, *Oral*, 20–21, citing appositely the demonstration by H. Schürmann of sayings on kingdom, repentance, judgment, love of enemy, eschatological preparedness, etc., which show no trace of post-Easter influence ("Die vorösterlichen Anfänge der Logientradition: Versuch eines formgeschichtlichen Zugangs zum Leben Jesu," in *Der historische Jesus und der kerygmatische Christus*, ed. H. Ristow and K. Matthiae [Berlin: Evangelische, 1962], 342–70).

42. Kelber, *Oral*, ch. 2. Unfortunately the overevaluation of the sayings source Q and the *Gospel of Thomas* in the neo-Liberal quest of the Jesus Seminar and J. D. Crossan (*The Historical Jesus: The Life of a Mediterranean Jewish Peasant* [San Francisco: Harper, 1991]) has continued to direct attention away from the importance of stories told about Jesus.

43. Kelber, *Oral*, 65–68.

44. Ibid., 91, 94.

45. The oral character of Mark's narrative has since been strongly emphasized by T. P. Haverly, "Oral Traditional Literature and the Composition of Mark's Gospel" (Ph.D. diss., Edinburgh, 1983), and especially by J. Dewey, "Oral Methods of Structuring Narrative in Mark," *Interpretation* 43 (1989): 32–44; eadem, "The Gospel of Mark as an Oral-Aural Event: Implications for Interpretation," in *The New Literary Criticism and the New Testament,* ed. E. S. Malbon and E. V. McKnight, Journal for the Study of the New Testament Supplement 109 (Sheffield: Sheffield Academic Press, 1994), 145–63. Note also Lord's earlier evaluation of "The Gospels as Oral Traditional Literature," in *Relationships,* ed. Walker, 58–84 (particularly 79–80, 82), 90–91. The conclusion of the symposium entitled *Jesus and the Oral Gospel Tradition* (ed. H. Wansbrough) can cut both ways: "We have been unable to deduce or derive any marks which distinguish clearly between an oral and a written transmission process. Each can show a similar degree of fixity and variability" (p. 12). Cf. Schröter, *Erinnerung,* 55, 60.

46. Kelber, *Oral,* 91–96, 130–31, 184–85 (quotations from 95, 98, 131).

47. See, e.g., Ø. Andersen, "Oral Tradition," in *Jesus,* ed. Wansbrough, 17–58, here 43–53.

48. The more serious danger in writing down a tradition, as Lord observed, is "when the singer believes that they (the written versions) are *the* way in which the song *should* be presented" (*Singer,* 79).

49. For this reason I often use the inelegant verbal noun formation "traditioning" to indicate a process of which "transmission" per se may be only a part.

50. Kelber, *Oral,* 96–105, 129 (quotations from 98, 99–100, 129).

51. Ibid., 141–51, 151–68.

52. Ibid., 185–99, 199–207 (quotations from 201, 207).

53. Ibid., 201.

54. Deut. 6:20–25: "*we* were Pharaoh's slaves . . . and the Lord brought *us* out of Egypt. . . ."

55. Kelber, *Oral,* 78–79.

56. K. E. Bailey, "Informal Controlled Oral Tradition and the Synoptic Gospels," *Asia Journal of Theology* 5 (1991): 34–54; reprinted in *Themelios* 20, no. 2 (1995): 4–11 (double column pages).

57. Ibid., 4–5.

58. Ibid., 6–7.

59. Ibid., 7–8.

60. Ibid., 8–9. To be noted is the fact that "community" here does not equate to "individual village," since the Evangelical community would be scattered over many villages.

61. Bailey, "Informal," 9–10.

62. The police accepted the community's version ("A camel stepped on him"), not because they did not know what had happened but because they accepted the community's judgment that the shooting was an accident.

63. Bailey notes that he had first heard the story twenty-eight years earlier, but the central core was "still indelibly fixed" in his mind because it was so firmly implanted in his memory that first week ("Informal," 9–10). If I may add my own pennyworth. I met Kenneth Bailey in 1976 or 1977, when he told me the same two stories. They made such an impression on me that I retold them several times during the intervening years. When I eventually came across the article cited (in 1998) I was fascinated to note that my own retelling had maintained the outline and the key features of the core elements, although in my retelling the supporting details had been reshaped. This oral transmission covered more than twenty years, after a single hearing of the stories, by one who normally forgets a good joke almost as soon as he has heard it!

64. Bailey, "Informal," 10.

65. Cf. A. B. Lord's examples of songs with a "more or less stable core" (*The Singer Resumes the Tale* [Ithaca, N.Y.: Cornell University Press, 1995], 44, 47, 61–62).

66. The three accounts of Paul's conversion in Acts are occasionally treated synoptically (e.g., C. W. Hedrick, "Paul's Conversion/Call: A Comparative Analysis of the Three Reports in Acts," *Journal of Biblical Literature* 100 [1981]: 415–32; C. K. Barrett, *Acts 1–14,* International Critical Commentary (Edinburgh: T & T Clark, 1994], 439–45), but their value as examples of the way oral tradition functioned has thus far not really been appreciated.

67. The passages are thus a good example of Lord's observation that even from the same singer, stability from one performance to another is likely to lie not at the word-for-word level of the text, but at the levels of theme and story pattern (*Singer,* ch. 5). Similarly Finnegan: "that variability is not just a feature of lengthy oral transmission through time and space but is inherent both in different renderings of one literary piece within the same group and period and even in texts by the same person delivered at no great interval in time. In such cases, memorisation of basic themes or plots is involved, but a generalised explanation of the oral poetry in terms of particular texts exactly memorised does not easily fit the abundant variability demonstrated in tape-recorded (as well as dictated) texts" (*Oral Poetry,* 57).

68. The point is simply assumed, e.g., by Bultmann (*History,* 39) and *The Complete Gospels,* ed. R. J. Miller (Sonoma, Calif.: Polebridge, 1994), 262–63.

69. To avoid the confusion that has been endemic in discussion of Q, I use "q" for the actual material common to Matthew and Luke, and "Q" for the hypothesized document from which q was drawn. The working assumption that Q = q is one of the major weaknesses in all Q research.

70. The most weighty consideration is that Matthew and Luke both agree in positioning the episode after the Sermon on the Mount/Plain (A. Harnack, *The Sayings of Jesus* [London: Williams & Norgate, 1908], 74; D. Lührmann, *Die Redaktion der Logienquelle,* Wissenschaftliche Monographien zum Alten und

Neuen Testaments 33; Neukirchen-Vluyn: Neukirchener Verlag, 1969], 57). Is that sufficient?

71. Contrast R. W. Funk et al., *The Five Gospels: The Search for the Authentic Words of Jesus* (New York: Macmillan; Sonoma, Calif.: Polebridge, 1993): "Since the words ascribed to Jesus vary, and since there is nothing distinctive about them, we must assume they were created by story-tellers" (p. 300). But the argument is self-defeating: would storytellers create such unmemorable words?

72. Funk's discussion is quite confused as to whether Matt. 8:11–12 could have existed separately from Matthew's narrative context (*Five Gospels*, 160) despite the recognition that its Q parallel (Luke 13:28–29) need not presuppose a Gentile mission (p. 348); J. S. Kloppenborg argues that the "tendentious development of the healing story into an apology for Gentile inclusion occurred already in the oral stage" prior to Q (*The Formation of Q* [Philadelphia: Fortress, 1987], 120).

73. Contrast the meticulous analysis of D. Catchpole, *The Quest for Q* (Edinburgh: T & T Clark, 1993), ch. 10, which assumes the literary paradigm throughout and evokes the picture of Matthew and Luke carefully editing an original Q more or less word by word.

74. See further C. H. Dodd, *Historical Tradition in the Fourth Gospel* (Cambridge: Cambridge University Press, 1963), 188–95; J. D. G. Dunn, "John and the Oral Gospel Tradition," in *Jesus*, ed. Wansbrough, 351–79, here 359–63.

75. For John's theology of different levels of faith, see, e.g., R. E. Brown, *The Gospel According to John*, 2 vols., Anchor Bible 29, 29A (New York: Doubleday, 1966), 1:530–31. Dodd saw the contrast as between the Synoptics' interest in the remarkable faith of a Gentile, whereas "in John the central interest lies in the life-giving power of the word of Christ" (*Historical Tradition*, 194). Crossan, however, overstates the contrast between the two versions (Matthew/Luke and John) when he talks of the story being pulled in "two contradictory directions" (*Historical Jesus*, 327).

76. Since Herod's army was modeled on the Roman pattern, the "centurion" of the Synoptic account could conceivably have been a Jew.

77. *Pace* F. Neirynck, who assumes that only redaction of literary sources can be invoked to explain the differences ("John 4.46–54: Signs Source and/or Synoptic Gospels," in *Evangelica II* [Leuven: Leuven University Press, 1991], 679–88).

78. See E. Haenchen, *Johannesevangelium* (Tübingen: Mohr-Siebeck, 1980), 260–61, summarizing his treatment in "Johanneische Probleme," in *Gott und Mensch* (Tübingen: Mohr-Siebeck, 1965), 82–90.

79. This remains the large consensus view among New Testament specialists, despite the continuing protests of a vocal minority.

80. It is widely recognized that the story is structured on the pattern of the story of Jonah, with the key lines distinctive to bring out the point, How much greater than Jonah is here! See, e.g., W. D. Davies and D. C. Allison, *Matthew 8-18*, International Critical Commentary (Edinburgh: T & T Clark, 1991), 70.

81. In particular Matthew's retelling emphasizes the themes of discipleship/ following (*akolouthein*—8:19, 22, 23) and of "little faith" (*oligopistos/ia*), distinctive to Matthew (8:26; cf. 6:30; 14:31; 16:8; 17:20).

82. Characteristic of discussion dominated by the literary paradigm is the assumption that variations between the two versions can be explained only in terms of conflation of sources; see, e.g., V. Taylor, *Mark* (London: Macmillan, 1952), 347.

83. Here again Taylor's discussion in terms of "fragments loosely connected at 35 and 36" and "fragmentary stories" (*Mark*, 403–4) betrays the assumption that there must have been an original story or original stories of which only fragments remain, and thus also his failure to appreciate the character of oral tradition.

84. The healing of Peter's mother-in-law (Mark 1:29–31/Matt. 8:14–15/Luke 4:38–39); the cleansing of the leper (Mark 1:40–45/Matt. 8:1–4/Luke 5:12–16); Jesus' true family (Mark 3:31–35/Matt. 12:46–50/Luke 8:19–21); precedence among the disciples (Mark 10:35–45 = Matt. 20:20–28; but Luke 20:24–27); the healing of the blind man/men (Mark 10:46–52/Matt. 20:29–34/Luke 18:35–43). Why do the lists of the twelve close disciples of Jesus vary as they do (Mark 3:16–19/Matt. 10:2–4/Luke 6:13–16)? Presumably because in the process of oral transmission confusion had arisen over the names of one or two of the least significant members of the group. The sequence of Mark 12:1–37/Matt. 21:33–46, 22:15–46/Luke 20:9–44 could be orally related, but the extent and consistency of verbal link suggest a primarily literary dependence of Matthew and Luke on Matthew. The constancy of verbal link between the three accounts of the feeding of the five thousand likewise probably indicates an editing rather than a retelling process (Mark 6:32–44/Matt. 14:13–21/Luke 9:10–17); but John's version (John 6:1–15), where almost the sole verbal links are the numbers (cost, loaves and fishes, participants, baskets of fragments), surely indicates oral retelling. The character of the sequel (Mark 6:45–52/Matt. 14:22–33/John 6:16–21) points clearly in the same direction. And though Matthew's dependence on Mark for the passion narrative is clear, the alternative version used by Luke may well indicate a tradition passed down orally independent of the Mark/Matthean (literary) version.

85. The linked stories of the Gerasene demoniac (Mark 5:1–20/Matt. 8:28–34/ Luke 8:26–39) and Jairus's daughter and the woman with the hemorrhage (Mark 5:21–43/Matt. 9:18–26/Luke 8:40–56) look like examples of heavy abbreviation of Marcan redundancy, especially by Matthew. Similarly with Matthew's treatment of the death of John the Baptist (Mark 6:17–29/Matt. 14:3–12), and with Matthew's and Luke's treatment of the healing of the epileptic boy (Mark 9:14–29/Matt. 17:14–21/Luke 9:37–43). Lord notes that performances of often very different lengths are a mark of oral tradition (*Singer of Tales*, 109–17).

86. E.g., Matt. 12:5–7, 11–12a adds precedents more apposite to the two cases of Sabbath controversy than were provided in Mark 2:23–28 and 3:1–5 (Matt. 12:1–8 and 9–14); cf. Luke 13:10–17.

87. E.g., the Matthean additions to explain why Jesus accepted baptism from the Baptist (Matt. 3:14–15), and in his presentation of Peter as the representative disciple (Matt. 14:28–31; 16:17–19); the Lucan addition of a second mission (of the seventy[-two]) in Luke 10:1–12, presumably to foreshadow the Gentile mission (cf. 14:23 below).

88. Cf., e.g., Mark 6:3a, 5a with Matt. 13:55a, 58; Mark 10:17–18 with Matt. 19:16–17. In both cases Matthew's respect for the Marcan wording is clear, even when he changed it presumably to prevent any unwelcome implication (see my *The Evidence of Jesus* [London: SCM, 1985], 18–22). See further J. C. Hawkins, *Horae Synopticae: Contributions to the Study of the Synoptic Problem*, 2nd ed. (1898; Oxford: Clarendon, 1909), 117–25.

89. It should be noted that this deduction from the tradition itself coheres with Papias's account both of Peter's preaching and of Mark's composition: that Peter "gave/adapted (*epoieito*—could we say performed) his teaching with a view to the needs (*pros tas chreias*—that is, presumably, of the audiences), but not as making an orderly account (*syntaxin*) of the Lord's sayings, so that Mark did no wrong in thus writing down some things (*enia*) as he recalled them" (Eusebius, *HE* 3.39.15).

90. It is probably significant that the two traditions of the same event which diverge most markedly are those relating to the death of Judas (Matt. 27:3–10; Acts 1:15–20); in comparison with the death of Jesus, the fate of Judas was of little historical concern.

91. It is more likely that Matt. 10:5 (restriction of the disciples mission to Israel) recalls Jesus' own instruction than that Jesus was known to commend a Gentile mission and Matt. 10:5 emerged as a prophetic protest within the Judean churches; in fact, Jesus' commendation of a Gentile mission is at best an inference to be drawn from certain episodes in the tradition.

92. Mark 5:35/Luke 8:49; Mark 9:17/Luke 9:38; Mark 10:17/Matt. 19:16/Luke 18:18; Mark 10:20; Mark 12:14, 19, 32/Matt. 22:16, 24, 36/Luke 20:21, 28, 39; Matt. 8:19; 9:11; 12:38; 17:24; Luke 7:40; 10:25; 11:45; 12:13; 19:39. It should be recalled that Jesus seems also to have been remembered as "a teacher of people" by Josephus (*Ant.* 18.63).

93. Mark 4:38; 9:38; 10:35; 13:1/Luke 21:7; Mark 14:14/Matt. 26:18/Luke 22:11; though it is noticeable that Matthew and Luke seem to have avoided the term (for the most part) on the lips of the disciples, presumably as not being sufficiently exalted.

94. See further my *The Theology of Paul the Apostle* (Grand Rapids: Eerdmans, 1998), 185–95.

95. This is by no means to deny that Jesus knew at least some Greek (in what language did any exchange between a Gentile[?] centurion and Jesus, or between Jesus and Pilate take place?), or even that he may have spoken in Greek on occasion. Meier's discussion of the subject is quite sufficient for our purposes (*A Mar-*

ginal Jew: Rethinking the Historical Jesus, Anchor Bible Reference Library, 2 vols. [New York: Doubleday, 1991, 1994], 1:255–68, 287–300). On the question of penetration of the Greek language into first-century Israel, see especially M. Hengel, *The 'Hellenization' of Judaea in the First Century after Christ* (London: SCM, 1989); S. E. Porter, "Jesus and the Use of Greek in Galilee," in *Studying the Historical Jesus,* ed. Chilton and Evans, 123–54. I see no reason to depart from the huge consensus which continues to maintain that Jesus gave at least the great bulk of his teaching in Aramaic; see particularly J. A. Fitzmyer, "The Languages of Palestine in the First Century A.D.," in *A Wandering Aramean: Collected Aramaic Essays* (Missoula, Mont.: Scholars Press, 1979), 29–56; idem, "The Study of the Aramaic Background of the New Testament" in the same volume (pp. 1–27, here 6-10), to whom Meier acknowledges his debt. Porter argues that possibly seven of Jesus' conversations took place in Greek: Matt. 8:5–13; John 4:4–26; Mark 2:13–14; 7:25–30; 12:13–17; 8:27–30; 15:2–5, each, apart from John 4, with parallels (*The Criteria for Authenticity in Historical-Jesus Research,* Journal for the Study of the New Testament Supplement 191 [Sheffield: Sheffield Academic Press, 2000], 157–63).

96. Note the warning of M. Casey, "The Original Aramaic Form of Jesus' Interpretation of the Cup," *Journal of Theological Studies* 41 (1990): 1–12, particularly 11–12.

97. Riesner estimates that "about 80 per cent of the separate saying units are formulated in some kind of *parallelismus membrorum*" ("Jesus as Preacher and Teacher," 202).

98. C. F. Burney, *The Poetry of our Lord* (Oxford: Clarendon, 1925).

99. M. Black, *An Aramaic Approach to the Gospels and Acts,* 3rd ed. (Oxford: Clarendon, 1967), 160–85; though note Fitzmyer's strictures (*Wandering Aramean,* 16–17). See also Riesner, *Jesus als Lehrer,* 392–404.

100. J. Jeremias, *New Testament Theology,* vol. 1, *The Proclamation of Jesus* (1971; Eng. trans. London: SCM, 1971), 3–29.

101. R. W. Funk talks of Jesus' "voice print," including antithesis, synonymous parallelism, reversal, paradox and others more distinctive to Funk's own approach (*Honest To Jesus* [Sonoma, Calif.: Polebridge, 1996], 144–45, 149–58).

102. As B. H. Streeter observed in his *The Four Gospels: A Study of Origins* (London: Macmillan, 1924), 277–78.

103. This possibility is widely acknowledged; see, e.g., U. Luz, *Matthäus 1-7,* Evangelisch-katholischer Kommentar zum Neuen Testament (Zurich: Benziger; Neukirchen: Neukirchener Verlag, 1985), 334; Crossan, *Historical Jesus,* 293; Meier, *A Marginal Jew,* 2:357–58; H. D. Betz, *The Sermon on the Mount,* Hermeneia (Minneapolis: Fortress, 1995), 370. In *Didache* 8.3 it is commended that the prayer be said three times a day (a good Jewish practice).

104. Orthodoxy still celebrates the liturgies of St. John Chrysostom and St. Basil of Caesarea.

105. See further Jeremias, *Proclamation,* 195–96.

106. Text-critical data in B. M. Metzger, *A Textual Commentary on the Greek New Testament* (London: United Bible Societies, 1971, corrected 1975), 16–17. *Didache* 8.2–3 indicates an intermediate phase when the doxology was only "Yours is the power and the glory forever."

107. Jeremias, *Proclamation,* 196–97.

108. The references in Rom. 8:15–16 and Gal. 4:6 confirm that Paul understood the "*Abba*" prayer as distinctive of Christians.

109. For example, the benediction over the meal begins, "Blessed art thou, Lord our God, king of the universe."

110. It goes back into good Aramaic; see, e.g., Jeremias, *Proclamation,* 196; W. D. Davies and D. C. Allison, *Matthew 1-7,* International Critical Commentary (Edinburgh: T & T Clark, 1988), 593.

111. Funk, *Five Gospels,* 148–50; the discussion is vitiated by the assumption of literary dependence.

112. Crossan, *Historical Jesus,* 294.

113. J. A. Fitzmyer notes that both forms can be retrojected into contemporary Aramaic "with almost equal ease and problems" (*The Gospel According to Luke,* 2 vols., Anchor Bible 28, 28A [New York: Doubleday, 1981, 1985], 1394–95); see again Casey, "Original Aramaic Form."

114. See further my *Unity and Diversity in the New Testament* (London: SCM, 1977, 2nd ed., 1990), 165–67, and those cited there in n. 23.

115. The fact that Paul ascribes the tradition to "the Lord" (1 Cor. 11:23) should not be taken to indicate a revelation given to Paul after his conversion (as particularly most recently H. Maccoby, "Paul and the Eucharist," *New Testament Studies* 37 [1991]: 247–67). The language is the language of tradition ("I received" —*parelabon*; "I handed on to you"—*paredōka*), and "the Lord" from whom Paul received it is "the Lord Jesus (who) on the night in which he was betrayed took bread . . ." (11:23). See further the still valuable discussion of O. Cullmann, "The Tradition," in *The Early Church: Historical and Theological Studies* (London: SCM, 1956), 59–75, who notes *inter alia* that 1 Cor. 7:10 also refers the tradition of Jesus' teaching on divorce to "the Lord" ("To the married I give charge, not I but the Lord . . .") (p. 68).

116. The silence of *Didache* 9 ("concerning the Eucharist") as to any "words of institution" need not imply that *Didache* reflects an earlier stage (than Mark or 1 Corinthians 11) in the liturgical development (as Crossan argues [*Historical Jesus,* 360–67]). It could well be that *Didache* assumes the traditional core and attests simply the addition of thanksgiving (*eucharistein*) prayers deemed appropriate in a more liturgically solemnized act (as also *Didache* 10). John's Gospel says nothing of a last supper, but reflects knowledge of bread and wine words in John 6:52–58. For a recent brief discussion and review (with bibliography), see W. D. Davies and D. C. Allison, *Matthew 19-28,* International Critical Commentary (Edinburgh: T & T Clark, 1997), 465–69.

117. Particularly Matthew's addition of the phrase "for the forgiveness of sins" (Matt. 26:28), the very phrase he seems deliberately to have omitted in 3:2 (cf. Mark 1:4/Luke 3:3).

118. Matt. 6:22–23/Luke 11:34–36; Matt. 6:24/Luke 16:13; Matt. 6:25–34/Luke 12:22–32; Matt. 7:1–2/Luke 6:37a, 38b; Matt. 7:3–5/Luke 6:41–42; Matt. 7:7–11/ Luke 11:9–13; Matt. 7:12/Luke 6:31.

119. Despite which, most discussions simply assume redactional use of Q; see, e.g., Fitzmyer, *Luke*, and Davies and Allison, *Matthew*, ad loc. Streeter recognized the likelihood of "oral tradition in more than one form," but argues that differences have to be explained by Matthew's "conflation" of Q and M—that is, by literary editing (*Four Gospels*, 251–53).

120. *Didache* 1.5 makes use of this last saying: "he will not get out from there, until he has paid back the last penny."

121. *Didache* 1.4–5 may well reflect knowledge of Matthew's version. In the *Gospel of Thomas* the saying has been formulated with a slightly different thrust: "If you have money, do not lend it at interest, but give it to someone from whom you will not get it back" (*Gos. Thom.* 95).

122. E.g., the reconstructions of Q by A. Polag (*Fragmenta Q: Textheft zur Logienquelle* [Neukirchen-Vluyn: Neukirchener Verlag, 1979]), seem to assume that sometimes Luke, sometimes Matthew has preserved Q; as a result he both masks the disparity between the two versions and still leaves it a puzzle why either or both diverged from the written text of Q. E.g., in the first case, on the usual literary redactional principles, it is more likely that Luke 14:34a echoes Mark 9:50a than that Luke = Q.

123. Matt. 8:19b–22/Luke 9:57b–60a; Matt. 11:7–11, 16–19/Luke 7:24–28, 31–35; Matt. 11:25–27/Luke 10:21–22; Matt. 12:43–45/Luke 11:24–26; Matt. 23:37–39/Luke 13:34–35; Matt. 24:45–51/Luke 12:42–46.

124. See again, e.g., Fitzmyer, *Luke;* and Davies and Allison, *Matthew*, ad loc.; Catchpole, *Quest*, 323–24.

125. The *Gospel of Thomas* has variant traditions of the first and last of the three examples above (Matt. 10:34–36/Luke 12:51–53/*Gos. Thom.* 16; Matt. 37–38/Luke 14:26–27/*Gos. Thom.* 55, 101 [but with typical *Thomas* embellishment]; Matt. 22:1–14/Luke 14:16–24/*Gos. Thom.* 64); Mark 8:34 also knows a variant version of Matt. 10:38/Luke 14:27/*Gos. Thom.* 55:2b, which Matt. 16:24 and Luke 9:23 follow. Whereas in the second example *Didache* again seems to know Matthew (*Did.* 15.3; Matt. 18:15–35), as probably does the *Gospel of the Nazarenes* 15 (Matt. 18:21–22).

126. Cf. Gerhardsson, who concludes that the differences between the parables (narrative *meshalim*) demonstrate "deliberate alterations of rather firm texts" ("Illuminating the Kingdom," 291–98), though the assumption of the literary paradigm should also be noted.

127. The judgments rendered by the Jesus Seminar on these passages well illustrate the highly dubious criteria and tendentious reasoning by which they

reached their conclusions, including a rather naïve idea of consistency (Matt. 10:34–36 seems to "contradict" Jesus' teaching on unqualified love); Jesus was less likely to echo scripture than the Christian community (reason unexplained); use made of material indicates its originating purpose (Luke 17:3–4 as the reflection of "a more mature community than is likely to have been the case with Jesus' followers during his lifetime"); the fallacy of "the original form" (the rationale of the procrustean bed of the literary paradigm) (Funk, *Five Gospels*, 174, 216–17, 362, 234–35). But to discuss authenticity by reference simply to such considerations as precise wording, tensions with other sayings, and appropriateness to later contexts totally fails to consider the implications of oral transmission: a saying, like a story, could retain its identity by constancy of theme and particular words or phrases, while at the same time being adapted and reapplied to developing situations in the ongoing life of the earliest churches.

128. Draper also argues that the thesis of some of Jesus' sayings "created entirely de novo . . . conflicts with the processes of oral transmission. Such entirely innovative 'words of the Risen Jesus' are inherently unlikely" (Horsley and Draper, *Whoever*, 183). Horsley, however, assumes that prophets would have been responsible for the celebration of the tradition (pp. 300–310) without inquiring what the role of teachers might have been.

129. B. W. Henaut is tendentiously concerned to argue the virtual impossibility of recovering any oral tradition behind the Gospels (*Oral Tradition and the Gospels: The Problem of Mark 4*, Journal for the Study of the New Testament Supplement 82 [Sheffield: JSOT Press, 1993]): all differences, no matter how great, can be explained in terms of literary redaction; and oral tradition was wholly fluid and contingent on the particularities of each performance. But his conception of the oral tradition process is questionable—as though it was a matter of recovering a history of tradition through a set of sequential performances (e.g., p. 118; here we see the problem in talking of "oral transmission"); and he gives too little thought to what the stabilities of oral remembrances of Jesus might be as distinct from those in the epics and sagas studied by Parry and Lord.

130. Cf. Horsley's scathing critique of liberalism's focus on the individual and of B. L. Mack's *The Lost Gospel: The Book of Q and Christian Origins* (San Francisco: HarperSanFrancisco, 1993) (Horsley and Draper, *Whoever*, 15–22). Crossan also seems to think of oral tradition solely in terms of individuals recollecting (J. D. Crossan, *The Birth of Christianity* [San Francisco: HarperSanFrancisco, 1998], 49–93).

131. Cf. the picture that P. S. Alexander adduces for the circle of disciples around a rabbi in the early tannaitic period forming a small, quasi-religious community, eating communally and with a common purse, being taught by him ("Orality in Pharisaic-Rabbinic Judaism at the Turn of the Eras," in *Jesus*, ed. Wansbrough, 159–84,166–67), a picture that may not be as anachronistic as might at first appear (pp. 182–84).

132. A strong body of opinion regarding Q sees the earliest stage of its collec-

tion/composition (Q¹?) as intended to provide guidance for itinerant missionaries on the pattern of Jesus' own mission; similarly Schürmann, "Vorösterlichen Anfänge."

133. The point has been argued by E. E. Ellis on several occasions, most recently in "The Historical Jesus and the Gospels," in *Evangelium—Schriftauslegung—Kirche*, Festschrift P. Stuhlmacher, ed. J. Ådna et al. (Tübingen: Mohr-Siebeck, 1997), 94–106, reprinted in his *Christ and the Future in New Testament History*, Novum Testamentum Supplement 97 (Leiden: Brill, 2000), 3–19; idem, *The Making of the New Testament Documents* (Leiden: Brill, 1999), 20–27; but Ellis weakens his case by unnecessarily questioning whether there was an initial oral stage of transmission (*Christ*, 13–14), and argues for "at least some written transmission from the beginning" (*Making*, 24), that is, already during Jesus' ministry (*Christ*, 15–16; *Making*, 32, 352). Similarly A. Millard argues that notes may well have been made by one or more of the literate among Jesus' hearers which could have served as sources for Mark (*Reading and Writing in the Time of Jesus* [Sheffield: Sheffield Academic Press, 2000], 223–29); though he also observes that Paul shows no awareness of any written records of Jesus' mission (p. 211). Ellis's conception of oral transmission is very restricted to a choice between "folkloric origin" and the "controlled and cultivated process" of the rabbinic schools (*Christ*, 14–15; cf. Millard, *Reading and Writing*, 185–92); and neither seems to be aware of Bailey's contribution. Millard's belief that "literacy was widespread in Palestinian Judaism" (p. 22) is challenged by counteropinions that literacy was low in Roman Palestine, perhaps only 3 percent (W. V. Harris, *Ancient Literacy* [Cambridge, Mass.: Harvard University Press, 1989]; M. Bar-Ilan, "Illiteracy in the Land of Israel in the First Centuries CE," in *Essays in the Social Scientific Study of Judaism and Jewish Society*, ed. S. Fishbane and S. Schoenfeld [Hoboken, N.J.: Ktav, 1992], 46–61).

134. It is not necessary to assume that the "Hellenists" only emerged after Easter; there may have been Greek-speaking disciples during Jesus' Galilean and Jerusalem missions (cf. Mark 7:26; John 12:20–22), and traditions already being transposed into Greek.

135. A repeated emphasis of Horsley and Draper, *Whoever*.

136. See again Schürmann, "Vorösterlichen Anfänge."

137. Horsley and Draper (*Whoever*, 161–64, 182) both draw on the work of J. M. Foley (*Immanent Art: From Structure to Meaning in Traditional Oral Epic* [Bloomington: Indiana University Press, 1991]; idem, *The Singer of Tales in Performance* [Bloomington: Indiana University Press, 1995]) on this point (Foley draws in turn on the literary theory of W. Iser and H. R. Jauss), and make much of the importance of "metonymic referencing" (elements that evoke a whole theme within the tradition), again in dependence on Foley (Horsley and Draper, *Whoever*, index "metonymic referencing").

138. Kloppenborg, following in the train of successive form-critical analyses, perceives the composition process as "the juxtaposition of originally independent

units" (*Formation*, 98). Funk assumes that "the imprint of orality" is evident only in "short, provocative, memorable, oft-repeated phrases, sentences, and stories"— "a sixth pillar of modern gospel scholarship" (*Five Gospels*, 4); "only sayings that were short, pithy, and memorable were likely to survive" (*Honest*, 40). This assumption predetermines that "the Jesus whom historians seek" will only be found in such brief sayings and stories. He lists 101 words (and deeds) judged to be "authentic" in his *Honest*, 326–35.

139. Matt. 10:38/Luke 14:27; Matt. 10:39/Luke 17:33; Matt. 10:33/Luke 12:9.

140. Matt. 5:15/Luke 11:33/*Gos. Thom.* 33:2; Matt. 10:26/Luke 12:2/*Gos. Thom.* 5.2, 6.4; Matt. 7:2/Luke 6:38b; Matt. 25:29/Luke 19:26/*Gos. Thom.* 41.

141. The fact that the *Gospel of Thomas* has a parallel only to Mark 3:27/Matt. 12:29 (not Luke 11:21-22 = Q?) (*Gos. Thom.* 35) would be consistent with the *Gospel of Thomas*'s de-eschatologizing tendencies.

142. Does the fact that *Thomas* has only two disjoint parallels (*Gos. Thom.* 14:2/Luke 10:8–9; *Gos. Thom.* 73/Matt. 9:37–38/Luke 10:2) imply a fading of a compulsion to mission?

143. Note particularly the severe criticisms at this point of C. M. Tuckett, *Q and the History of Early Christianity* (Edinburgh: T & T Clark, 1996), 52–82.

144. In H. Koester's view the apocalyptic material "conflicts" with the emphasis of the wisdom and prophetic material (*Ancient Christian Gospels: Their History and Development* [London: SCM; Philadelphia: Trinity Press International, 1990], 135). Kloppenborg speaks of "aporiae created by redactional activity," or of a group of sayings "modified by the insertion of a secondary expansion or commentary . . ." (*Formation*, 97, 99); but that simply begs the question, as Kloppenborg seems to realize (*Formation*, 99).

145. Horsley in Horsley and Draper, *Whoever*, 23–24, 61–62, 83–93, 148. This is in effect an extension of a strong trend to recognize "complexes of logia" or "collections of aphoristic sayings" behind Q (D. Zeller, *Die weisheitlichen Mahnsprüche bei den Synoptikern*, Forschung zur Bibel 17 [Würzburg: Echter, 1977]; R. A. Piper, *Wisdom in the Q-tradition: The Aphoristic Teaching of Jesus*, Society of New Testament Studies Monograph Series 61 [Cambridge: Cambridge University Press, 1989]; similarly Kloppenborg, *Formation*).

146. See particularly H. W. Kuhn, *Ältere Sammlungen im Markusevangelium* (Göttingen: Vandenhoeck & Ruprecht, 1971). Worthy of note is Lord's observation that "[o]ral traditional composers think in terms of blocks and series of blocks of tradition" ("Gospels," in *Relationship*, ed. Walker, 59).

147. Bultmann, *Jesus*, 12–13.

148. As again by Crossan in his talk of "scientific stratigraphy" (*Historical Jesus*, xxviii, xxxi–xxxii). Funk also envisages "the historical Jesus" being "uncovered by historical excavation" (*Five Gospels*, 3).

149. I have struggled to find a suitable image to replace that of layers (edited editions) and have played with the model of forms somewhat like space satellites circling around the remembered Jesus, with the forms of the 60s and 70s not nec-

essarily further from Jesus than those of the 40s and 50s. The image is not very good, but it can be elaborated to depict John's Gospel as on a higher orbit, or to include the possibility of forms drifting out of the gravity of the remembered Jesus, or being caught by a countervailing gravity. The earlier image of a trajectory could be fitted to this also—e.g., Q material on a trajectory leading to the *Gospel of Thomas* no longer held within the original gravity field.

150. This point was already being made by H. Koester in his first monograph —*Synoptische Überlieferung bei den apostolischen Vätern* (Berlin: Akademie-Verlag, 1957).

151. R. Bauckham provides a number of examples ("For Whom Were the Gospels Written?" in *The Gospels for All Christians: Rethinking the Gospel Audiences*, ed. R. Bauckham [Grand Rapids: Eerdmans, 1998], 13–22). He suspects that "those who no longer think it possible to use the Gospels to reconstruct the historical Jesus compensate for this loss by using them to reconstruct the communities that produced the Gospels" (p. 20). See also S. C. Barton's strictures in the same volume ("Can We Identify the Gospel Audiences?" pp. 173–94) on the use of "community" and on our ability to identify beyond generalizations the social context in which the Gospels were written.

152. Kloppenborg, *Formation*, 25; "Q represents a theologically autonomous sphere of Christian theology" (p. 27), "a discrete group in which Q functioned as the central theological expression" (p. 39). Koester, *Ancient Christian Gospels*: "Both documents (*Gospel of Thomas* and Q) presuppose that Jesus' significance lay in his words, *and in his words alone*" (p. 86, my emphasis).

153. See particularly Koester, "One Jesus and Four Primitive Gospels"; idem, "The Structure and Criteria of Early Christian Beliefs," in *Trajectories through Early Christianity*, ed. J. M. Robinson and H. Koester (Philadelphia: Fortress, 1971), 205–31; Lührmann, *Redaktion*, 95–96; Mack, *Myth*, 83–97. Koester's reflections on "The Historical Jesus and the Historical Situation of the Quest: An Epilogue," in *Studying the Historical Jesus*, ed. Chilton and Evans, 535– 45, indicate how dubious the reasoning has become. (1) "The history of Christian beginnings *demonstrates* that it was most effective to establish and to nurture the community of the new age without any recourse to the life and work of Jesus of Nazareth" (p. 535, my emphasis). *Assumption*: "the community of the new age" did not know or value any Jesus tradition. (2) "There were followers of Jesus, who were not included in the circle of those churches for which the central ritual and the story of Jesus' suffering and death was the unifying principle. Instead, they believed that their salvation was mediated through the words of wisdom that Jesus had spoken. In the Synoptic Sayings Source a community appears that had combined this belief in Jesus with the expectation of his return as the Son of Man" ("Historical Jesus," 537). *Assumptions*: one document per church; silence regarding means ignorance of means opposition to; differing emphases are irreconcilable in a single document. (3) Some of those addressed in 1 Corinthians seem to have understood Jesus' sayings "as the saving message of a great wisdom teacher"; the earliest

compositional strata of Q seem to have understood "Jesus' words of wisdom as a revelation providing life and freedom" ("Historical Jesus," 540). *Assumptions*: Corinthian "wisdom" was based on Jesus' teaching, and implies a Christology; 1 Cor. 1–4 requires more than a rhetorical and sociopolitical understanding of that wisdom; Q wisdom was soteriological rather than parenetic.

154. Bauckham, "For Whom?" 1.

155. Ibid., 28–30; "Why should he go to the considerable trouble of writing a Gospel for a community to which he was regularly preaching?" (p. 29).

156. Ibid., 30–44; also M. B. Thompson, "The Holy Internet: Communication Between Churches in the First Christian Generation," in *Gospels,* ed. Bauckham, 49–70. Bauckham justifiably asks, "Why do scholars so readily assume that the author of a Gospel would be someone who had spent all his Christian life attached to the same Christian community" (p. 36).

5

The Word Was Made Flesh and Dwelt among Us:

Jesus Research and Christian Faith

Elizabeth A. Johnson, C.S.J.

S INCE THE BIRTH OF MODERN BIBLICAL SCHOLARSHIP some two hundred years ago, scholars have been using the best empirical methods they can hone to explore concrete details of the life of Jesus of Nazareth along with the way his memory was shaped and passed on by the early communities of disciples. By employing classical tools of historical and literary research to place Gospel texts in their contexts, this work has yielded a wealth of insight into the story of Jesus and the origins of Christianity in the specific circumstances of first-century Palestine. As this new millennium dawns, we are experiencing a fresh renaissance in Jesus studies thanks to newer methods drawn from the social sciences—cross-cultural, economic, and political analysis—plus expanding knowledge of first-century Judaism and the Greco-Roman world due to both discoveries of ancient scrolls and recent archaeological excavations.[1] The papers presented during this symposium are excellent examples of this craft, made more powerful by our presence here in this land where the gospel events took place.

The empirical knowledge that results from these scholarly studies inevitably gives rise to existential religious questions within a community of faith. To the extent that we personally experience its impact, we ask how it might shape our own discipleship and relationship with the mystery of the living God mediated through Jesus Christ. Insofar as this knowledge impinges on the corporate, public identity of the church, we ask about its meaning for the community's faith and practice.

Theology, as distinct from biblical scholarship, grapples with these hermeneutical questions. It aims to bridge the time between the first century and the twenty-first with meaningful connections, so that the tradition remains a living tradition rather than an ossified one. At the start of the second millennium, the medieval theologian Anselm defined theology as *fides quaerens intellectum*, or faith seeking understanding—a lively, open-ended definition. As a scholarly discipline, theology seeks to interpret the meaning of faith for different communities in historically changing times and places.

Distinct from the other papers of this colloquium, this paper is an act of theology in the systematic sense just described. It grapples with the significance that this research into Jesus in his own time, place, and culture may have for what Christians believe and do today. Let us be clear at the outset that we are dealing with an issue that is relatively new for faith. The church has lived for most of its two thousand years without any "quest for the historical Jesus."[2] Indeed, the very notion of history that undergirds this quest, namely, history itself as the record of "what really happened," emerged only during the latter part of the Enlightenment in eighteenth- and nineteenth-century Europe. Thus this is a fresh conversation in the living tradition. Insofar as many of the insights about Jesus generated by biblical scholarship are genuinely new to people who have lived with the Gospel texts as sacred scripture, these new data pose challenges to traditional patterns of thought. Insofar as vast numbers of contemporary people operate with a type of thinking marked by a "literal" rather than "legendary" understanding of history, this research also offers opportunities to answer basic questions about the meaning of Christian faith.

THREE DISPUTED OPTIONS

In my judgment, contemporary Jesus research is a blessing for the church. Not everyone would agree. The question of whether and to what extent Jesus research even should impact the life of faith is highly controversial. At least three positions have emerged.

One trajectory, traceable from Reimarus in the eighteenth century through David Friedrich Strauss in the nineteenth to some, though certainly not all, members of the Jesus Seminar in our day, takes delight in using Jesus research to puncture what it considers the overinflated balloon of christological doctrine.[3] Given the difference between what the Gospel texts portray and what "really" happened, the Gospels are mere pious fabrications, goes the early argument—or outright deceptions concocted by the disciples. The probability that Jesus ever said most of what the Gospels attribute to him is minimal, goes the recent argument, making his teaching unreliable. The doctrine that holds he is the incarnate Word of God has no grounding in the historical record; the best we can do is think of him as a failed prophet or a misguided revolutionary. Thus are critical historical methods used to debunk the faith response that Christians offer toward Jesus as the Christ who mediates divine mercy and love. Here Jesus research triumphs at the expense of faith.

By way of criticism to this onslaught, an opposite trajectory develops. Traceable with different nuances from Martin Kähler in the nineteenth century to Luke Timothy Johnson in our day, this position basically holds that the "real" Jesus is not the person who lived in history per se but the historic biblical Christ of the Gospel texts.[4] There one encounters the living figure of the risen Christ and is challenged existentially to place one's trust in him. While some historical knowledge may be legitimate and even necessary—for example, that Jesus actually existed and that he was crucified under Pontius Pilate—the ever-shifting sands of historical research and its results are not terribly relevant for faith. Rather, the witness of the biblical text provides a "storm-free region" for the saving act of faith, made in view of the risen Christ's continuous and powerful presence in the church here and now. Here faith triumphs by diminishing, if not outright dismissing, the impact of critical inquiry into the pre-Easter Jesus.

A third trajectory, shared over the years by many biblical scholars for whom piety matters, by numerous theologians, and, I dare say, by the participants of this conference, opts for a both-and approach. This third viewpoint finds the skeptical "history-alone" idea deficient insofar as it does not respect the interpretive power and dynamism of faith in peoples' lives. But this third stance also finds the devout "faith-alone" defense lacking insofar as it does not respect the importance of critical thinking in the lives of contemporary Christian people. Correlating history and faith, this third position instead allows a kind of mutual light to be shed back and forth between historical reasoning and trust in God through Jesus Christ. Here it is not thought in some simplistic way that history "grounds" faith or gives rise to faith, which is always a gracious gift from God. But when received in a faith context, historical research can indeed strengthen as well as challenge faith, for divine presence and action in the world are not so intangible as to leave no discernible historical traces. In terms of the relevance of Jesus research to Christian faith, if God became a human being, it is not unimportant what kind of concrete human being God became.

The First Vatican Council—yes, the First—addressed the potential conflict between the insights of human reason and the truths of faith in a most helpful way. Drawing on ancient catholic tradition, it argued in the decree *Dei Filius* that there can never be any real discrepancy between faith and reason because the same God is the source of both, revealing the truths of faith and also gifting the human mind with the power of reason. If a contradiction between the two does seem to break out, it is due either to the doctrines of faith not having been rightly understood or to what are in fact opinions being taken for the final verdicts of reason. Furthermore, not only are faith and reason not at odds, but they can be of mutual help. Faith enlightens reason as to the true purpose of human life in the world. When, enlightened by faith, reason seeks to understand this carefully, devoutly, and calmly (*sedulo, pie, et sobrie*), it can arrive at insights that are most fruitful. By making analogies with things already known and crafting new connections between faith and human life, reason can serve a positive purpose in promoting understanding of the mystery of God, who, however, always remains beyond human understanding (*Dei Filius* 43, 44).

This nineteenth-century council spoke of reason as an abstract, logical power and concentrated on scientific reason, which studied the natural world to unlock the ways the world works (evolution being an especially contentious point). Its insight holds equal validity, I think, for other kinds of reason including that which conducts historical investigation. In this spirit, the third, "both-and" position regarding Jesus research and Christian faith holds faith and historical reason to be capable of being partners rather than enemies. This is the conviction that shapes this lecture. I hope to affirm the significance of historical research into the life and times of Jesus for the intelligibility and liberating practice of the faith of persons in the contemporary world, where historical consciousness is part of the air we breathe and where the hunger and thirst for justice impel our conscience.

The title holds the key to my starting point: "the Word was made flesh and dwelt among us" (John 1:14). I am assuming rather than defending Christian faith, although the precise meaning of incarnation itself, to say nothing of resurrection, has been a matter of fierce theological debate in recent years. Setting out from this home base, my thesis proposes that Jesus research affects faith mainly by changing Christian imagination. Because recasting the image of the one who is at the center of belief and practice has far-reaching results, this paper will then explore the impact of the shift in imagination in four areas: the person of Jesus, his saving work (salvation), the church that follows him, and the mystery of God revealed in and through the event of his life and destiny.

CHANGING IMAGINATION

The image of Jesus is crucially important in the life of Christian faith. Since no one any longer meets Jesus of Nazareth in the flesh, he is encountered since his death through a memory image which mediates his living presence through the power of the Spirit. Down through the centuries, this image, drawn together in various ways from scripture, doctrine, religious and ethical practice, and available human experience, functions at the very center of Christian life. Existentially, it is the means by which believers come to know and relate to Jesus Christ, whether as children or adults. Corporately, it shapes the church's creeds, ethics, doctrines and theology, liturgical celebration and preaching, spirituality and practices of piety, catechesis and public values. Theologically, set within a narrative framework, the *memoria vitae, passionis, mortis, et resurrectionis Jesu Christi* ensures that the content of *Jesus* in the confession that Jesus is the Christ is not reduced to a cipher or a projection but remains a gracious, challenging gift from God. Subtract the memory of Jesus from the church, and the whole life of faith implodes.[5]

In a dramatic way, especially for churches that have traditionally lived by a high doctrinal Christology supported by a literal reading of the Gospels, Jesus research is changing this memory image. It is painting new pictures of how Jesus interacted with his world and providing new categories by which he can be understood. Jesus the Jew;[6] a marginal Jew;[7] a prophet of Israel's restoration;[8] a Spirit-filled leader, compassionate healer, subversive sage, and founder of a revitalization movement within Judaism;[9] a Mediterranean Jewish peasant;[10] an eschatological prophet proclaiming the dawning of the reign of God and paying the price with his life[11]—these various profiles are changing the traditional Christian imagination regarding the dynamic of Jesus' life and destiny. Granted, they are not all the same, and real contradictions exist between various scholarly methods, use of sources, and reading of the evidence. Still, taken singly or together, these depictions encapsulate an awareness of the figure at the origin of Christianity different from that of the doctrinal Christ of traditional piety. This is not to say that these images are opposed to doctrine, but they do give rise to a different appreciation. Obviously the images emerging from contemporary studies do not exhaust the reality of the actual Jesus who lived. But I would argue that given the critical tools being utilized, this changed imagination arguably approximates aspects of the first disciples' memory of Jesus more closely than the church's memory image has done for many generations.

This changed imagination is affecting understanding in at least four significant areas that we will now explore, albeit too briefly to do justice to the full range of Jesus research's impact.

THE PERSON OF JESUS CHRIST

Classical doctrine, hammered out in Hellenistic terms by early church councils, affirms that Jesus' identity as the one "Christ, Son, Lord" involves a double relationality. He is "one in being with the Father as to his divinity" and "one in being with us as to his humanity" (Council of Chalcedon 451). Truly divine and truly human: much subsequent theology used philosophical methods to shed light on the meaning of this two natures doctrine, attempting to explain how the incarnation of the Word of God results in a genuine human being. Despite these efforts, the genuine humanity of Jesus has rather regularly been neglected or slipped from view. Ironically, this is particularly the case with highly orthodox Christology. Its benchmark of truth is the confession that "Jesus is truly God," while equal importance is not attached to the belief that "Jesus is truly human," that is, "a real, genuine, limited human being with his own experience, an obedient human being, like us in all things except sin."[12]

Indeed, the doctrinal tradition of Christology is plagued by a mysterious monophysite undercurrent whereby the divine nature swallows up the human nature, thus undermining the fullness of the confession it seeks to protect. Why this should be the case has been the subject of some speculation. Intellectual dualism that prizes spirit over matter, body over soul, and thus pure divinity over enfleshed humanity is one contributing factor. A competitive model of God's relation to the world whereby the infinitely powerful One overwhelms the puny integrity of the creature is another. A political power structure that privileges an elite group over the grubby masses, absorbing Christ into the glorified image of the ruling emperor is yet another. It may also be the case that we are so little at home in our own skins that the idea of God's truly entering into our earthy condition becomes seriously unimaginable.

Precisely here, Jesus research refreshes the imagination of the church about the genuine humanity of the eschatological prophet from Nazareth. Fed by Jesus research, a clearer grasp of Jesus' historical humanity now provides Christology with a new yet ancient starting point. Instead of beginning in heaven and tracing a descending pattern as the Word becomes flesh (Christology from above, modeled on John's Gospel), leading edges of contemporary Christology begin on earth with Jesus of Nazareth and trace an ascending pattern from life through death to resurrection into glory (Christology from below, modeled on the Synoptic Gospels).[13] As aspects of this paradigm shift to an ascending pattern are explored, the full humanity of Jesus becomes harder and harder to ignore.

And here is a key point. Jesus research affects the imagination of faith about the true humanity of the Word made flesh not by generalizing but by *particularizing*. Jesus of Nazareth is not a generic human being but a specific one. His human nature is not an abstraction but a concrete human life shaped by a real history in the world. He is situated in time and place, namely, first-century Palestine. Like everyone else, he descends from a line of ancestors—in his case the people of Israel. He is Jewish, both culturally and religiously, and his worldview is fed by that stream of human tradition. His human identity is shaped by his relationships to a quite specific family, society, and God. He is no stranger to the passions of red-blooded humanity but experiences the vagaries of the flesh in his own circumstances. Despite his many gifts he is limited in knowledge and needs to grow in self-awareness and discernment of his vocation. His career is not pre-programmed but is the result of free decisions, not always easily made, about his ministry and its focus. Even a few such details change the imagination and feed the rediscovery of the "truly historical human" dimension of christological belief. It becomes harder to maintain a "Superman" model of Jesus' life: mild-mannered worker in wood and stone on the outside, with secret, souped-up powers on the divine inside, as if his mind and will were not utterly affected by his finite, social location in history.

While it may be easy to admit that Jesus' body was real flesh that could experience pleasure and pain, and while it may even be admissible that he thought and spoke in Jewish categories, resistance to the impact of Jesus research often draws a line in the sand over Jesus' own self-consciousness. Such resistance finds it difficult to allow that the one confessed as Lord and Christ actually experienced nescience and exercised genuine human free will. One of the earliest theologians to grapple with this issue was Karl Rahner, whose 1961 essay continues to shed a helpful light. Far from being an actor reciting lines already written, or a puppet whose strings were pulled by a heavenly power, Jesus' self-knowledge and decision making had a "truly human" character. How is this thinkable?[14]

Taking a page from transcendental philosophy, Rahner proposes that human self-consciousness is structured around two related poles. At one pole, the subjective one, we enjoy a wordless, pre-thematic, intuitive grasp of who we are. Here we "know" ourselves by being fundamentally present to ourselves as the person we are. This deep self-presence guides how we typically conduct daily life, react to emergencies, make major life decisions. Obviously, this sense of who we are can never be totally expressed in words. Rather, it is a continuous, subliminal self-knowledge that grounds and pervades all we do as human subjects. At the other pole, the objective one, we "know" who we are by means of words and facts. Our name, age, and vital statistics, our heritage, likes and dislikes, conscious choices, all are forms of self-knowledge that we can articulate out loud and communicate to others. Knowledge of ourselves at this objective pole is a matter of definition. Since this knowledge can never spell out who we are in the depths of our person at the subjective pole, there is always a sense in which we both know and don't know ourselves at the same time.

Throughout our historical lives various experiences provide the occasion to translate our intuitive self-awareness at the subjective pole into self-defining words and concepts at the objective pole. Reflective people do this more than others, but all do it to some degree. Success and failure, experiences of love or rejection, temptations we wrestle with, choices we make, skills we develop, and so on—all help us to spell ourselves out in a more concrete way as life goes on. This is a lifelong process, with new experiences enabling us to get a more secure handle on our identity as time goes by, so that people enjoy a more articulated knowledge of themselves at the age of forty than when they were twenty. Since there is no limit to learning about ourselves, the process of self-interpretation through life experience continues all the way up to the moment of death.

What is true for human beings in general is also the case with Jesus of Nazareth. He experienced a living history of interpreting himself to himself as a result of his life experience: "and Jesus grew in wisdom and age and grace before God and human beings" (Luke 2:52). At the subjective pole of self-knowledge he grasps himself nonverbally as the person he is, namely, the Word made flesh. This self-consciousness, however, is not explicit but preconceptual, intuitive. One could argue that it is the source that propels his own adult assumption of teaching authority, his profound relation with the mystery of God whom he called *"Abba,"* and his compassionate connection to the dispossessed. But this self-knowledge is not a clear and distinct definition. Jesus does not wake up in the morning reciting the Prologue of John's Gospel or the formula of Chalcedon. Rather, it takes his whole lifetime with all its experiences for him to grasp himself in concrete terms. It takes the events of his ministry, of those who love or reject him, of those who ask "Are you the Christ?," all the way up to and including the moment of his agonized death when he felt abandoned even by the God whom he had passionately served.

Did Jesus know he was God? Rahner concludes: yes and no. Yes at the subjective pole of self-awareness where we intuitively grasp who we are. No at the objective pole of self-awareness where we define ourselves in concrete terms. To put the question another way: Did this first-century Jewish man think he was Yahweh? Of course not. The very parameters of the faith in which he worshiped forbad such a self-definition. In later years Christians would have to develop the very concept of God into trinitarian terms in order to make this identification.

Allowing for nescience, psychological development, and genuine, situated freedom in Jesus of Nazareth is an acid test of how radically "one with us as to his humanity" we are prepared to allow him to be. The bipolar structure of human self-consciousness operating in history is simply one theological construct that permits us to think how this could "work." If one holds to a position that considers Jesus a "mere man," even if an extraordinary Jewish one, then the impact of Jesus research on Christian imagination is not so dramatic. But if one holds deeply to the classical confession of faith, this scholarship brings to birth a renewed appreciation of just how radical the incarnation really is. God with us and for us under the conditions of genuine human existence, which is inevitably particular and limited—How much further could Love go?

SALVATION THANKS TO JESUS CHRIST

Changing the memory image of the actual historical life of Jesus is also broadening ways of understanding the redeeming impact of his life and destiny. "For us and for our salvation": thus does the Nicene Creed sum up faith in the overflowing, beneficent results that flow to needy humankind thanks to Jesus Christ. How can this be understood? In the decades after Jesus' death and resurrection, early Christians ransacked their religious heritage and their everyday dealings to find metaphors and analogies that would express what had transpired and continued to transpire in their new experience of God's grace coming to them through Jesus in the Spirit. The New Testament is rich with their imaginative expressions. They appealed to business metaphors of buying, redeeming, or ransoming something for a price. They employed medical metaphors of healing and being made whole again. They called into play legal metaphors of justification, someone on trial being declared not guilty; political metaphors of being liberated, delivered, set free; and military metaphors of victory over the powers of evil. Experience of animal sacrifice in the temple provided them with the cultic metaphor of sacrificial atonement. Experience of a peaceful end to personal and corporate animosity helped them frame relational metaphors of reconciliation, breaking down walls that divide, and being brought near. Paul uses the family metaphor of being adopted children to describe their new relationship to God, while John envisions the even more profound relationship of being verily born of God.

Unlike conciliar declarations that clarify, however doxologically, the inner constitution of Jesus Christ in particular terms of natures and person, language about his saving work was never subject to such dispute and definition. In the course of time, however, especially in Western Christianity, one metaphor came to predominate, namely, that of sacrificial atonement. Reflecting the feudal context in which he wrote, Anselm's treatise *Cur Deus Homo* gave logical precision to how this metaphor works.[15] Sin deeply offends the honor of God. In order to restore the order of the universe, satisfaction must be paid. But human beings, being finite, can never make such satisfaction, which, because of the nature of the Person offended, must be infinite. So God becomes a human being to accomplish this end. How is it done? As a human being Jesus owes God loving obedience at every moment, so his simply living a perfect life is not enough. Because he is sinless, however, there is one thing that by rights he should not suffer, namely, death, which is a punishment for sin. So Jesus Christ dies on the cross, giving God something that is truly "unowed." He thereby earns infinite satisfaction, which, because he does not need it, he distributes to us sinners.

Anselm intended this inquiry into "why God became a human being and died" as a demonstration of the mercy of God, who did for humankind what we could not do for ourselves. Thanks to Jesus' sacrificial death, the debt of the rest of humanity is paid: we are freed from sin and restored to right relationship with God. But this satisfaction theory soon took on darker colors in the hands of lesser thinkers and the growing juridical power of the medieval church. Despite Thomas Aquinas's efforts to tone down the *necessity* of a bloody, sacrificial death, the metaphor promoted a heavily sinful view of the world and forgetfulness of the free grace liberally poured out in Christ. Despite Scotus's critique of the metaphor's image of God as a mighty Lord concerned mainly with his own honor, preachers promoted the notion of God as an offended, even angry Father who needs to be placated by the blood of his precious Son (compare this to the idea of God present in the major parables of Jesus). The metaphor's narrative focus on the cross, moreover, leads to the idea that death was the very purpose of Jesus' life. He came to die; the script was already written before he stepped onto the world stage. This not only robs Jesus of his human freedom, but it sacralizes suffering more than joy as an avenue to God. It tends to glorify violent death as somehow of value. Liberation theologies note how, as a result, the cross can be used wrongly to inculcate passivity in the face of unjust, unnecessary suffering rather than action to resist, because one is supposed to imitate the Suffering Servant who died obediently and opened not his mouth.[16] Bringing the experience of domestic abuse into the conversation, particularly the abuse of children, feminist theologies critique this model's notion of a father who allows or even needs the death of a child, no matter what benefit might accrue to others. Our salvation is no excuse for cosmic child abuse.[17]

The difficulties that have accrued around the sacrificial atonement metaphor of salvation, exacerbated by its almost exclusive use for centuries, do not negate the importance of the cross or the power of redemptive suffering. Rather, new theological interpretation is called for that will head debilitating complications off while doing justice to the centrality of Jesus' death "for us." By setting the cross in its historical context, Jesus research contributes to this needed solution. It offers a new imagination with which to appreciate the Messiah's saving work.

1. The view of salvation fed by Jesus research links the cross with the ministry that preceded it and the resurrection that followed it in an *essential* way, rather than let the cross stand alone as the saving act of atonement.

Now we see that salvation, restoring people to wholeness in their relationship with God and each other, begins in the public ministry itself. Jesus' preaching of the approaching reign of God, by turns joyful and challenging, coupled with his healings, exorcisms, inclusive table fellowship, and partisanship for marginalized people, already offers a foretaste of the world in which God reigns, a world without tears. In his company diverse people experience new community with God: sinners, the sick, women, men, young, established, seekers, poor of all kinds. In those days, separation of religion and state was not something anyone had yet conceived of. Thus the Jesus movement was politically dangerous in a time of mass movements against Roman occupation. In addition, driving home his vision with prophetic passion, Jesus performed a symbolic action against the temple in Jerusalem during the feast of Passover, overturning the tables and freeing the animals meant for sacrifice. Thereby he earned the animosity of the entrenched priestly class, the priestly aristocracy, who would prove to be formidable enemies.

In historical perspective, Jesus' death on the cross is the price he paid for his prophetic ministry. His violent, tortured, bloody end is the consequence of the kind of activity he engaged in. Historically it was not foreordained; if he had changed course it probably would not have happened. But he opted for fidelity to his vocation, preaching the reign of God, and enacting God's compassion to the poor. As his movement proved a thorn in the side of the powers that be, they removed him. Repressive regimes do this all the time. He was put to death in the prime of life, his movement in tatters, his promises mocked, to all intents and purposes even abandoned by the God whose merciful drawing near he had so passionately proclaimed.

Such darkness puts into high relief the power of the resurrection, restoring it to the pivotal role it has in early Christian preaching and the New Testament itself. The resurrection of Jesus into glory is not a codicil to his life story nor a natural, expected outcome, but an irreplaceable turning point. God raised him up. Herein lies the saving power of this event: death does not have the last word. The crucified one is not annihilated but brought to new life in the embrace of God, who remains faithful in surprising ways. Thereby the judgment of earthly judges is reversed and Jesus' own person, intrinsically linked with his preaching and praxis, is vindicated. This event unleashes a new Spirit into history, the Spirit of life. Through the presence of Jesus, the crucified who is now the Living One, a future is offered to all others who have come to grief, even as crosses keep on being set up in history.

2. As a result of this historical, narrative approach to the cross in relation to public ministry and resurrection, the view of salvation fed by Jesus research gives rise to an interpretation of the death of Jesus as the destiny of the prophet sent from God.

As an event shaped by the forces of history, his death did not happen with ironclad necessity but was the result of contingent circumstances and free human decisions. Promoting the coming reign of God in word and deed, Jesus and his movement ran afoul of the interests of ruling powers in his corner of the world. Knowing his life was in danger, he continued nevertheless to preach and act in accord with the burning passion of his life—God's drawing near as salvation for all, especially the poor and marginalized people—in hope that his ministry would succeed. Our own era presents living examples of this dynamic: Oscar Romero, Martin Luther King, the four North American churchwomen Ita Ford, Maura Clark, Dorothy Kazel, and Jean Donovan, and others who have given outstanding witness to the point of their death. They are seeking not death but a transformation of heart with social ramifications in the name of God. In an antagonistic world, they are crushed. Then others who are affected begin to feel the power of their memory and interpret their deaths, in continuity with their lives, as redemptive suffering for others.

So too, and uniquely so in view of the resurrection, with Jesus of Nazareth. Subsequent to the traumatic events of the end of his life, the women and men who followed him sought to interpret what happened as somehow connected with God's merciful plan. They developed the language of this having been done "for us," and retrojected their new understanding back into their oral retelling of events of the ministry. His love, which caused him to risk all and end up in unholy suffering, mediated the gracious compassion of God over human misery. But as the events actually unrolled in history, there was no prior necessity for this bloody outcome. To put it simply, Jesus, far from being a masochist, came not to die but to live and help others live in the joy of divine love. To put it boldly, God the Creator and Lover of the human race did not need Jesus' death as an act of atonement but wanted him to flourish in his ministry of the coming reign of God. Human sin thwarted this divine desire yet did not defeat it. The unjust, tormented death of this marginalized Jewish victim of state punishment becomes, for faith, the opening for a new, surprising, healing and liberating presence of God in the world.

3. Flowing from this interpretation of the cross as the historical death of the prophet sent from God, an interpretation rooted in Jesus' ministry and completed in the resurrection, the view of salvation fed by Jesus research shifts theological emphasis from a sole, violent act of atonement for sin before an offended God to an act of suffering solidarity that brings the compassionate presence of God into intimate contact with human misery, pain, and hopelessness.

Part of the difficulty with the atonement/satisfaction metaphor, especially as it has played out in a juridical context, lies in the way it valorizes suffering. Rather than being something to be resisted or remedied in light of God's will for human well-being, suffering is seen as a good in itself or even an end necessary for God's honor. It is true that in the course of human life a measure of suffering can teach wisdom and helps to mature character. Its presence can also call forth responses of enormous charity and care for the weak and vulnerable, thereby developing the virtue of those not personally suffering. While suffering is a genuine mystery whose meaning can never be fully elucidated, all of the world's religious traditions seek to connect this experience with the ultimate power of the universe in some way, helping people to cope and promising release.[18] However, the particular angle taken by the construal of Jesus' death as juridical atonement makes suffering in itself a good. Not only has this led to masochistic tendencies in piety (which are far removed from genuine asceticism), but as this has played out in the public sphere it has promoted acceptance of suffering resulting from injustice rather than energizing resistance.

In the light of what Edward Schillebeeckx calls the "excess" of suffering in our world, in the light of the unjust, bloody deaths of millions of people in the twentieth century and the continued unjust suffering of multitudes of people because of poverty, oppression, and violence, the cross cannot be used to valorize continued misery. Hence the theology of salvation that argues that the depth of suffering Jesus experienced on the cross, the wretched suffering as such, is not *in itself* salvific. Indeed, speaking from the historical point of view, numerous theologians today do not hesitate to call his execution a tragedy, a disaster, a fiasco, an unmitigated failure. Rather than being an act willed by a loving God, it is a strikingly clear index of sin in the world, a wrongful act committed by human beings. What may be considered salvific in such a situation is not the suffering endured but only the love poured out. The saving kernel in the midst of such negativity is not the pain and death as such but the mutually faithful love of Jesus and his God, not immediately evident.

Such a view brackets any idea of God as a sadistic Father, Jesus as a passive, sacrificial victim, his death as a payment for our benefit, and human misery as willed by God as penalty for sin. Rather, Jesus' suffering, a fate resulting from his free, loving fidelity to his prophetic ministry and his God, is precisely the way our gracious God has chosen to enter into solidarity with all those who suffer and are lost in this broken world. Now even the most meaningless suffering, the most anti-divine experience, while remaining essentially unfathomable, does not separate the sufferer from the love of God. Divine participation in Jesus' suffering, coupled with the outpouring of the Spirit of life in his resurrection, gives assurance of new life in, through, and beyond sin, misery, guilt, and death. And so we hope.[19] Rather than endorsing apathetic indifference, this interpretation impels Christians to enter the list of those who struggle against injustice for the well-being of those who suffer, for this is where God is to be found, trying to bring about joy in the beloved creation even here and now.

4. Finally, the view of salvation fed by Jesus research allows the rich tapestry of metaphors found throughout the New Testament to be brought back into play. Being liberated, healed, ransomed and set free, justified, reconciled, adopted or born as God's very own children, all augment the sense of being forgiven thanks to a precious sacrifice. No one image and its accompanying theology can exhaust the experience and meaning of salvation through Jesus Christ. Taken together these metaphors correct distortions that arise when one alone is overemphasized and promote the growth of a plurality of soteriologies fitting for different times and places.

THE CHURCH: FOLLOWING JESUS CHRIST

As the community of disciples graced by the Spirit who follow Jesus the Christ, Christians take their cue for right action, belief, and relationship from their memory image of him.

Originally the community in Palestine was comprised of Jewish disciples, male and female, who in the light of the resurrection increasingly interpreted Jesus as the expected Messiah, the Christ. Far from giving them any reason to leave their Jewish religion, this encouraged their continued observance while they preached the good news to their fellow Jews. They engaged in some distinctive acts such as baptism and gathering in each other's homes for the breaking of the bread while continuing their pattern of Jewish prayer and temple worship. Over time, the success of their preaching to the Gentiles widened their membership demographically, creating fierce tensions about observance of Torah. As the number of Gentile Christians grew, the number of Jewish Christians declined, but it was decades before the latter communities split from—or were put out of—the synagogue.

As was the case with Jesus' historical life, there was no blueprint to follow in those earliest years. Did Jesus found the church? Only in the sense that he gathered a group of women and men disciples to follow him and imbued them with a certain style of life and prayer in view of the coming reign of God. In changing circumstances they faced new issues, nor could the particularities of Jesus' own life be duplicated. Empowered by the Spirit, they had to improvise, discerning how the truth of his message and presence could best be embodied in new times and places. They followed Jesus not by slavish imitation but by creative application of his values, imprinting his presence in new situations as best they could.

Ever since, through a terribly messy history, the core dynamic has been the same. In the community of the church, the future of what Jesus started is being lived out. In the dramatic words of Edward Schillebeeckx, "The living community is the only real reliquary of Jesus."[20] Down through the centuries we keep alive the "dangerous" memory of Jesus; we follow in his footsteps; we embody his presence in word and sacrament and also in actions of healing and compassionate justice that mediate fragments of salvation into the world here and now.

> By following Jesus, taking our bearings from him and allowing ourselves to be inspired by his Spirit, by sharing in his Abba experience and his selfless support for the "least of these," and thus entrusting our own destiny to God, we allow the history of Jesus, the Living One, to continue in history as a piece of living christology, the work of the Spirit in the world.[21]

The church as a piece of living Christology—herein lies the link with Jesus research. For new understandings of Jesus' own historical story lead to critique of some of the church's patterns of discipleship, prayer, and praxis and inspire new directions. Three critical examples:

~ How could the church ever have persecuted the Jews if we had remembered the Jewish character of Jesus' own ethnic and religious identity? I recall visiting a museum in Munich, Germany, that presented the history of Christmas cribs. As the nineteenth century progressed, mother and baby grew increasingly blond and blue-eyed until they were icons of the master race. Jewishness was bleached away. Renewed emphasis on the historical Jewishness of Jesus functions now as one element in growth toward mutual respect and right relations between Jewish and Christian peoples.

~ How can economically well-off Christians continue patterns of consumption that contribute to the destitution of millions of exploited poor people struggling for life? Renewed emphasis on Jesus' prophetic preferential option for the poor in the name of God summons our conscience to action on behalf of justice that will transform oppressive structures in keeping with his loving, liberating intent. Latin American theologian José Miranda states the challenge with singular directness: "No authority can decree that everything is permitted, for justice and exploitation are not so indistinguishable. And Christ died so that we might know that not everything is permitted. But not any Christ. The Christ that cannot be co-opted by the comfortable is the historical Jesus."[22]

~ How can the hierarchical church continue to relegate women to second-class status governed by male-dominated structures, law, and ritual? Renewed emphasis on Jesus' praxis of the reign of God with an eye to its gender inclusivity calls for the institution's conversion to the full dignity of women as human beings made in the image of God and baptized in the image of Christ. Jesus had women disciples who were faithful witnesses of his death and burial and commissioned witnesses of the risen Christ. Even apart from myriad Gospel examples of Jesus' relationship with women, his rejection of any relationship patterned on domination/subordination and his vision of a new humanity of mutual service and empowerment challenge the church to new praxis on behalf of women in partnership with men.[23]

As a piece of living Christology, the church is awakened and challenged by Jesus research to a new faithfulness.

THE LIVING GOD

Since Christians believe Jesus to be the Word, Wisdom, and revelation of God, truly divine, then what scholarship turns up about the specificity of this particular first-century Jewish human being has great import for understanding the character and intent of the living God. Under the rubric of a high and confessionally orthodox Christology, recovering the history of Jesus becomes a route to recovering aspects of divine mystery generally submerged by classical doctrine. That doctrine, drawn from philosophical theism apart from revelation, conceives of God as an absolute, self-subsistent being with attributes of infinite perfection such as omnipotence, immutability, and impassibility, and so constituted as to have no real relation to the world or its history. Reversing direction, theology today seeks to think the reality of God from the history of Jesus Christ. If Jesus belongs to the definition of God, what does the concrete shape of the history of this human being reveal about the incomprehensible divine mystery? So strongly is this work being done that many claim that nothing short of a "revolution" is occurring in the concept of God.[24]

The being of God as triune self-relation, truly related to the world, able in freedom to self-empty and become, able in love to suffer with beloved creation, powerfully compassionate over the pain of the world, willing to be its liberator from evil—such insights are now on the table. Leander Keck states the logic simply: "whom God vindicates discloses the character of God."[25] In Jesus, God vindicates a prophet who proclaims the compassionate rule of the living God who is coming to overturn evil and set the world free from powers that enslave; God vindicates a preacher and teacher who liberates people from a constricting view of this God, understanding that divine mystery draws near to seek the lost; God vindicates a lively, Spirit-filled human being who in gracious acts of inclusive table community, forgiveness, and healing lives out his own message in the concrete. In this way of thinking, Jesus not only teaches parables about God. He is concretely the parable God is telling in this historical world.

These narratives fuse into a symbol of God's character. Theology dares to extrapolate from the words and actions of Jesus to the conception of God's own being as fundamentally and essentially Love (1 John 4:8). God is the lover of the earth and human beings who desires the well-being of all. That places God in total opposition to whatever degrades or destroys the beloved creatures. It makes God particularly partisan toward those who are powerless and suffering. Far from being allied with forces or structures that oppress, God's liberating love opposes them and seeks their transformation so that the downtrodden might be released into fullness of life, the singular precondition for all human beings to dwell in new community. It follows that to know and love God, then, is to hunger and thirst for justice, to ally oneself compassionately with the cause of God in solidarity with those who suffer in this world. Understanding God as the ever-coming, liberating God of life is yet another result of theology's reception of Jesus research.

CONCLUSION

Some might object that too much scholarly probing into the life and times of Jesus of Nazareth robs his story of mystery and therefore of its capability of serving faith. In truth, the opposite is occurring. Not only can research never exhaust the reality of a person, any person, whose depths remain unreachable. But historical study succeeds in placing Jesus so care-

fully in first-century Palestine that he becomes helpfully strange to contemporary, first-world persons. The inveterate tendency to domesticate
him, making him like unto ourselves, is upended when his own historical
concreteness is asserted. Completing his study of the first hundred years or
so of Jesus research, Albert Schweitzer used the startling image of a swing-
ing pendulum to describe what had happened.[26] Research had loosed the
bands by which Jesus had been riveted to "the stony rocks of ecclesiastical
doctrine," and rejoiced to see his figure begin to live and move again. The
historical Jesus advanced to meet the modern world. "But he does not stay;
He passes by our time and returns to His own." To its dismay, theology
could not keep him in its own era but had to let him go. "He returned to
His own time, not owing to the application of any historical ingenuity, but
by the same inevitable necessity by which the liberated pendulum returns
to its original position." Jesus of Nazareth's historical particularity stands
as a block to the perennial temptation to co-opt him for our own purposes,
whether ecclesiastical or tribal or personal.

At the same time that scholarly research protects the enigmatic reality
of Jesus in time and place, it also feeds the quest for greater understanding.
By giving us clues that Jesus of Nazareth was one kind of person and not
another, taught specific things about God and human life and not something else, lived a certain life and died one kind of death and not another,
called people to one kind of response and not another, Jesus research is
providing new imaginative fodder for Christian life and practice. Neither
history that is skeptical of faith nor faith that exists in an a-historical vac-
uum will suffice to satisfy questions asked in the spirit of our age. But history and faith in mutual relationship open fruitful new paths.

As we sit here on the shore of the Sea of Galilee pondering these things,
I would like to conclude with a paraphrase of a famous statement with
which Schweizer concluded his massive work on Jesus research nearly a
century ago. Granted, he wrote with a theological point of view different
from that which I am proposing in this paper. Still, his insight about the
spiritual power flowing from the actual Jesus of history to our time provides a fitting summation for this colloquium:

> He comes to us as one unknown, without a name, as of old, by the lake-side,
> he came to those who knew him not. He speaks to us the same word: "Fol-
> low thou me!" and sets us to the tasks that he has to fulfill for our time. He
> invites. And to those who respond, whether they be wise or simple, he will
> reveal himself in the toils, the sufferings, the joys they shall pass through in
> his fellowship; and, as an ineffable mystery, they shall learn in their own
> experience who he is. [27]

NOTES

1. For the early quest, see Albert Schweitzer, *The Quest of the Historical Jesus* (New York: Macmillan, 1968; original 1906). For later work, see Marcus Borg, *Jesus in Contemporary Scholarship* (Valley Forge, Pa.: Trinity Press International, 1994).

2. In colloquial, uncritical usage, the "historical Jesus" refers to the real Jesus as he actually lived, acted, and spoke in history. Technically, however, the "historical Jesus" designates the picture of Jesus reconstructed by scholarship, which picture may vary owing to the methods and commitments of researchers. See the helpful discussion in John Meier, *A Marginal Jew: Rethinking the Historical Jesus,* Anchor Bible Reference Library, 2 vols. (New York: Doubleday, 1991, 1994), 1:21-40.

3. H. S. Reimarus, *Reimarus: Fragments,* ed. Charles Talbert (Philadelphia: Fortress, 1970); David Friedrich Strauss, *The Life of Jesus Critically Examined,* ed. Peter Hodgson (Philadelphia: Fortress, 1972); Robert Funk et al., eds., *The Five Gospels: The Search for Authentic Words of Jesus* (New York: Macmillan, 1993). One member of the Jesus Seminar whose work argues eloquently for the benefit of this research for faith is Marcus Borg; see his *Jesus: A New Vision* (San Francisco: HarperSanFrancisco, 1987); idem, *Meeting Jesus Again for the First Time* (San Francisco: HarperSanFrancisco, 1994).

4. Martin Kähler, *The So-Called Historical Jesus and the Historic Biblical Christ,* ed. Carl Braaten (Philadelphia: Fortress, 1964); Luke Timothy Johnson, *The Real Jesus: The Misguided Quest for the Historical Jesus and the Truth of the Traditional Gospels* (San Francisco: HarperCollins, 1996).

5. See discussion of the importance of the Jesus image in Leander Keck, *A Future for the Historical Jesus : The Place of Jesus in Preaching and Theology* (Philadelphia: Fortress, 1980); and Elizabeth Johnson, "The Theological Relevance of the Historical Jesus: A Debate and A Thesis," *The Thomist* 48 (1984): 1–43.

6. Geza Vermes, *Jesus the Jew* (Philadelphia: Fortress, 1973).

7. Meier, *A Marginal Jew.*

8. E. P. Sanders, *Jesus and Judaism* (Philadelphia: Fortress, 1985).

9. Borg, *Jesus: A New Vision.*

10. John Dominic Crossan, *The Historical Jesus: The Life of a Mediterranean Jewish Peasant* (San Francisco: HarperCollins, 1991).

11. Edward Schillebeeckx, *Jesus: An Experiment in Christology* (New York: Seabury Crossroad, 1979).

12. Karl Rahner, "I Believe in Jesus Christ: Interpreting an Article of Faith," in *Theological Investigations IX,* trans. G. Harrison (London: Darton, Longman & Todd, 1972), 166.

13. For a thoroughgoing Christology from a historical perspective, see Roger Haight, *Jesus Symbol of God* (Maryknoll, N.Y.: Orbis, 1999).

14. Karl Rahner, "Dogmatic Reflections on the Knowledge and Self-

Consciousness of Christ," in *Theological Investigations V,* trans. Karl Kruger (New York: Seabury Crossroad, 1975), 193–215.

15. Anselm, *Cur Deus Homo,* in *Saint Anselm: Basic Writings,* trans. S. N. Deane (La Salle, Ill.: Open Court, 1974), 171–288.

16. Ignacio Ellacuría and Jon Sobrino, eds., *Mysterium Liberationis: Fundamental Concepts of Liberation Theology* (Maryknoll, N.Y.: Orbis, 1993); Gustavo Gutiérrez, *On Job: God-Talk and the Suffering of the Innocent,* trans. Matthew O'Connell (Maryknoll, N.Y.: Orbis, 1987).

17. Joanne Carlson Brown and Rebecca Parker, "For God So Loved the World?" in *Violence against Women and Children: A Christian Theological Sourcebook,* ed. Carol Adams and Marie Fortune (New York: Continuum, 1995), 36–59; Rita Nakashima Brock, *Journeys by Heart: A Christology of Erotic Power* (New York: Crossroad, 1988).

18. John Bowker, *Problems of Suffering in Religions of the World* (Cambridge: Cambridge University Press, 1970); William Cenkner, ed., *Evil and the Response of World Religion* (St. Paul, Minn.: Paragon, 1997); Edward Schillebeeckx, *Christ: The Experience of Jesus as Lord,* trans. John Bowden (New York: Crossroad/Seabury, 1980), 670–723.

19. Johann Baptist Metz, *A Passion for God: The Mystical-Political Dimension of Christianity,* trans. Matthew Ashley (New York: Paulist Press, 1998); Leonardo Boff, *Passion of Christ, Passion of the World,* trans. Robert Barr (Maryknoll, N.Y.: Orbis, 1987); Jon Sobrino, "The Risen One Is the One Who Was Crucified: Jesus' Resurrection from among the World's Crucified," in Sobrino, *Jesus in Latin America* (Maryknoll, N.Y.: Orbis, 1987), 148–58.

20. Schillebeeckx, *Christ,* 641.

21. Ibid.

22. José Miranda, *Being and the Messiah* (Maryknoll, N.Y.: Orbis, 1977), 9.

23. Maryanne Stevens, *Reconstructing the Christ Symbol: Essays in Feminist Christology* (New York: Paulist Press, 1993).

24. The claim to revolution is made by Jürgen Moltmann, Hans Küng, Walter Kasper, Jon Sobrino, and Leander Keck, among others. See discussion in Elizabeth Johnson, "Christology's Impact on the Doctrine of God," *Heythrop Journal* 26 (1985): 143–63.

25. Keck, *A Future for the Historical Jesus,* 234.

26. Schweitzer, *Quest of the Historical Jesus,* 399.

27. Ibid., 403 (paraphrased). Schweitzer is more skeptical than I about the relevance of historical Jesus research for faith; he thinks with a much more monarchical understanding of God; consequently he uses command and obedience rather than invitation and response to describe the relationship between Jesus and the believer.